FROM WALKING TOURS

Paris

2nd Edition

Lisa Legarde

MACMILLAN • USA

ABOUT THE AUTHOR

Lisa Legarde was born in New Orleans and graduated from Wellesley College with a B.A. in English. She has traveled extensively in Europe and North America and is the author of *Frommer's Walking Tours: San Francisco* as well as guides to Amsterdam; New Orleans; New Mexico; and Santa Fe, Taos, and Albuquerque. She is also co-author of *Frommer's New England.*

MACMILLAN TRAVEL

A Simon & Schuster Macmillan Company
1633 Broadway
New York, NY 10019

ISBN 0-02-860469-5
ISSN 1081-3381

Editor: Ron Boudreau
Map Editor: Douglas Stallings

Design by Amy Peppler Adams—designLab, Seattle
Maps by Ortelius Design and John Decamillas

SPECIAL SALES

Bulk purchases (10+ copies) of Frommer's Travel Guides are available to corporations at special discounts. The Special Sales Department can produce custom editions to be used as premiums and/or for sales promotion to suit individual needs. Existing editions can be produced with custom cover imprints such as corporate logos. For more information write to: Special Sales, Simon & Schuster, 1230 Avenue of the Americas, New York, NY 10020.

Manufactured in the United States of America

CONTENTS

LIST OF MAPS

The Walking Tours

An Invitation to the Reader

In researching this book, I discovered many wonderful places. I'm sure you'll find others. Please tell us about them, so we can share the information with your fellow travelers in upcoming editions. If you were disappointed with a recommendation, we'd love to know that, too. Please write to:

Lisa Legarde
Frommer's Walking Tours: Paris
Macmillan Travel
1633 Broadway
New York, NY 10019

An Additional Note

Please be advised that travel information is subject to change at any time. The authors, editors, and publisher cannot be held responsible for the experiences of readers while traveling. Your safety is important to us, however, so we encourage you to stay alert and be aware of your surroundings. Keep a close eye on cameras, purses, and wallets—all favorite targets of thieves and pickpockets.

PARIS: CITY OF LIGHT

The City of Light has always aroused the varying passions of its visitors. Charles Dickens wrote that Paris is the "most extraordinary place in the World." To Henry James it was the "greatest temple ever built to material joys and the lust of the eyes." Hemingway described it as a "moveable feast," believing that if you were lucky enough to experience Paris as a young person it would stay with you for the rest of your life. Others have been less positive. Mark Twain said, "The French talk funny, eat frogs, and don't bathe. One shouldn't trust the water and all French women can become spectacles of depravity. The streets were cleaner in St. Louis." For D. H. Lawrence Paris was "a nasty city," and Virginia Woolf found it a "hostile brilliant alien city." Still, they felt compelled to visit.

Happily, millions of people remember Paris as Oscar Hammerstein did: "The last time I saw Paris, her heart was warm and gay. I heard the laughter of her heart in every street café."

Whether people love or hate Paris, something about this city and its citizens always draws them back.

From the Middle Ages, when students came to listen to the great philosopher Abélard, to the 20th century, when expatriate Americans discovered the Left Bank, Paris has always drawn writers, painters, poets, and philosophers with its beauty, intellectual ferment, and devotion to art and ideas. Its renowned joie de vivre translates daily life into an art form—as any visit to a charcuterie, pâtisserie, florist, milliner, jeweler, chocolatier, or street market will confirm.

This peek at the past and how Paris grew into what you see today should help orient you before you begin strolling the streets and making your own acquaintance with the city. Paris consists of 20 *arrondissements* (districts), each with its own character and ambience, situated on either the *Rive Gauche* (Left Bank) or *Rive Droite* (Right Bank) of the river Seine. Many arrondissements contain what were once separate villages, like Auteuil and Passy. For more information, see "City Layout" under "Essentials & Recommended Reading" at the end of this book.

Paris's growth can be traced in a series of concentric circles radiating from the original nucleus on the Ile de la Cité. The first wall around the island was built in the late 3rd century, and the walls of Philippe II in the 1180s, Charles V in the 1370s, and Louis XIII in the 1630s marked the city's expanding perimeter. Only remnants of the first wall can still be seen—in the Marais and St-Paul—but an outline of the later ones can be traced from the Bastille to the Louvre's Cour Carrée.

Under Louis XIII the walls were extended to embrace the Tuileries. When Louis XIV, the "Sun King" who dominated Europe, felt secure enough to tear down these walls, they were replaced by the *Grands Boulevards:* des Capucines, des Italiens, and de la Madeleine, to name only three. Another wall, punctuated by 52 tollgates designed by Claude-Nicolas Ledoux, was built between 1784 and 1789 by the Fermiers Généraux, import-tax collectors. This hated wall became one of the insults to the common people that helped foment the Revolution; it was demolished several decades later, along with most of the toll-gates. Between 1841 and 1845, Louis-Adolphe Thiers built a wall that followed the route of the present boulevard des Marechaux; it failed the test of the Franco-Prussian War, and its parts were ceded to the city of Paris or destroyed.

Today, a circle of boulevards—for the most part coinciding with the ramparts of the 14th, 16th, and 17th centuries—encloses all of old Paris except for a southern portion extending beyond the boulevard St-Germain. Outside the Grands Boulevards lie the *faubourgs* (old suburbs), around which runs another circle of boulevards corresponding to the 18th-century ramparts. Beyond those stretch still other suburbs to the boulevards that line the late 19th-century fortifications.

FROM GALLIC-ROMAN LUTETIA TO MEDIEVAL PARIS

The Seine has always played a major role in the city's life. Indeed, the river was the crucible of the early city, for here on the Ile de la Cité a small Gallic trading post, Lutetia Parisiorum, was established at the end of the 3rd century B.C. The city's birth by the river is still remembered in its coat of arms: a boat with the inscription *Fluctuat Nec Mergitur* ("It floats and does not sink"). The river, however, did not protect Lutetia from the armies of Julius Caesar, who defeated the Gallic leader Vercingetorix in 52 B.C.; Caesar made the settlement an urban outpost of the Roman Empire, located on the main trading routes between Mediterranean and northern Europe.

These trade routes traveled the same paths as today's rue St-Jacques on the Left Bank and rue St-Martin on the Right Bank. The Romans expanded the city across the river to the Left Bank, particularly on and around the Montagne Ste-Geneviève. Two monuments from this period that can still be seen are the baths at Cluny and the Arènes de Lutèce, where you can imagine gladiators battling before audiences seated on the ring of tiered stone seats.

Some of the most enduring elements of French culture emerged in Paris as the Roman Empire waned and the Middle Ages began. Christianity was introduced around A.D. 250 by St. Denis, the first bishop of Paris; his persecution and martyrdom are recalled in the name *Montmartre* (see Walking Tour 9 for more details). As the Roman presence declined, the city was increasingly threatened by barbarian invasion, so a wall almost 8 feet thick was erected in the late 3rd century to protect the Ile de la Cité. The 5th century brought fears of attacks by the Huns, and legend has it that only the prayers of Geneviève, patron saint of Paris, saved the city. In 486 France began to stabilize as an independent kingdom when the first Merovingian king, Clovis I, defeated the last Roman governor and turned back the Visigoths and the Alemanni.

In 508 Clovis made Paris his capital. Clovis's death brought on a period of fratricidal strife arising from the division of his kingdom. The dynasty collapsed, and the Carolingians usurped the throne. Their first king, Charles Martel, defeated the Saracens on a battlefield between Tours and Poitiers in 732. He was succeeded by his son Pépin the Short, who was followed by his son, the great Charlemagne, who established an extensive empire but spent most of his time in Aix-la-Chapelle, which he made his capital. After the death of Charlemagne's son Louis I, the kingdom was rent by more strife, and Carolingian might declined to the point that Norsemen besieged Paris in 885 and 886.

When the Carolingian dynasty ended in 987, the nobles chose as king Hugh Capet, comte de Paris and duc de France, who again made Paris the capital and began the new Capetian dynasty. His 11th- and 12th-century successors—Robert II, Henri I, Philippe I, Louis VI, and Louis VII—went on to solidify and extend the monarch's power. During the reign of the Capetians, a series of village settlements began to form around several abbeys—such as St-Germain-l'Auxerrois, St-Germain-des-Prés, Ste-Geneviève, and Notre-Dames-des-Champs. Under Philippe II (1180–1223) these settlements were enclosed within a rampart dating from 1190 on the Right Bank and from about 1210 on the Left Bank. Streets were laid out, a fort was built (the Louvre), and construction on several churches, including Notre-Dame, was begun.

Meanwhile, four mendicant orders established themselves on the Left Bank: the Jacobins in 1219, the Cordeliers in 1230, the Augustin friars in 1293, and the Carmelites in 1319. Numerous schools were also established in the late 13th and 14th centuries, including the Sorbonne, founded by Robert de Sorbon in 1253, which became a fountainhead of theological learning, legendary for its great scholars Albertus Magnus and St. Thomas Aquinas. This revival of learning reached its height in the 13th century as scholars and students from all over Europe arrived in Paris's intellectual center with Latin as their *lingua franca*—hence the Latin Quarter.

The city's reputation as a leading theological center was enhanced by the role France played in the Crusades—a role personified by St. Louis (Louis IX, 1226–70), who built Paris's brilliant "jewel box," the Sainte-Chapelle, to store such treasures from the Holy Land as the Crown of Thorns (now housed in the Treasury of Notre-Dame and shown once a year on Good Friday). His successors, Philippe III (1270–85) and Philippe IV (1285–1314), further strengthened the monarchy, but the rest of the 14th century was consumed by the Hundred Years' War (1337–1453).

The seeds of this strife between England and France had been sown in 1152 when Eleanor of Aquitaine, whose marriage to Louis VII had been annulled, married Henry Plantagenet, duc de Normandie and comte d'Anjou, the future Henry II of England. Her dowry had included vast French lands, and so the battle for France had been enjoined. The Burgundians joined the English; famine and the Black Death made things worse; the English entered Paris, crowned Henry VI king of England and France in Notre-Dame, and occupied the country from 1419 to 1436. The situation deteriorated until Joan of Arc, driven by "voices" telling her to rid her country of the English, bolstered Charles VII's courage and led the French army (unsuccessfully) against the English in 1429. Two years later she was captured by the Burgundians and sold to the English, who burned her at the stake as a heretic.

PARIS IN THE 16TH CENTURY

After the long interruption of the Hundred Years' War, the consolidation of power resumed under Louis XI (1461–83), Charles VIII (1483–98), Louis XII (1498–1515), and most of all François I (1515–47). France's first great Renaissance king, François I transformed the Louvre fort into a magnificent palace to which the monarchy later moved permanently (although he set about embellishing the capital, François preferred to maintain his court in the Loire Valley).

Henri II's solemn entry into Paris in 1549 on François I's death marked the triumph of both the Renaissance and Paris, which became the undisputed capital. Expansion of the Louvre continued, and in 1563 Catherine de Médicis began the construction of the Tuileries. The city slowly took on the look we now know as streets were straightened, house facades were built of durable stone, quays were constructed, and the pont Neuf was begun; theaters were also introduced.

Unfortunately, this stability was not to last, for the Wars of Religion (1562–98) did not spare Paris during the reigns of the last two Valois kings, Charles IX (1560–74) and Henri III (1574–89). The 1572 St. Bartholomew's Day Massacre saw the city awash in the blood of thousands of Protestants; on the 1588 Day of the Barricades, Henri III was forced to flee the city. His legal heir, Protestant Henri of Navarre, laid siege to the city and was violently opposed by the Catholic League, led by the Guise family. Henri defeated the League though was forced to convert to Catholicism before being allowed to enter Paris on March 22, 1594, when he is rumored to have said "Paris vaut bien une messe" (Paris is well worth a Mass).

Henri IV (1589–1610) was one of France's most beloved kings, and he and his minister, the duc de Sully, were responsible for building the place Royale (later place des Vosges), the cornerstone of the 17th-century development of the Marais as the aristocratic quarter. Henri also laid out the place Dauphine, built the quai de l'Horloge, and enlarged the Louvre's Cour Carrée to four times its size, adding the Grande Galerie and Pavillon Henri IV. France's prosperity was restored and religious tolerance encouraged.

FROM LOUIS XIII TO LOUIS XVI

Upon Henri IV's assassination by a Catholic fanatic, Louis XIII (1610–43) became king, though his mother, Marie de Médicis, acted as regent during his minority. She went on to commission the Palais du Luxembourg (1615) and, west of the Tuileries, the cours de la Reine, a favorite route for fashionable carriages.

When Louis assumed the throne, he expanded the city even more. He combined two unoccupied islands in the Seine into the Ile St-Louis, laid out the Jardin des Plantes, and encompassed the Tuileries by extending Charles V's walls. Louis XIII's brilliant and ruthless minister, Cardinal Richelieu, established the Académie Française and built the Palais-Cardinal (now Palais-Royal), all the while destroying the power of the Huguenots. Richelieu was followed by the equally brilliant Cardinal Mazarin, who endowed the Collège Mazarin in the Hôtel de l'Institut, now home to the Académie Française. Today the Bibliothèque Nationale occupies Mazarin's palace.

The monarch's power was further centralized under the flamboyant Louis XIV (1643–1715), who became king at age nine. In 1649, the Fronde protest (led by *parlement* and nobles) and the resulting disturbances forced the court to leave Paris. Louis returned to the city in 1652 but moved his court first to St-Germain-en-Laye and later to his new Versailles. Aided by his two great ministers, Colbert and Louvois, he made France a military power feared throughout Europe.

Although he shunned Paris, Louis gave much to the city, adding the magnificent colonnade to the Louvre and laying out the Grands Boulevards along the axis traced by Louis XIII's earlier walls. The Tuileries palace was completed and sumptuously decorated, and its gardens—redesigned by André Le Nôtre—were expanded along the tree-lined Champs-Elysées (1667). He was also responsible for the construction of the places Vendôme and des Victoires, the pont Royal, the Hôtel des Invalides (a retreat for invalid soldiers), the Observatory, and the Gobelins tapestry factory. Louis XIV's desertion of Paris alienated its citizens and prepared the ground for the ideas that kindled the Revolution. Although when Louis' reign ended France was still feared throughout Europe, the many wars that had established its hegemony had also severely weakened its financial strength.

Louis XV (1715–74) continued the three trends his predecessor had developed: expansion, war, and financial decline. The place Louis XV (later place de la Concorde) was laid out; the rue Royale created in 1732; and the Madeleine church begun in 1764. The boulevards began to be lined with opulent mansions and houses, as well as such theaters as the Comédie-Italienne (1780), which occupied the site of today's Opéra Comique, and the Théâtre-Français (1782). On the Left Bank the Ecole Militaire and the Champ-de-Mars date from 1751; St-Sulpice was completed, and a new church begun on the site of the Panthéon. People flocked to the gardens of the Palais-Royal and to its new galleries, which had been added in 1761 to house cafés, shops, and a waxworks.

During the 18th century, the financial strain of pomp, glamour, and military conquest began to claim its toll. The treasury continued to be drained by wars—the War of the Austrian Succession (1740–48) and the Seven Years' War (1756–63), as well as the American Revolution, which Louis XVI (1774–92) supported. Monetary problems became so acute that in 1789 he was forced to summon the States General—the old parliamentary assembly—for the first time since 1614. Unfortunately for Louis, what began as a rational discussion of the nation's finances soon turned into a movement for radical reform.

FROM THE REVOLUTION TO THE SECOND EMPIRE

The summoning of the States General, which was transformed into the National Assembly in 1789, set into motion the chain of events that led to the Revolution. In July 1789 a Paris mob stormed the Bastille (which held only two or three prisoners), and three days later, at the Hôtel de Ville, Louis XVI was forced to kiss the new French tricolor. In October Louis and his queen, Marie Antoinette, were hauled from Versailles to the Tuileries, and a constitutional monarchy was established in 1791. War with much of Europe followed, accompanied by the growth of radical factions in France. When revolutionary troops and a Parisian mob stormed the Tuileries on August 10, 1792, the king and queen were removed and thrown into prison; five months later they were guillotined in the place de la Révolution (now place de la Concorde). Robespierre presided over the rest of the Reign of Terror until its end in July 1794. The next year a new constitution was ushered in, the Directoire (Directory), but it was terminated by Napoléon Bonaparte's 1799 coup d'état, which ushered in the Consulate.

First Consul Napoléon and his wife, Joséphine, quickly moved into the Tuileries, and for their convenience the rue de Rivoli arcades were introduced. At his 1804 coronation in Notre-Dame, Napoléon crowned himself emperor and Joséphine empress, then embarked on a series of campaigns that took him to Egypt and Moscow until his 1815 defeat at Waterloo.

Napoléon was responsible for many of the city's most grandiose monuments. He started construction of the Arc de Triomphe and completed construction of the Madeleine, which was meant to serve as a "temple of glory." He commissioned his favorite architects, Percier and Fontaine, to build the Arc de Triomphe du Carrousel. And the Bourse des Valeurs (1808–26) was begun in the style of a Greek temple. It was also Napoléon who truly set the Louvre on its course as an art museum: The art booty he acquired during his military campaigns was displayed there and became the core of the museum's collection.

In 1814 Louis XVIII (1814–24) was restored to the throne, and the city began its enormous 19th-century growth. By 1841 the population numbered 935,000, up from 547,000 in 1801; in 1861 it soared to 1,696,000 and by 1881 it reached 2,270,000.

Industrialization took hold and exhibitions were held; the first railway arrived in Paris in 1837. This was a period of great social change and democratization, which may have helped cause two revolutions. The first one, in 1830, replaced Charles X, who tried to restore absolute monarchy, with Louis-Philippe (1830–48). The second, in 1848, brought Louis-Napoléon Bonaparte (nephew of Napoléon I) to power, first as president of the Second Republic and then, in 1852, as Emperor Napoléon III of the Second Empire.

Napoléon III (1852–70) authorized his Préfet de la Seine, Baron Georges-Eugène Haussmann, to completely reshape Paris, and the prefect razed whole neighborhoods to cut the starburst network of wide boulevards and avenues Parisians walk along today. The new gates of the city were the rail stations—Gare de Lyon, Gare du Nord, Gare Montparnasse, and Gare St-Lazare—and Haussmann laid out boulevards and avenues for their easy access, including the boulevard de Strasbourg and rue de Rennes. In the process, magnificent crossroads were created, such as the rue de l'Etoile and the place de l'Opéra. In addition, 24 parks—including the Bois de Boulogne, parc de Monceau, and parc des Buttes-Chaumont—were created; a system of horse-drawn omnibus transportation was begun; Les Halles was constructed; and a sewage system was laid.

In this Paris lived and worked the intellectual giants of the day—Balzac, Baudelaire, Dumas, Hugo, Sand, Chopin, Berlioz, Delacroix, Ingres, Daumier, and Manet were only a few who frequented the boulevards with their cafés, music halls, and theaters (including the Opéra—now called the Opéra Garnier—which was relocated to its present site in 1875). Offenbach and Gounod were opera favorites; theater crowd pleasers were comedies by Dumas and Labiche.

Famous courtesans reveled in their social prominence, capturing the hearts of even the emperor. One of these was La Paiva, who amassed such a vast fortune that she was able to build a palace on the Champs-Elysées. Everyone came to Paris for pleasure—the French from the provinces came to shop, go to the theater, and sit in the plush red cafés lit with gilt chandeliers, and the English came to indulge every pleasure and then go home to complain. The animated life that filled the boulevards is what comes to mind still when people think of Paris.

Here were concentrated the most fashionable cafés, theaters, and restaurants—above all, the Café Tortoni at the corner of rue Taitbout, where Manet lunched practically every day before walking in the Tuileries, and to which everyone who was anyone in Paris repaired before and after the theater. The city was the art capital of Europe, and its achievements were showcased in the International Exhibitions of 1855, 1867, 1878, 1889, and 1900, the occasions for the building of the Trocadéro (1878), Eiffel Tower (1889), and Grand Palais and Petit Palais (1897–1900). Everyone came to admire this Paris—the modern city par excellence.

FROM THE PARIS COMMUNE TO WORLD WAR I

The Empire ended disastrously in the Franco-Prussian War (1870–71). Paris was besieged for four months, then taken over by the Germans. Napoléon III was taken prisoner at the Battle of Sedan, and upon the German withdrawal a communist uprising took place; it was quickly and bloodily suppressed, yet not before the mob had torched the Tuileries, burning to the ground all but the Pavillon de Flore. The last of the Communards were executed at Père-Lachaise Cemetery. The Third Republic was declared, and it lasted for 60 years; new cabinets came and went while the country underwent more rapid social and industrial change, which in turn spawned revolutionary cultural and artistic movements.

Under the Third Republic French painters made their country the world center of art. The transformation from the Romantic to the modern era was clearly marked with the 1885 death of writer Victor Hugo, who had been the great romantic symbol of 19th-century France. His body lay in state under the Arc de Triomphe for 24 hours, and thousands flocked to pay their last respects. However, change had been coming for a while, as evidenced in the works of such realist painters as Manet and Courbet and in the novels of Zola, which had been stirring great controversy.

In particular, Manet's *Le Déjeuner sur l'herbe,* shown at the 1863 Salon des Refusés (created by Napoléon III to display works rejected by the Salon, the annual exhibition sponsored by the Académie Française), had shocked viewers with its subject matter and technique. In 1874 Manet, Renoir, Cézanne, Monet,

Morisot, Degas, Pissarro, Sisley, and 21 other artists, calling themselves the Société Anonyme, held their first exhibition. Their paintings were dismissed as mere muddy scrapings and the artists described as madmen. Louis Leroy, in *Charivari*, dubbed the show the "Exhibition of the Impressionists," and the name stuck.

In 1876 a second exhibition was held, showing 24 works by Degas, 12 by Pissarro, 18 by Monet, and 15 each by Sisley and Renoir. Again the critics howled. Albert Wolff described the show as a "horrifying spectacle," its artists as five or six lunatics afflicted with the madness of ambition. He complained vehemently about each artist, recommending that someone "try to explain to M. Renoir that a woman's torso is not a mass of decomposing flesh with those purplish green stains which denote a state of complete putrefaction in a corpse." Only one or two enlightened critics, including Charpentiers and Chocquet, realized that 19th-century life called for new art and new literature.

By the 1890s the impressionists had arrived—at least in Paris. Similar experimentation was occurring in music by such composers as Fauré, Debussy, Ravel, and Dukas; in the sciences by Berthelot, Pasteur, and the Curies; and in literature by Proust, who in 1913 published the first volume of his revolutionary novel, *A la recherche du temps perdu.* In 1898 Samuel Bing opened his shop, Art Nouveau, and its name became synonymous with the fluid, sinuous decorative style that dominated the first decade of the century. This style can be seen today at such grand restaurants as Maxim's (1890) or on the street at the one or two remaining Hector Guimard entrances to the Métro (which opened in 1900).

France's transformation to a modern industrial nation also produced a far more democratic society, giving rise to an urban proletariat that flocked to the cafés, restaurants, café-concerts, and dance halls. These were the people who the impressionist and realist painters documented in their art. By the turn of the century Paris boasted 27,000 cafés, about 150 café-concerts, and thousands of restaurants—a phenomenal number considering there were only 50 at the end of the 18th century. The city's cultural life centered on the cafés along the Grands Boulevards and in Montparnasse and Montmartre. For example, Manet,

Zola, Fantin-Latour, Nadar, Monet, Pissarro, and Renoir gathered at the Café Guerbois in Montmartre from 1869 to 1873 and later at the Nouvelle-Athènes in the place Pigalle.

The café-concert was one of the late 19th-century inventions that contributed to the city's reputation for gaiety and sociability. People came here when they liked, dressed as they liked, ate and drank as they watched the show, commented throughout, and joined in the singing. Maurice Chevalier and Mistinguett both started their careers in such places. On the boulevards there were the Eldorado and the Scala, while in Montmartre was the Moulin Rouge (1889), immortalized by Toulouse-Lautrec and host to many a famous artist, including Colette, La Goulue, and Jane Avril. It had a large ballroom with tables in the gallery as well as a garden where one could watch the "girls" riding donkeys.

The Folies-Bergère, originally the Café du Sommier Elastique, became famous throughout Europe in the 1890s. Poets and painters frequented Montmartre's Le Chat Noir and Aristide Bruant's Le Mirliton. However, the frivolity of the café-concerts and dance halls was forced to die down for a while when in August 1914 the troops marched off singing "La Marseillaise."

FROM 1918 TO THE PRESENT

During World War I the Germans failed to reach Paris, yet France bore the brunt of the fighting, and at the end of the war premier Georges Clemenceau won heavy war reparations and imposed a tough treaty on the Germans at Versailles. Postwar Paris bounced back and became a magnet for young Americans. In 1919 Prohibition had been passed in the United States, and nativism and isolationism dominated American politics; Paris, on the other hand, was tremendous fun and also the world's art capital. It had already given birth to impressionism and art nouveau in the 19th century, and those were followed in the 1920s by cubism (1907–14), dadaism (1915–22), and surrealism and art deco. Americans came in droves from the early twenties to the late thirties, gathering in the cafés of Montparnasse—Café du Dôme, Le Sélect, and La Coupole. In the forties and fifties, the bohemians moved to the boulevard St-Germain, where they frequented Deux-Magots, Café de Flore, and Brasserie Lipp, all still thriving.

In the 1930s the economic depression throughout Europe and the rise of Hitler and his Nazis led to the outbreak of World War II. Hitler's troops eventually broke through the Maginot Line to occupy Paris on June 14, 1940, establishing their headquarters at the Hôtel Lutetia. Marshal Pétain's Vichy government in theory ran unoccupied France (while collaborating with the Nazis), while Gen. Charles de Gaulle became leader of the Free French and organized *le maquis* ("the Resistance") throughout the country. The Allies landed in Normandy in June 1944, and Paris was finally liberated on August 25, 1944; the next day General de Gaulle paraded down the Champs-Elysées. By the end of the year the Germans had been expelled from France. De Gaulle headed a provisional government prior to the official proclamation of the Fourth Republic.

The Fourth Republic saw the violent end of colonial French rule around the world—in Madagascar, Indochina, and North Africa, where the Algerian liberation war led to the collapse of the republic. In 1958 de Gaulle was recalled to head the Fifth Republic and resolve the crisis created when an Algerian right-wing military coup threatened France. In 1962, after a French referendum, Algeria gained its independence. The decade ended with more turmoil: In May 1968 workers went out on strike around the country as Parisian students took to the streets to rebel against France's antiquated educational system.

In 1969 Georges Pompidou became president. During his tenure the Centre Pompidou, or Beauborg, was launched, along with the Tour Montparnasse. The tower was a preview of what was to come as the 1980s transformed Paris's architectural unity with the addition of the avant-garde Centre Pompidou and Forum des Halles, the Institut du Monde Arab, the Opéra de la Bastille, I. M. Pei's controversial glass pyramid at the Louvre, the Grande Arche de la Défense, and the Cité des Sciences et de l'Industrie at La Villette.

François Mitterrand, France's first socialist president, was elected in 1981 and reelected in 1988; in May 1995 conservative Jacques Chirac became the new president. In 1989 Paris celebrated two monumental birthdays: the bicentennial of the Revolution and the centennial of the Eiffel Tower. They have become symbols of hope, progress, and change that express our ability to renew our spirits—and Paris's unique ability to transform itself into a new City of Light for each generation.

The Tours at a Glance

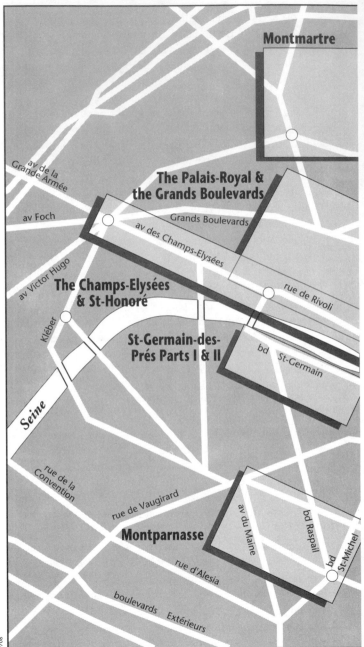

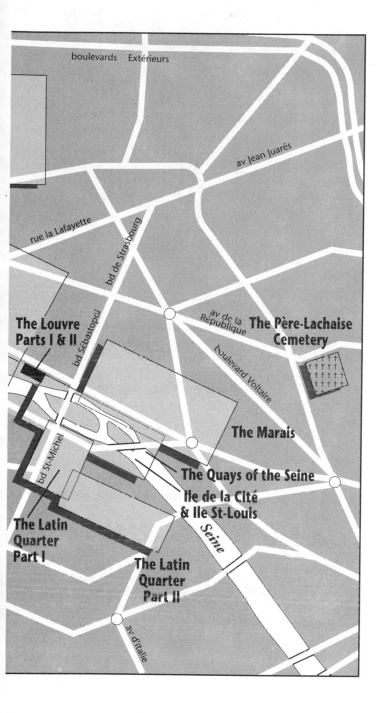

boulevards Extérieurs

av Jean Juarés

rue la Lafayette

bd de Strasbourg

**The Louvre
Parts I & II**

bd Sébastopol

av de la
République

**The Père-Lachaise
Cemetery**

boulevard Voltaire

The Marais

bd St-Michel

The Quays of the Seine

**Ile de la Cité
& Ile St-Louis**

Seine

**The Latin
Quarter
Part I**

**The Latin
Quarter
Part II**

av d'Italie

The Quays of the Seine

Start: The intersection of rue des Prêtres-St-Germain-l'Auxerrois and rue de l'Amiral-de-Coligny (Métro: Louvre-Rivoli or Pont-Neuf).

Finish: Pont Neuf.

Time: Two to three hours, depending on how much time you spend in churches, shops, and museums.

Best Time: Any time of day, but if you're interested in shopping at the bookstalls along the quay—or in any of the shops, for that matter—it's best to go in the early afternoon.

A relatively straightforward short walk along the Seine is probably just what you need on your first day in Paris. You'll get your bearings by visiting parts of both the Right and the Left Bank neighborhoods bordering the river, and you'll get to see some of the loveliest views in all of the city.

This romantic stroll takes you by interesting shops, wonderful mansions, and the oldest church in Paris. As you walk, try imagining what the riverbanks were like before the quays were built—when houses overhung the Seine and the river was the center of trade and commerce.

• • • • • • • • • • • • • • • •

From where you're standing, go into place du Louvre, where at no. 2 you'll find:

1. **St-Germain-l'Auxerrois,** a church named for Germain, the bishop of Auxerre, a "healer" who was so good at curing people he is said to have raised disciples from the dead.

    Of the original Romanesque structure, only the 12th-century tower still stands. Note the gothic porch on the west side of the church, one of only two of its kind in the entire city (the other is on the Sainte-Chapelle). Given the number of churches in Paris, this is somewhat amazing. Also note the bell tower, whose 38-bell carillon was the only one in Paris saved from the Revolution's melting pots. It was this very same carillon (along with the Tour de l'Horloge on the Ile de la Cité) that rang out the signal beginning the St. Bartholemew's Day Massacre, when the Catholics butchered more than 3,000 Huguenots.

    The interior's organ case came from the Sainte-Chapelle and was constructed in 1756. The royal pew, canopy and all, was made by Charles Le Brun for the royal family in 1684.

    Architect Louis Le Vau and sculptor Antoine Coysevox are buried within the church. Playwright Molière was married here, and this is also where he had his son baptized.

    Continue around and back out to the quai du Louvre. Turn left along the quay and on your right you'll see the Musée du Louvre. (You won't be going into the Louvre on this tour—see Walking Tour 11.) Go left across the:

2. **Pont des Arts,** a pedestrian bridge. By all means stop in the middle of it and enjoy the views in both directions (Notre-Dame is on your left as you cross).

    The bridge, which took its name from the Palais des Arts (the Louvre's original name), was built between 1801 and 1803 by engineers Louis-Alexandre de Cessart and Jacques Lacroix-Dillon as a pedestrian toll bridge (around

1848 the toll was *un sou*, or five centimes). The first cast-iron bridge in Paris, it was a pleasure to walk across then because of the wonderful gardens maintained on it. You're not standing on the original bridge, which was closed in 1970 because it was considered unsafe; it was reopened in 1984 after a two-year restoration project. The only major differences are that this new bridge is built of steel and has fewer, wider arches, making it more navigable for boats and barges. The original arches were only 56 feet wide.

Just as you come across the bridge, directly in front of you is the:

3. **Palais de l'Institut de France,** at 23 quai de Conti. Louis Le Vau is responsible for this masterwork, which he designed specifically to line up with the Cour Carrée across the pont des Arts. It took nearly 30 years to construct (1663–91) but was well worth the wait.

One of the academic groups that calls this palace home is the Académie Française, founded by Cardinal Richelieu in 1635 specifically to compile a dictionary of the French language. Membership cannot exceed 40 members (all male), and a new member can be elected only when a current member dies—the electee then must write the eulogy for his predecessor. Many people imagine members of the Académie have included France's best writers, yet that's not necessarily true—Baudelaire, Proust, and Flaubert were never admitted. In fact, it's rare for a great writer to be admitted at all.

In the same building is Mazarin's library. Cardinal Mazarin's money paid for the Palais de l'Institut de France, and his books are housed in the East Pavilion. Mazarin's private library became France's first public library when in 1643 he decided to open it to scholars initially once a week and eventually daily. Surprisingly, during the Revolution the collection was enlarged because any books confiscated from private collections or churches were added to Mazarin's already grand collection. It's next to impossible to gain access to the library unless you're a student or permanent scholar there, but do walk around and view the architectural design elements within the building, especially the magnificent staircase.

Next door (to the right if you're facing the river) is the:

4. **Hôtel de la Monnaie** (the Mint), at 11 quai de Conti. The quai de Conti, built between 1650 and 1760, was named for a family of princes that used to live in a building that occupied the spot on which the Mint now stands.

The Hôtel de la Monnaie, built between 1771 and 1777 in Louis XVI style, was architect J. D. Antoine's first important work; in fact, he lived in the building from the time it was completed until his death in 1801. In front rise enormous Ionic columns and six allegorical statues representing Prudence, Might, Justice, Trade, Peace, and Plenty. Thestatues were sculpted by Pigalle, Mouchy, and Lecomte.

From about 1878 to 1973 all French coins and medals were minted here. Currently only two active ateliers (workshops) produce commemorative coins, and you can go in and visit if you're interested in how it's all done. Guided tours explaining the minting process are offered.

Continue straight ahead on the quai de Conti. At no. 1 is the spot known as the:

5. **Curie intersection,** so-called because scientist Pierre Curie, husband of Marie Curie, was killed on this spot in 1906 by a runaway horse and carriage. This was also the location, at the corner of quai de Conti and rue Dauphine, of a favorite hangout of English writers: the original Café Anglais, the first Paris establishment to offer English-language newspapers and pamphlets.

Continue ahead onto the oldest quay in Paris, the:

6. **Quai des Grands-Augustins.** Built in 1313 under Philippe le Bel, the quay was named for one of France's largest monasteries.

Established in the 13th century by St. Louis, the St-Augustin friars settled in the area in 1293. In 1588 a papal reform divided the monastery into the Grands and Petits Augustins. The Petits Augustins were forced to leave, but the Grands Augustins remained. Unfortunately, the monastery and its gothic church were destroyed in 1797 during the Revolution.

At no. 51 note the:

7. **Restaurant Lapérouse,** dating from the end of the 18th century. The restaurant's history states that the beautiful women who dined here used to engrave their initials on the mirrors of the dining rooms with diamonds given to them by their admirers to immortalize their love. At the end of the 19th century, the tradition was still practiced; however, it was Dumas, Zola, Hugo, Maupassant, and many others from the world of art and literature who frequented the salons of Le Lapérouse. The restaurant is still considered one of the finest in Paris.

   When you reach the place St-Michel, to your right will be the:

8. **Pont St-Michel,** named for the no-longer-extant Palace Chapel (dedicated to the Archangel Michel) in which Philippe III was baptized in 1165.

   Look from the bridge to the right as you walk along the river, across the place St-Michel, and you'll see **Gabriel Davioud's fountain** depicting St. Michel slaying the dragon (1856–60). The fountain is 75 feet high and 15 feet wide.

   Continue along and you'll be headed onto the:

9. **Quai St-Michel.** Built between 1812 and 1816, the quai St-Michel supplanted some row houses that used to overhang the river. Matisse had his studio at **no. 19,** and it was from his window in 1914 that he painted several famous views of Notre-Dame, the petit-pont, and the top of the Sainte-Chapelle.

   Just a bit farther along the quai St-Michel, on the right, is the alley **rue du Chat-qui-Pêche** ("Street of the Fishing Cat"). There's nothing to see here, except for some garbage cans, but it does happen to be Paris's narrowest street and existed even before the quay was built. Legend has it that before the quay the Seine sometimes rose above its banks, flooding the cellars of the mansions that stood here, and an enterprising neighborhood cat took advantage of its good fortune and went fishing within the confines of the cellars—hence the street's name.

   Continue to the end of the quai St-Michel and you'll be at the:

10. **Petit-pont,** aptly named because at 131 feet it's the shortest bridge in Paris. Built under the direction of Bishop

Maurice de Sully in 1186, the petit-pont was destroyed 11 times by fire and flood; the present bridge has been standing since the 19th century. It's interesting to note that for hundreds of years the petit-pont was one of only two bridges that connected the Left Bank and the Right Bank.

After passing the petit-pont you'll be on the:

11. **Quai de Montebello,** built between 1811 and 1813 to commemorate Maréchal Lannes, duc de Montebello, who was killed in 1809 at Essling, Austria. At the beginning of the 19th century, the houses here were frequently occupied by washerwomen who worked on the *bateaux-lavoirs*.

While walking, look to your right for the current **Shakespeare & Company,** which carries on the legacy of Sylvia Beach's original (for more about Shakespeare & Company, see Walking Tour 4, Part II, stop 3). This cramped store stocks a wide selection of books in English and (up a very steep, very narrow flight of stairs) part of Beach's personal library. You're welcome to sit up there on the makeshift sofas and browse for as long as you like.

Turn right when exiting Shakespeare & Company and walk a few steps down on your right to **St-Julien-le-Pauvre**, one of the oldest churches in Paris. Next door to that is the square René-Viviani, in which there's a **false acacia** that's supposedly the oldest tree in Paris (you'll know it by the concrete blocks holding it up).

Just beyond the square René-Viviani is the:

12. **Pont au Double,** so named because of the double toll that was once imposed on those visiting the sick wards of the Hôtel Dieu, which occupied part of the bridge—one toll as they entered, another as they departed. As you can imagine, back then the river was a convenient spot in which to dump hospital waste. Thankfully, the hospital wards were gone by 1835. The present cast iron bridge dates from 1847.

Continue on the quai de Montebello, along which you'll see some of the:

13. *Bouquinistes,* or booksellers. Situated on the banks of the Seine, these green bookstalls represent one of Paris's oldest markets. (They were originally located on the pont Neuf but were evicted in 1650.) Here you'll find every-

The Quays of the Seine

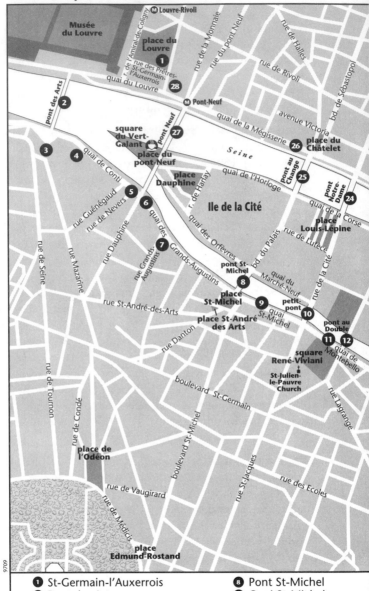

- **1** St-Germain-l'Auxerrois
- **2** Pont des Arts
- **3** Palais de l'Institut de France
- **4** Hôtel de la Monnaie
- **5** Curie intersection
- **6** Quai des Grandes-Augustins
- **7** Restaurant Lapérouse
- **8** Pont St-Michel
- **9** Quai St-Michel
- **10** Petit-pont
- **11** Quai de Montebello
- **12** Pont au Double
- **13** *Bouquinistes*
- **14** Quai de la Tournelle

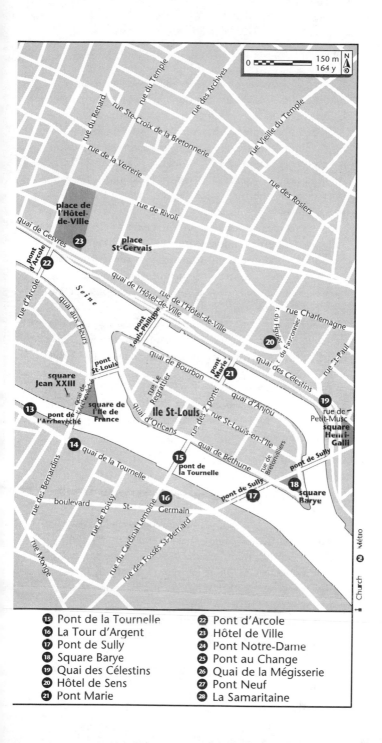

Map labels:

- rue du Renard
- rue du Temple
- rue Ste-Croix de la Bretonnerie
- rue des Archives
- rue Vieille du Temple
- rue de la Verrerie
- rue des Rosiers
- **place de l'Hôtel-de-Ville**
- rue de Rivoli
- quai de Gesvres
- **23**
- **place St-Gervais**
- **Pont d'Arcole**
- **22**
- rue d'Arcole
- *Seine*
- quai de l'Hôtel-de-Ville
- rue de l'Hôtel-de-Ville
- rue Charlemagne
- quai aux Fleurs
- **Pont Louis-Philippe**
- r. du Figuier
- r. de Fauconnier
- **20**
- quai de Bourbon
- **Pont Marie**
- rue St-Paul
- **pont St-Louis**
- **square Jean XXIII**
- rue Le Regrattier
- **21**
- quai des Célestins
- **13**
- **pont de l'Archevêché**
- **square de l'île de France**
- quai d'Orléans
- **Ile St-Louis**
- rue St-Louis-en-l'Ile
- rue des 2 ponts
- quai d'Anjou
- **19**
- rue de Petit-Musc
- **square Henri-Galli**
- **14**
- quai de la Tournelle
- quai de Béthune
- **15**
- **pont de la Tournelle**
- rue de Bretonvilliers
- **pont de Sully**
- rue des Bernardins
- boulevard St-Germain
- rue de Poissy
- **16**
- **pont de Sully**
- **17**
- **18**
- **square Barye**
- rue du Cardinal Lemoine
- rue des Fossés St-Bernard
- rue Monge
- ✝ Church
- **Ⓜ** Métro

Scale: 0 — 150 m / 164 y, N

Legend:

- **15** Pont de la Tournelle
- **16** La Tour d'Argent
- **17** Pont de Sully
- **18** Square Barye
- **19** Quai des Célestins
- **20** Hôtel de Sens
- **21** Pont Marie
- **22** Pont d'Arcole
- **23** Hôtel de Ville
- **24** Pont Notre-Dame
- **25** Pont au Change
- **26** Quai de la Mégisserie
- **27** Pont Neuf
- **28** La Samaritaine

thing from picture postcards to the works of Balzac. Most of the bouquinistes sell the things they like, which means they're generally very knowledgeable about their stock—some even have a specialty, although many shoppers lament that the bouquinistes are not what they used to be.

The first bouquinistes hawked their wares on foot, walking through the streets carrying their books in willow baskets suspended by straps around their necks. In 1578, at the beginning of Henri III's reign, the bouquinistes were ordered to find permanent places from which to sell their books; however, it wasn't until the beginning of the 17th century that they set up shop on the quays.

Even so, a host of famous writers and artists have haunted these stalls. Imagine wandering through and spying Balzac, Apollinaire, or Stendhal picking through the stalls. Hemingway was spotted here on many occasions—it was one of his favorite spots in the whole city.

Note that the bouquinistes usually open after 11am and close before 7pm, so if they're closed, try to stop back later in the day or on another day because the quay is a lot more active and exciting when they're open.

As you continue along you'll come to the **pont de l'Archevêché,** which provides one of the best, if not *the* best, view of Notre-Dame. After passing the pont de l'Archevêché you'll be on the:

14. **Quai de la Tournelle.** Built in 1554 as the quai des Bernaldins, in 1750 it became the quai de la Tournelle, named after the tower that was part of Philippe III's wall in the Middle Ages.

On your right at no. 47 is the **Musée de l'Assistance Publique** (Museum of Public Health and Welfare). Housed in a 17th-century mansion, the museum was once used as the central pharmacy for all Parisian hospitals. In 1934 the museum was established; it holds an interesting collection of old pharmaceutical containers and implements, including apothecary jars and surgical kits (Dupuytren's among them). Its displays of historical documents and various paintings will give you a good idea of how hospitals developed and were run—and will probably make you grateful for modern medicine.

Head along to the:

15. **Pont de la Tournelle,** which like many of the city's bridges was originally built of wood. When in 1656 it was washed away by the Seine's rising waters, a plan for a stone bridge that aligned with the pont Marie was implemented. It was later widened, and in 1928 the tower with the statue of Ste. Geneviève (Paris's patron saint) was erected.

On your right at 15 quai de la Tournelle, just past the bridge, is the famous restaurant:

16. **La Tour d'Argent.** Opened during the reign of Henri III and in 1582 named after the Conciergerie's tower on the Ile de la Cité across the river, La Tour d'Argent is still one of Paris's most prestigious restaurants. The wine cellars here are legendary, and so are the prices (a mere $120 for a slice of pâté de foie gras). The dining room, on the upper floor, offers a panoramic city view.

Since La Tour d'Argent has been open for 400 years, it's only fitting that a gastronomic museum is open on the ground floor.

Continue along the quai de la Tournelle to the:

17. **Pont de Sully.** The most interesting thing about the pont de Sully, named for Maximilien de Béthune, duc de Sully, is that it's actually two separate metal bridges resting on the tip of the Ile St-Louis, and it's the only one constructed in that way. *Note:* If you're a fan of modern sculpture, continue on a little farther to the **Musée de la Sculpture en Plein Air** (Open-Air Sculpture Museum) before crossing the pont de Sully.

On your right before you cross the pont de Sully is the **Institut du Monde Arabe**—one of few examples of modern architecture in Paris. When you reach the other side of the first bridge, note the small park on your right, called the:

18. **Square Barye,** named for Antoine-Louis Barye (1796–1875), best known for his animal sculptures. He acquired most of his knowledge of animals while employed by a goldsmith who required him to make models of animals at the Jardin des Plantes between 1823 and 1831. Barye

particularly enjoyed sculpting animals in an aggressive, violent, or tense posture—a tradition of the Romantic movement.

Go left after crossing the second bridge, around the square Henri-Galli, and onto the:

19. **Quai des Célestins,** built in the late 14th century under Charles V. Its original name was the quai des Ourmetiaux; it was renamed in 1868 for the Célestin convent destroyed during the Revolution.

    On the corner of rue du Petit-Musc is the **Ecole Massillon** (formerly the Hôtel Fieubet), an extraordinary building guarded by the first sphinxes ever seen in Paris and decorated with other sculptural accents, including fruit andfloral garlands. A bit farther on is **no. 4**, where Antoine-Louis Barye died in 1875.

    Continue walking along the quai des Célestins. At rue St-Paul is an interesting **garden shop** that sells outdoor sculpture and furniture, among other things. Stop in and take a look.

    When you get to rue du Fauconnier, go right and head up to rue du Figuier. Go left to no. 1, the:

20. **Hôtel de Sens.** With its gothic portal, framed by two turrets, this is a prime example of medieval Parisian civic architecture. Built between 1474 and 1475 as a "fortified mansion," it's one of the oldest structures in the city. Originally used as a stronghold for La Ligue (a group that unified the Catholics against the Calvinists), then owned by the bishops of Sens, it was later rented to art students and jam makers, who practically destroyed the interior. In 1916 the city took it over, and finally in 1936, after much controversy, a restoration project was begun that took 26 years to complete. Presently the Hôtel de Sens houses the Bibliothèque Forney. Open Tuesday through Saturday, the library specializes in the fine arts, including decorative arts, crafts, and architecture. Exhibitions featuring the library's collection are held frequently. Even if you're not interested in the books, enter the gate into the courtyard and have a look at the ornate stone decoration.

    Go back the way you came to the quai des Célestins. Turn right and walk past the:

21. **Pont Marie,** a humpback bridge with five arches. Originally the bridge had some houses built along its sides, but in 1658 two of the arches collapsed and 22 houses disappeared into the river with them. Since 1788 there have been very few changes to the bridge.

    After you pass the pont Marie you'll be on the quai de l'Hôtel-de-Ville. Continue past the pont Louis-Philippe and on your left note the:

22. **Pont d'Arcole,** named for a young man who was killed during an 1830 protest outside the Hôtel de Ville (see below). As he was dying he begged, "Remember that my name is d'Arcole." Somebody remembered, but it wasn't until 68 years later that the bridge was renamed. Built as a pedestrian suspension toll bridge in 1828, it was replaced by an iron footbridge in 1954.

    To your right is the place de l'Hôtel-de-Ville. Head into the place de l'Hôtel-de-Ville and you'll be in front of the:

23. **Hôtel de Ville,** Paris's grand city hall. The place de l'Hôtel-de-Ville (originally place de Grève) was a prime site for many of the executions carried out from 1313 to 1830. Catherine de Médicis, apparently not satisfied with the thousands already killed in the St. Bartholomew's Day Massacre, had two Huguenot leaders hanged here. This was also the place where Henry IV's murderer, Ravaillac, was executed (he was quartered) and where witches were burned alive. Throughout history, this building has seen all kinds of celebrations, rebellions, and strikes.

    After coming back out of the Hôtel de Ville, continue around the quays on quai de Gesvres (which used to be the place where butchers came to slaughter their animals) along to the:

24. **Pont Notre-Dame,** which was once Paris's most fashionable bridge. There were two reasons for this: It was here that Paris made its first attempt at a numbering system and, as a result, all the bridge houses were stylishly numbered in gold. Also, this was the royal entryway into Paris.

    Continue along to the:

25. **Pont au Change,** so named because it was rebuilt in 1141 by the city's moneychangers and goldsmiths, at the orders

of Louis VII. It was originally known as the King's Bridge because it was the royal route to Notre-Dame, and when the king crossed the bridge the bird sellers from the nearby bird-and-flower market would release thousands of birds to honor his presence.

At the pont au Change the quai de Gesvres turns into the:

26. **Quai de la Mégisserie.** For 500 years, city tanners came here to cure their leather. There are still bird-and-flower markets here, and as you walk you can check out the various types of birds, from chickens to doves, and the garden and flower shops—perhaps you'd like to purchase some tulip bulbs direct from Holland.

At the end of the quai de la Mégisserie you'll come to the:

27. **Pont Neuf,** the oldest (even though its name means "New Bridge") and most famous bridge in Paris. Henri III laid the first stone on May 31, 1578, yet was long gone by the time it was finished and officially opened by Henri IV 29 years later. It was the first stone bridge built that wasn't lined with houses. With a total of 12 arches, the pont Neuf is actually two bridges (they don't quite line up)—one stretching from the Right Bank to the Ile de la Cité, the other stretching from the Left Bank to the island. Originally the pont Neuf served as a lively social center where Parisians went to do their banking, be entertained by jokers and street performers, and even have their teeth pulled.

The tour is almost over and you're probably ready for a little refreshment and relaxation.

Take a Break   Go left to the middle of the pont Neuf and on your left will be the **Taverne Henri IV,** 13 place du pont-Neuf, a 17th-century building housing one of Paris's most famous wine bars. Named after the statue of Henri IV you can see in the middle of the pont Neuf, this place serves bistro-style food at moderate prices, as well as a full selection of wines.

From the tavern, go back across the bridge to the quai de la Mégisserie. Then turn left and proceed to:

28. **La Samaritaine,** the biggest department store in Paris. It was named after the pont Neuf water pump that used to carry water to the Jardin des Tuileries (the pump was named and decorated in honor of the Samaritan woman who offered Jesus a drink of water). La Samaritaine has everything and anything—from hats to belts and kitchenware to bath accessories.

The architectural history of the buildings comprising the store spans from 1900 to 1930, but the real attraction in the glass- and iron-front main store is the art nouveau ironwork staircase. From the ninth floor you'll get a spectacular panoramic view of the city.

When you've finished shopping, leave the department store and either go right back to where this tour started or head over the pont Neuf and begin the next walking tour, an exploration of the Seine islands.

ILE DE LA CITÉ &
ILE ST-LOUIS

Start: Métro station at the pont Neuf.

Finish: Square Barye.

Time: About three hours.

Best Time: Any time during the day.

As you begin your walk on the Ile de la Cité, you'll be following in the footsteps of the men and women responsible for the city's beginnings. This is where the Romans put down their roots, the place out of which the wonderful city of Paris exploded.

On the Ile de la Cité the spires of two of the world's most incredible churches—the Sainte-Chapelle and Notre-Dame—soar to the sky. You can visit yesterday's royal prisons and today's courts of law, walk through a huge flower-and-bird market, and stand on the spot marking the very center of Paris.

As you cross from Ile de la Cité to Ile St-Louis, you'll pass by Notre-Dame's flying buttresses and be able to visit a moving monument to the victims of the Holocaust.

The Ile St-Louis will transport you back to a time when Paris was far more quiet and residential. This walk will take you by some of Paris's most sought after real estate, and you'll come across current residents who rarely even step off the island. On the Ile St-Louis are the places where Baudelaire's hashish club met, where Chopin played, and where James Jones once lived.

When you finish this tour you should feel as if you've gotten a taste of the way Paris once was and be thankful that on these small islands a good deal of the past still remains intact.

• • • • • • • • • • • • • • • •

From the Métro station, walk about halfway out on the pont Neuf. Go left down the stairs behind the statue of Henri IV (erected by Louis XVIII using bronze melted down from a statue of Napoléon that once stood atop the column in the place Vendôme) into the:

1. **Square du Vert-Galant.** *Vert Galant,* or "Gay Blade," was Henri IV's nickname. This is a great place to sit and have a picnic—you'll be just about as close to the river as you can get without actually being in it. A crusty baguette, some Brie or other cheese, a few tidbits from a charcuterie, and a bottle of wine in this shady, secluded park—what could be better? On summer weekend afternoons crowds can fill the park, but for the most part you'll find enough privacy. Absorb the view of the Louvre and the Hôtel de la Monnaie (see Walking Tour 1, stop 4, for more information about the latter). Tourist boats *(vedettes)* that'll take you on a trip along the Seine also depart from here.

Come back up the stairs and cross the pont Neuf. Going between the buildings will bring you to the:

2. **Place Dauphine,** which many believe to be Paris's most quaint square. Originally the Ile de la Cité was three separate islands. When those islands were joined in 1607, the result was the place Dauphine. Laid out by Henri IV, it was named for the dauphin who later became Louis XIII. Have a little walk around the square—you won't find a quieter one in all the city. Note that Ludovic Halévy, the French author who was the librettist of *Carmen,* died at **no. 26** in 1908. Imagine yourself here in 1660, when Louis XIV and

his queen, Marie-Thérèse, visited the Ile de la Cité to find a gateway made entirely of sugar placed in the place Dauphine, along with a carousel, specifically to honor their visit.

Another significant event that occurred here was in 1728, when Jean-Baptiste-Siméon Chardin (1699–1779), one of the greatest French masters of the still life, first showed *La Raie* (*The Skate,* now at the Louvre—see Walking Tour 11, Part II, stop 10).

Ahead of you is the Palais de Justice. Turn left on rue de Harlay and walk to the quai de l'Horloge, then go right. Look up at the various towers on the side of the:

3. **Palais de Justice and the Conciergerie,** on the right side of the street as you walk.

The Palais de Justice began as the Palais de la Cité, the palace for France's medieval kings. Philippe III was born here, and Philippe le Bel enlarged it. By the mid-14th century, the king was spending less time here and more at the Louvre; the move was made permanent when in 1358 Charles V's entire staff was killed by a mob led by Etienne Marcel. After Charles fled, the palace was used as the royal prison and court. In 1618 and 1776 the buildings were ravaged by fire; the only remaining medieval structure is the Sainte-Chapelle (see below).

The first tower on your right is the **Tour de Bonbec,** known as the "babbler" because the torture inflicted here was so intense. Prisoners had their legs squeezed between two planks or ropes tied progressively tighter around different parts of their bodies until they cut into the skin. The oldest form of torture used here was a trap door that opened into a pit of razor-sharp spikes.

The second tower, the **Tour d'Argent,** is where the crown jewels were stored at one time. And the third tower, the **Tour de César,** is where Ravaillac, Henry IV's assassin, was held—and presumably tortured—while awaiting execution.

This building's prisons, now called the Conciergerie, were used as holding cells for the Revolution's tribunals. Marie Antoinette was held here before her execution; others imprisoned here prior to execution included Robespierre and Danton. The entrance to the Conciergerie, where you can see the old prisons, is at 1 quai de l'Horloge.

On the corner of the quai de l'Horloge and boulevard du Palais is the **Tour de l'Horloge,** the site of Paris's first public clock. (The nonworking one you see today is not the original.) The Tour de l'Horloge is also the tower from which the bells sounded signaling the St. Bartholomew's Day Massacre. At the alarm, Catholics ran through the streets, killing several thousand sleeping Protestants.

Go right at the corner to the entrance of the Palais de Justice—the site of the present-day courts of law. Turn right into the **cour du Mai** (May Courtyard), named for the trees from the royal forest that were planted here (they're long gone). This is the exact spot where such prisoners as Marie Antoinette and Robespierre had to wait before being led to the place de la Révolution (now place de la Concorde) for their executions. Visitors are allowed to enter the present courtrooms.

To your left you'll see the:

4. **Sainte-Chapelle.** This Holy Chapel is the oldest part of the Palais de Justice complex and was built by St. Louis to house two significant religious artifacts—a piece of the cross on which Christ was crucified and the Crown of Thorns (both have been moved to Notre-Dame and are on view only on Good Friday). It's said that to acquire these artifacts St. Louis paid nearly triple the amount required for the entire church's construction. Most of what you see today doesn't date from the church's completion over 700 years ago (1248), but tombstones set in the floor do date from the 14th and 15th centuries; much of the sculptures, spire, doors, and paintings are from the 19th century.

However, the real reason to visit the Sainte-Chapelle (well worth standing in the long line that always forms in front) is to see the 15 astonishing 50-foot-high by 14-foot-wide stained-glass windows. About half the glass in these windows dates to the 13th century; the rest is an extremely careful 19th-century restoration. The windows actually contain 1,134 stunning scenes that illustrate the Bible from Genesis to the crucifixion. To "read" them chronologically would likely take several years, but if you do make the attempt, start to the left of the entrance and move clockwise around the church, reading each window from the bottom to the top. Some of the windows show the construction of the church, and the great Rose Window is meant to depict the Apocalypse.

As you come out of the Sainte-Chapelle, cross boulevard du Palais diagonally to your left. You'll be at rue de Lutèce, where you should turn right and walk to the:

5. **Cité Métro station,** on your left. This original art nouveau dragonfly "Métropolitain" station, which looks sort of like the entrance to the Bat Cave, dates back to 1900. Designed by Hector Guimard (1867–1942), the plantlike cast-iron forms are considered to be Guimard's most inspired works. There are only a few originals left.

Located just beyond the Métro station is the:

6. **Place Louis-Lépine,** where on Monday through Saturday from 8am to 6pm a flower market is held. There are very few flower markets left in Paris where you'll find such a wide variety of species. On Sunday from 8am to 7pm the flower market becomes a bird market, carrying on the long tradition of bird sellers in Paris. Take a leisurely stroll through here, whether it's bird day or flower day.

After you've gone through the market, you'll end up on rue de la Cité. Turn right and on your left will be the:

7. **Hôtel Dieu.** Built by Diet from 1866 to 1878 in neo-Florentine style, the Hôtel Dieu is the main hospital for central Paris. This site had been previously occupied by several buildings. The original 12th-century Hôtel Dieu was an entirely different structure, running the entire width of the island, touching both banks of the river. In the 15th century, Paris's first cabaret—La Pomme de Pin—opened here. Then an orphanage occupied the location, until it was demolished to make way for the present Hôtel Dieu.

As you continue along, on your right you'll see the:

8. **Préfecture de Police.** Here in the Palais de la Cité's old barracks the police joined the resistance against the Nazis in 1944 by twice locking themselves inside—first on August 19, then on August 26. Almost 300 were killed.

When you get to the corner, go left into another square and on your right will be the entrance of the:

9. **Crypte du Parvis-Notre-Dame.** If you're interested in archaeology, visit the excavations of what used to be the Ile de la Cité's central square (discovered during excavations for an underground parking lot), which include Roman walls dating from approximately A.D. 300.

    To help you visualize the kinds of buildings that once stood here, there are scale models showing how Paris grew from a small settlement to a Roman city.

    Emerge from the Crypte and head toward Notre-Dame. You are in the:

10. **Place du Parvis-Notre-Dame.** To your right is a statue of Charlemagne that dates from approximately 1882.

    In 1768 it was announced that a spot at the far end of the place du Parvis, in front of Notre-Dame, would be the starting point of all the national highways connecting Paris to other points in France. It's since been called *kilomètre zéro*. You're literally standing at the center of Paris.

    Continue through the square up to the:

11. **Cathédrale Notre-Dame.** In 1160, Maurice de Sully, then the bishop of Paris, had an idea to build one immense, incredible church to replace two—old Notre-Dame and St-Etienne. Three years later work began on the cathedral you see today, which took almost 200 years to complete; construction ended in 1359.

    Unfortunately, few of the original interior furnishings remain because Notre-Dame was badly damaged and stripped of its valuables during the Revolution. Some time during this period the stained-glass windows were replaced with clear glass and the walls whitewashed. It wasn't until the 1830s that anyone thought about restoring the cathedral. Victor Hugo's *The Hunchback of Notre-Dame* (1831) played a large role in generating public interest in the church and, finally, stimulating Louis-Philippe to order a restoration project in 1844. (You'll notice that Notre-Dame's exterior is again being cleaned and restored.)

    Inside, you can't miss the rose windows (some stained glass inside was salvaged and dates from the 13th century). Look for the Coustou and Coysevox sculptures in the choir; Robert de Cotte's choir stalls (on the backs of which are bas-reliefs including scenes depicting the Virgin Mary's

Ile de la Cité & Ile St-Louis

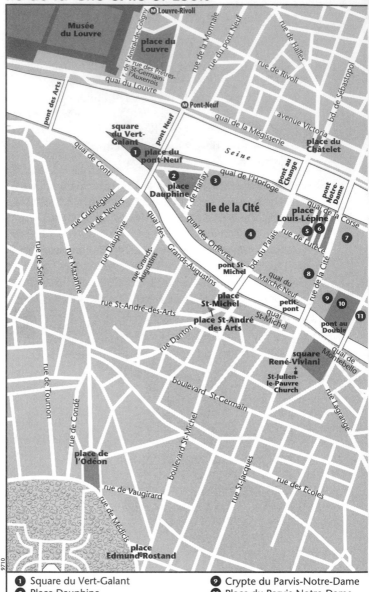

1. Square du Vert-Galant
2. Place Dauphine
3. Palais de Justice and the Conciergerie
4. Sainte-Chapelle
5. Cité Métro station
6. Place Louis-Lépine
7. Hôtel Dieu
8. Préfecture de Police
9. Crypte du Parvis-Notre-Dame
10. Place du Parvis-Notre-Dame
11. Cathédrale Notre-Dame
12. Mémorial des Martyrs Français de la Déportation de 1945
13. Nos. 18–20 quai d'Orléans
14. No. 12 quai d'Orléans
15. No. 10 quai d'Orléans

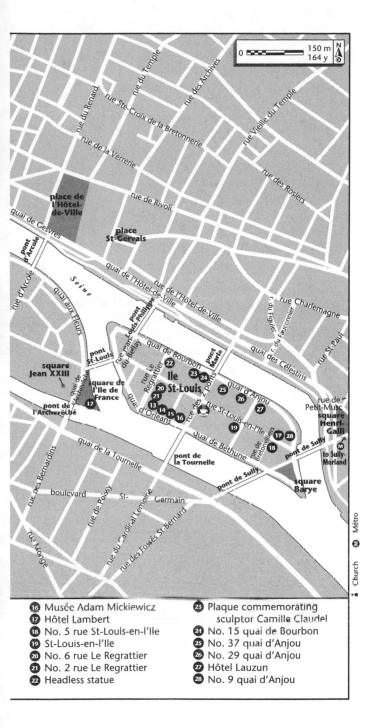

16 Musée Adam Mickiewicz

17 Hôtel Lambert

18 No. 5 rue St-Louis-en-l'Ile

19 St-Louis-en-l'Ile

20 No. 6 rue Le Regrattier

21 No. 2 rue Le Regrattier

22 Headless statue

23 Plaque commemorating sculptor Camille Claudel

24 No. 15 quai de Bourbon

25 No. 37 quai d'Anjou

26 No. 29 quai d'Anjou

27 Hôtel Lauzun

28 No. 9 quai d'Anjou

† Church   Ⓜ Métro

life); and Cliquot's organ (1730). In the Treasury of Notre-Dame the gold, enamel, and jeweled relics brought back from the Crusades by St. Louis can be viewed for a small fee. You should also go upstairs and take in Paris from aloft—the view is unparalleled.

Throughout the ages Notre-Dame has served as Paris's central meeting place. Wonderfully extravagant banquets were often held inside; the church's doors were always open to weary travelers who needed a place to stay. Philippe le Bel once even rode into the church on horseback, and it was here in 1431 that Henri VI was crowned king. In 1779, Louis XIV dowered 100 young women and married them off here en masse. In 1793, during a particularly impious period, a belly dancer was placed on the high altar and the saints in the niches were replaced by statues of the likes of Voltaire and Rousseau. And, of course, it was here in 1804 that Napoléon Bonaparte, usurping the role of Pope Pius VII, lifted the imperial crown from the altar and crowned himself emperor and Joséphine empress.

The sheer beauty and force of the building, with its sculpture-encrusted facade, gargoyles, and flying buttresses (erected in the 14th century), have brought many a wayward Catholic back to his or her religion. The sense of awe felt all over the world for this great gothic work of art crosses all religious lines.

Come back out of Notre-Dame and, facing away from the cathedral, turn left, then pass several street portraitists and caricaturists. Go left through the gate into the square Jean XXIII and around to the back of the cathedral, where you can view the flying buttresses up close. At the end of the square Jean XXIII is the quai de l'Archevêché (you'll know it from the rows of tour buses parked along it). Cross the quai de l'Archevêché and head into the square de l'Ile de France, a park on the tip of the Ile de la Cité. Stroll through the park to the:

12. **Mémorial des Martyrs Français de la Déportation de 1945.** To reach the memorial, descend the stairs (you'll see the iron spikes that block the opening at the very tip of the island), then turn left at the bottom and pass through the narrow opening. Inside is an eternal flame dedicated to

the 200,000 French who died in Nazi concentration camps during World War II.

Designed by G. H. Pingusson in 1962, the memorial is constructed around 200,000 quartz pebbles, symbolic because in the Jewish religion it's traditional to place a stone or pebble on a grave. There's one pebble for each person who died. Also inside are several other small tombs holding bits of soil from each of the concentration camps.

You won't have to do too much meditating in here to experience the intended effect: The iron spikes and bars coupled with the red scrawl on the walls and the small rooms give you the feeling that you're imprisoned. It's one of the city's most stirring monuments.

When you've finished paying your respects, come back up to the park and, for variety, go up the stairs on the other side (the ones you didn't descend). Go through the gate, exiting the small park, and cross the pont St-Louis onto the Ile St-Louis. After crossing the bridge, go right on the quai d'Orléans to:

13. **Nos. 18–20 quai d'Orléans,** on the left side. Walter Lippmann (1889–1974) lived here with his wife for a short time in 1938. A journalist/editor who worked for *The New Republic, The Washington Post,* and New York *Herald Tribune,* Lippmann was a 1958 Pulitzer Prize recipient.

Continue on to:

14. **No. 12 quai d'Orléans,** where Harry and Caresse Crosby (Caresse's real name was Mary Phelps Jacob—Caresse was a nickname) spent the summer of 1923. The Crosbys were the founders of Black Sun Press, and they spent a good deal of time and money publishing their own poems as well as books of letters by well-known writers (such as Proust, Henry James, and D. H. Lawrence). The Crosbys came to Paris in hopes of joining the fun other expatriates were reportedly having, and they enjoyed themselves more than they ever thought possible. The publishing company was no more than a way for them to gain access to Paris's literary and artistic circles.

While living here Harry kept a rowboat tied up on the Seine near his apartment building so he could row across the river and then walk to work.

Next door is:

15. **No. 10 quai d'Orléans,** where James Jones lived from
1958 to 1975. Jones, author of *From Here to Eternity* (1951),
hosted a constant parade of famous people: Mary McCarthy,
James Baldwin, Sylvia Beach, the ever-present-for-a-free-
drink-or-meal Henry Miller, Man Ray, Gene Kelly, Arthur
Miller, Art Buchwald, Alice B. Toklas, and Thornton Wilder,
to name a few. It's said that after *From Here to Eternity*'s
publication Jones carried around a bunch of envelopes, each
containing 67 cents. Every time he found out that a friend
had purchased a copy of his book he'd give him or her an
envelope: "That's my royalty on each copy," he'd explain. "I
don't want to make money on my friends."

At no. 6 quai d'Orléans is the main attraction on this
quay, the:

16. **Musée Adam Mickiewicz,** dedicated to the exiled poet
known as the "Byron of Poland." The second-floor museum houses mementos as well as a library. On the ground
floor is an entire room dedicated to Chopin—it even holds
his old armchair. The museum has very limited hours (2 to
6pm on Thursday only) and is closed for two weeks during
Christmas and Easter, but if you happen to get here when
it's open, you should definitely go in.

Continue straight onto the quai de Béthune. At **no. 24**
is the apartment building in which Helena Rubinstein
resided while in Paris. Go left on rue Bretonvilliers and
under the archway to rue St-Louis-en-l'Ile. Go right to
no. 2 rue St-Louis-en-l'Ile, which is the:

17. **Hôtel Lambert.** This 17th-century residence was Louis
Le Vau's masterpiece, built in 1645 for Nicolas Lambert de
Thorigny, president of the Chambre des Comptes. Then
for a century this *hôtel particulier* (private mansion) was the
home of Poland's royal family, the Czartoryskis, who were
lucky enough to have entertained Chopin (or, rather, were
lucky enough to have been entertained by him).

At one time, Voltaire was a resident of the Hôtel Lambert with his mistress, Emilie de Breteuil, marquise de
Châtelet. They had such raucous fights that they were talked
about all over Europe. Unfortunately, this magnificent home
is rarely open to the public.

Across the street at:

18. **No. 5 rue St-Louis-en-l'Ile** lived literary agent William Aspenwall Bradley, who represented Katherine Anne Porter, Edith Wharton, Gertrude Stein, and John Dos Passos. He and Alfred Knopf encouraged Sylvia Beach to write her memoirs, though, incredibly, omitting any mention of James Joyce, the French, and Gertrude Stein. It wasn't until many years later that Beach wrote her memoirs, naturally discussing all her Paris friends.

    Retrace your steps, crossing rue Bretonvilliers. At no. 19 bis rue St-Louis-en-l'Ile is the church:

19. **St-Louis-en-l'Ile.** Built between 1664 and 1726 in Jesuit Baroque style, according to Louis Le Vau's original designs, this church has been and still is the site of many Parisian weddings. Inside you'll find a wonderful glazed terra-cotta statue of St. Louis, as well as a 1926 plaque reading, "In grateful memory of St. Louis in whose honor the city of St. Louis, Missouri, USA, is named." The interior decoration is stunning. Note the iron clock at the church entrance as well as the iron spire, dating from 1765.

    Take a Break On your left at no. 31 rue St-Louis-en-l'Ile is **Berthillon,** considered the best ice cream and sorbet parlor in all of Europe. The ice cream flavors range from standard chocolate and vanilla to Grand Marnier and mocha; the sorbets range from lime to rhubarb.

    Note: Berthillon is closed from late July to early September (which is a testament to how good the product here is:

Louis Le Vau

Louis Le Vau (1612–70) was the chief architect on some of the most significant building projects commissioned by Louis XIV. He made the Ile St-Louis his home, and on it he built the Hôtel Lambert and the Hôtel Lauzun. In 1655 he became the head architect for the Louvre, then went on to design the palace at Versailles (in collaboration with Charles Le Brun).

Imagine an ice cream business that can support itself without the summer rush!).

Continue along and when you get to rue Le Regrattier walk to:

20. **No. 6 rue Le Regrattier,** where Baudelaire's mistress, Jeanne Duval (the "Black Venus"), lived.

Farther down the street is:

21. **No. 2 rue Le Regrattier,** where poet Nancy Cunard lived. Cunard was the daughter of Lady Cunard, who was described by Janet Flanner (writing under her famous pen name, Genêt) as "one of London's greatest American hostesses." She assembled a marvelous collection of African art pieces and, in 1929, set up Hours Press to publish new limited editions (signed by the authors) on an 18th-century Belgian handpress.

When you get to the end of rue Le Regrattier you'll be back on the quai d'Orléans. Turn right. This walk along the quay affords a spectacular view of the back of Notre-Dame.

Follow the quai d'Orléans to rue Jean-du-Bellay. Turn right on rue Jean-du-Bellay to the quai de Bourbon. Then go right on the quai de Bourbon to the intersection of rue Le Regrattier and the quai de Bourbon, where you'll see the:

22. **Headless statue** that gave rue Le Regrattier its original name: "rue de la Femme Sans Teste"—"street of the Headless Woman." In actuality, the statue is thought not to be of a woman at all but of St. Nicolas, the patron saint of boatmen.

At no. 19 you'll see:

23. **A plaque commemorating sculptor Camille Claudel,** who from 1899 to 1913 lived and worked in the ground-floor apartment that faces the courtyard.

Unfortunately, Claudel is one of those very talented woman artists who was unknown for many years. Recently, with the help of the film *Camille Claudel* (in French with English subtitles), she's been rediscovered—not just because she was the student and lover of Auguste Rodin (many years her senior) but also because she was an incredible sculptor in her own right. Some of her work—including my favorite, *La Petite châtelaine*—is on display at (ironically) the Musée Rodin. The Musée d'Orsay has a couple of pieces, including a remarkable sculpture of an old woman, *Clotho*. Regrettably, Claudel destroyed much of her own work during a mental breakdown caused by her breakup with Rodin and her paranoia that he was trying to sabotage her career. Claudel was able to spend only half her life sculpting—the other half was spent in an asylum where, sadly, she did no sculpting and eventually died.

Just a couple of doors down is:

24. **No. 15 quai de Bourbon,** where French painter/writer Emile Bernard (1868–1941) lived. A contemporary of van Gogh and Toulouse-Lautrec, he and Louis Anguetin developed the technique of *cloisonnism*, an emulation on canvas of cloisonné enamel. From 1888 to 1891 he worked closely with Gauguin at Pont Avon and in Paris, but shortly thereafter his writing took precedence.

Continue along the quai de Bourbon onto the quai d'Anjou, where:

25. **No. 37 quai d'Anjou** was home to John Dos Passos in 1921, about the time his novel *Three Soldiers* was published. Popular with the French, Dos Passos was considered the most "American" of the expatriates living in Paris at that time.

A few buildings down is **no. 33,** the former location of Le Rendezvous des Mariners, a favorite dining spot of Dos Passos. He often met Hemingway here for meals.

Still farther along is:

26. **No. 29 quai d'Anjou,** where in 1922 William Bird established Three Mountains Press. Hemingway met Bird that year at the Genoa Economic Conference, where they were working as journalists, and not long after Bird suggested that Hemingway do some writing for him. In 1924 he was able to publish Hemingway's experimental work. Ezra Pound worked as Bird's editor, and in 1923 Pound's was the first title published by Three Mountains.

Unfortunately, the books Bird published were not profitable, and the whole operation, despite its beautiful hand-built 17th-century printing press, folded by 1929.

Continue ahead to no. 17 quai d'Anjou, the:

27. **Hôtel Lauzun,** another Louis Le Vau masterpiece. The exterior of this *hôtel particulier* doesn't look like much, but the interior is a splendid amalgamation of the plans of a group of architects, including Le Vau, Le Brun, Lepautre, and Sebastien Bourdon. The painted ceilings and intricately carved wood paneling *(boiserie)* have been preserved, along with some statues, tapestries, and paintings. *Note:* To visit the interior you must make arrangements well in advance.

The mansion was built from 1656 to 1657 for Charles Gruyn des Bordes. In 1682 it was sold to the duc de Lauzun, who resided here for only three years. Then it had several other famous tenants, among them Baudelaire and Théophile Gautier. In fact, Baudelaire and his hashish club did the research for *Les Paradis artificiels* (loosely translated, "drug-induced states of fantasy") here in 1834.

Lauzun was the brother-in-law of Louis de Rouvroy, duc de St-Simon, who in his famous diary described Lauzun as the kind of person who was never happy, was ill-tempered, and enjoyed spending most of his time alone. However, history shows that he had a mischievous side as well: Once he hid under a bed in which Louis XIV and Madame de Montespan were making love and later reported to her exactly what he'd heard. (One wonders, however, how Lauzun fit under the bed at all since he was known to have had a gluttonous appetite.) Other notable inhabitants have included Rainer Maria Rilke and Richard Wagner.

Be sure to note the wrought-iron balcony and the fish pipes on the exterior facade.

Just a little farther down the quay is:

28. **No. 9 quai d'Anjou,** where sculptor/painter/caricaturist Honoré Daumier once lived. (See Walking Tour 10, stop 29, for more about Daumier.)

As you follow the quay to the end, you'll be at the pont de Sully. Turn right into the square Barye for a brief rest before heading out to continue your explorations. The square Barye was once part of the terraced gardens of the duc de Bretonvilliers.

To reach the Métro, cross the pont de Sully to the Right Bank and head for the Sully-Morland station.

MONTPARNASSE

Start: Gare Montparnasse.

Finish: Intersection of boulevard Raspail and boulevard Edgar-Quinet.

Time: Three to four hours.

Best Time: Between 10am and 4pm on Tuesday through Sunday, when the Musée Bourdelle is open.

riginally nicknamed Mount Parnassus by a group of students, the "mount" was flattened when the boulevard du Montparnasse was laid out. Not long after, with the openings of cafés and cabarets, the boulevard began to grow.

By the 1920s Montparnasse had become the Left Bank home of the Lost Generation. Stein, Hemingway, Duncan, and many other expatriates gathered in this bohemian paradise to drink, philosophize, and dance. They mixed and mingled with Simone de Beauvoir and Jean-Paul Sartre, as well as with Russian political exiles like Trotsky and Stravinsky.

Following a recent massive redevelopment project, Montparnasse has lost a lot of its old-world charm; however, if you can overlook the neon, movie theaters, and modern night-clubs you should be able to imagine what it was like for

Modigliani and Malvina Hoffman to live and work here. Perhaps you can conjure the Montparnasse of the 1920s and see Hemingway under a lilac bush at La Closerie des Lilas with his friend John Dos Passos or see James Joyce in his favorite restaurant singing an old Irish ballad with his friends.

• • • • • • • • • • • • • • • • •

Begin your tour in the:

1. **Gare Montparnasse.** Opened in 1974, this rail station is the Paris terminal serving Brittany, Mayenne, and Basse-Normandie. Inside is the St-Bernard chapel, which was made from a railway sleeper car.

   Come out of the station into the place R. Dautry and you'll be facing the:

2. **Tour Montparnasse,** a 688-foot-high tower dwarfing the surrounding buildings as it's the highest structure around. Even though it was built in a curved shape to "soften" its otherwise harsh architecture, many consider it an eyesore. Saul Bellow described it as "something that had strayed away from Chicago and had come to rest on a Parisian street corner." On the 56th floor is an observatory with a bar and restaurant, and on a clear day you can see for approximately 30 miles.

   Go left out of the plaza and cross boulevard de Vaugirard onto avenue du Maine. Follow avenue du Maine and turn left onto rue Antoine-Bourdelle. Continue to the:

3. **Musée Bourdelle,** on the right side of the street. Considered a small treasure by avid art lovers, Musée Bourdelle is actually the former home, garden, and working studio of sculptor Emile-Antoine Bourdelle (1861–1929).

   Born in Montauban, Bourdelle learned sculpting by helping out in the workshop of his cabinetmaker father. In 1876 he studied at Toulouse's Ecole des Beaux-Arts and won a scholarship to attend Paris's Ecole des Beaux-Arts in 1884. Not long afterward he became Rodin's head assistant, but his work was frequently ignored because it was overshadowed by that of the "Master." Later he became a teacher and started an atelier (studio) that became a school known as La Grande Chaumière.

In 1912 Bourdelle did the sculptures of Isadora Duncan on the facade of the Théâtre des Champs-Elysées, and they're among his finest work. Some of the most interesting pieces in the museum are his busts of Rodin and numerous portraits and studies of Beethoven.

Go back out to rue Antoine-Bourdelle, turn left to avenue du Maine, then turn left. As you walk along avenue du Maine, notice the specialty-food shop **Landes et Gascogne** on your left—you can purchase some interesting and unique items here. Cross avenue du Maine and turn right on rue d'Alençon. Look to your right for **Kitchen Bazaar,** a shop whose window displays a wonderful selection of old-fashioned toasters (newly manufactured). When you reach boulevard du Montparnasse, turn right and look across the street for:

4. **No. 60 bd. du Montparnasse,** where Alexander Calder (1898–1976), the American sculptor/painter who invented the mobile, stayed for several months in 1926. According to Calder, his interest in art began in 1922 as a result of his study of mechanical engineering, rather than through the work of his father and grandfather, both sculptors.

   In 1923, Calder attended the Art Students League in New York City, where he used to sit outside and make rapid drawings of passersby. This drawing method helped develop his skill at showing movement with one unbroken line. Wire sculptures were a logical next step, and in 1927 he began making toys for the Gould Manufacturing Company. Calder's abstract works became extremely popular in both the United States and Paris, and he has since been acknowledged as a pioneer in the field of kinetic art.

   As you continue walking, take a quick peek into the spectacular art nouveau interior of the **Bistro de la Gare**. Soon you'll come to the:

5. **Place du 18 Juin 1940,** named for the date on which Charles de Gaulle ordered continuing resistance against the Nazis. James Joyce's favorite eatery, Restaurant Trianon, was located at no. 5 place du 18 Juin 1940. One of his most frequent dinner companions was John Dos Passos.

   As you head back along boulevard du Montparnasse, look on your left for:

6. **No. 81 bd. du Montparnasse,** the former atelier of Carolus-Duran. He opened a school here in 1872 to teach painting, not the basics of anatomy and life drawing. Since it departed from traditional art instruction, his school was thought of as "cutting edge," but if artists didn't already have drawing skills before they entered it was difficult for them to produce work of any significance.

John Singer Sargent (1856–1925), an American born in Florence, Italy, came to work here in 1874 at the age of 18. Already highly skilled in life drawing, Sargent was able to jump to the head of the class shortly after he joined; as a result, he spent some time as Duran's assistant. By 1878 Sargent was out working on his own.

Sargent had the privilege of growing up internationally schooled and influenced. William Starkweather once described him as "an American born in Italy, educated in France, who looks like a German, speaks like an Englishman, and paints like a Spaniard." It should then come as no surprise that he was a great lover of Velázquez's work.

On the left-hand corner of rue du Montparnasse and boulevard du Montparnasse you'll pass the church of **Notre-Dames-des-Champs.** Continue along boulevard du Montparnasse to the corner of rue Vavin, where at no. 99 you'll find:

7. **Le Sélect.** This café, one of the most popular in Paris in the 1920s, was frequented by Ernest Hemingway and Joan Miró (1893–1983), among others.

It was here that Isadora Duncan held an impromptu "demonstration" supporting anarchists Sacco and Vanzetti, who had been convicted of murder. A fight with another of Le Sélect's patrons, journalist Floyd Gibbons, over whether or not Sacco and Vanzetti's lives should be spared prompted her to lead a small march to the American embassy to protest their impending executions.

Continue along boulevard du Montparnasse and on your right, at no. 102, will be:

8. **La Coupole.** This café opened in December 1927 and became a favorite spot of Russian exiles and emigrées (including Leon Trotsky and Igor Stravinsky) both before and after the Bolshevik Revolution. It also hosted the area's

Montparnasse

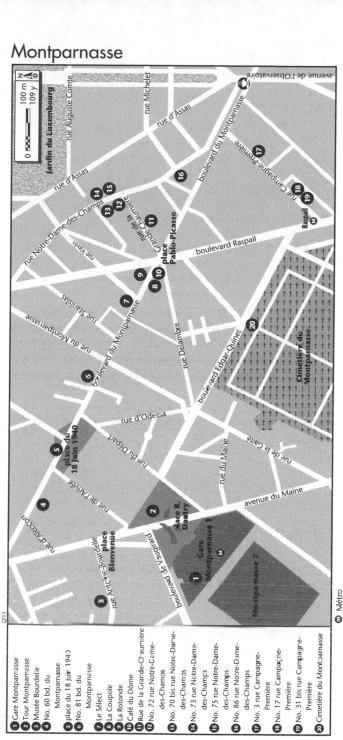

1. Gare Montparnasse
2. Tour Montparnasse
3. Musée Bourdelle
4. No. 60 bd. du Montparnasse
5. place du 18 juin 1940
6. No. 81 bd. du Montparnasse
7. Le Sélect
8. La Coupole
9. La Rotonde
10. Café du Dôme
11. Rue de la Grande-Chaumière
12. No. 72 rue Notre-Dame-des-Champs
13. No. 70 bis rue Notre-Dame-des-Champs
14. No. 73 rue Notre-Dame-des-Champs
15. No. 75 rue Notre-Dame-des-Champs
16. No. 86 rue Notre-Dame-des-Champs
17. No. 3 rue Campagne-Première
18. No. 17 rue Campagne-Première
19. No. 31 bis rue Campagne-Première
20. Cimetière du Montparnasse

Ⓜ Métro

artistic community, including Josephine Baker, Sartre, Matisse, and Kiki de Montparnasse and her lover, photographer Man Ray.

The 12 columns inside were painted (in exchange for a meal) by—among others—Brancusi, Gris, Léger, Chagall, Soutine, and Delaunay; they're registered as a historic monument.

At the intersection of boulevard du Montparnasse and boulevard Raspail, note the controversial **Auguste Rodin bust of Balzac.** Before continuing on, look for:

9. **La Rotonde,** 103–105 bd. du Montparnasse, a café housed at no. 105 when it opened in 1911. This was more than just a café. Stanton MacDonald Wright, an American painter who frequented La Rotonde, described it as "a gathering place of most American and German artists; André, the waiter there, lent the boys [the artists] money and treated many as a father would." He also said that the café at that time contained "a small zinc bar in a long narrow room with a terrace where [they] drank and warmed [themselves] at great porcelain stoves."

Kiki de Montparnasse

Born illegitimate and raised by her grandmother in Burgundy, Kiki (?–1953) was called to Paris by her mother, who put her to work—first in a printing shop, then in a shoe factory, and finally in a florist's shop on rue Mouffetard, where she was discovered by a sculptor. So began her career as an artists' model. At age 14, after her mother disowned her, she became a nightclub dancer at the Jockey-Bar (Montparnasse's first nightclub). Kiki was a voluptuous, seductive nonconformist who would bare her breasts to anyone who'd pay her three francs. She is most closely associated with Montparnasse since she spent 20 years frequenting Café du Dôme, Le Sélect, and La Rotonde. As she got older, her quality of life deteriorated and she began abusing drugs and alcohol, which ultimately caused her death.

Around 1924 La Rotonde had become popular enough to warrant expanding it next door to no. 103. Apollinaire, Max Jacob, Picasso, and Modigliani enjoyed spending time in the café and nightclub. There was an artists' gallery located on the premises as well. Edna St. Vincent Millay, the American romantic poet, was often found here during her 1922 visit.

On the opposite side of the street, at no. 108, is the:

10. **Café du Dôme,** which opened in 1897. Like the others, this café was quite popular with Americans and various other expatriates in the 1920s. Hemingway and Sinclair Lewis both frequented the Dôme.

Go left up the:

11. **Rue de la Grande-Chaumière.** Check out the sculpture in the window of **Art et Buffet Restaurant.** At no. 14 bis, on your left, is the **Académie de la Grande-Chaumière,** the art school begun by Antoine Bourdelle. On the right side (now the Best Western Villa des Artistes), no. 9 was once the **Hôtel Liberia,** the haunt of many artists and writers. Among them was Nathanael West (1903–40), an American novelist born Nathan Weinstein, who moved to

---

Edna St. Vincent Millay

A graduate of Vassar College, Edna St. Vincent Millay (1892–1950) was born in Rockland, Maine. Around the time she was born her uncle survived a life-threatening stay at New York's St. Vincent Hospital, and so her mother gave her the middle name St. Vincent. Not long after her college graduation, Millay headed for New York City and set up home in Greenwich Village. For a while, to support herself, she wrote articles for *Vanity Fair* magazine under the pseudonym Nancy Boyd. As her poetic career flourished, she came to be well respected by her contemporaries and well liked by her popular audience. In 1922 she won a Pulitzer Prize for her poem "The Ballad of the Harp Weaver."

Paris in 1926 and lived here for two years. He was fascinated with the idea of the American dream, and his best-known work is *Miss Lonelyhearts* (1933). West worked as an editor for several magazines, and two years after the publication of *Miss Lonelyhearts* he moved to Hollywood to become a scriptwriter.

Sculptor Malvina Hoffman (1887–1966; see below) also took furnished rooms somewhere on this street, which around 1920 was fondly referred to as the "rabbit hutch." Hoffman described the sounds of rue de la Grande Chaumière as a veritable cacophony of "the calls of the knife sharpeners and mattress makers, the pan pipes of vendors of goats while leading their bleating flocks."

At **no. 8,** on your left, is the old studio of Amedeo Modigliani (see Walking Tour 10, stop 15).

Take a quick detour to the left on rue Notre-Dame-des-Champs to:

12. **No. 72 rue Notre-Dame-des-Champs,** on your left. A second-floor apartment in this building was Malvina Hoffman's first studio, and its only running water was from a tap down the hall.

This is where she worked on her first commission—a bust of the American ambassador to France, Robert Bacon. While living here she met Rodin and visited his studio. One day he asked her to pick out one of the sculptures displayed in his studio and study it carefully until he came back. Knowing this to be a test, Hoffman intensely studied the one she'd chosen. Rodin returned about 20 minutes later and took her to another room. He gave her some clay and instructed her to sculpt from memory the head she'd studied. He walked out, locked the door, then came back a while later to find she'd done an excellent job. He proceeded to take her to lunch, and that's how she was accepted as his student.

Only five years after she began working with Rodin, Hoffman achieved national recognition for her *Pavlova La Gavotte* and *Bacchanale russe.* She is also responsible for the creation of the Hall of Man at Chicago's Field Museum.

Also on the left is:

13. **No. 70 bis rue Notre-Dame-des-Champs,** where in 1921 Ezra Pound and his wife, Dorothy, moved into an apartment overlooking the courtyard and garden. Though all his furniture was made out of boxes and various discarded items, the place was charming. It didn't matter that he was poverty-stricken: He loved to throw parties, and just about everyone who was anyone during the time he lived in Paris visited this apartment. Hemingway often spent time here boxing and writing with Pound.

Katherine Anne Porter (1890–1980) lived in the very same apartment in 1934. She came to Europe on a Guggenheim grant and joined Sylvia Beach's Shakespeare & Company Library in 1933. Porter remained in Paris until 1936 and is acclaimed for her collection of short stories, *Flowering Judas* (1930), and her novel *Ship of Fools* (1962).

Across the street on your right is:

14. **No. 73 rue Notre-Dame-des-Champs,** where John Singer Sargent once shared a studio with Carroll Beckwith. Here he completed his first major commission—a portrait of playwright Edouard Pailleron.

Also look for:

15. **No. 75 rue Notre-Dame-des-Champs,** the home of Alice B. Toklas and Harriet Levy. Toklas first came to Paris with her friend and fellow San Franciscan Levy, and they moved into an apartment here. In 1912 Levy moved back to the United States, though Toklas decided to stay and moved in with Gertrude and Leo Stein (she'd been typing manuscript pages for Gertrude since her arrival). When Leo moved to Italy in 1914, Toklas stayed and stayed—for 32 years.

Turn around, cross the intersection of rue de la Grande-Chaumière (the same street you took to get to rue Notre-Dame-des-Champs), and follow along rue Notre-Dame-des-Champs to:

16. **No. 86 rue Notre-Dame-des-Champs,** James Abbott McNeill Whistler's studio. A painter/graphic artist, Whistler (1834–1903) was active mainly in England. He began his training as an artist after he left West Point Military Academy. In 1855 he moved to Paris and, like many before

and after him, spent a great deal of time making copies of works in the Louvre. Four years later he decided to settle in London but returned to France frequently. Whistler was a great friend of Oscar Wilde and, like him, a believer in art for art's sake. He particularly enjoyed describing his works in musical terms and often gave them musical titles. From his studio window he had a lovely view of the Luxembourg Gardens.

Follow rue Notre-Dame-des-Champs to the end. Turn right at the corner.

Take a Break   At no. 171 bd. du Montparnasse is **La Closerie des Lilas,** a pleasant place to stop for a drink. This was the favorite neighborhood hangout of Hemingway, Lenin, Trotsky, and Fitzgerald. Every morning Hemingway would come here and write—in fact, he did some rewriting of *The Sun Also Rises* here. Often he could be found contemplating the statue of Maréchal Ney (Napoléon I's marshal of France, who was shot for treason) standing outside on the spot where Ney was killed. He often came with John Dos Passos, and the two would sit outside under the lilac bushes and read the New Testament to each other.

Go right as you come out of La Closerie des Lilas and walk to rue Campagne-Première. Turn left on rue Campagne-Première and proceed to:

17. **No. 3 rue Campagne-Première,** a new building on the site of the one in which Whistler stayed while studying under Swiss painter Charles Gabriel Gleyre (1808–74). In 1843, when historical painter Paul Delaroche closed his studio, a number of his students went to work with Gleyre, who encouraged outdoor painting. Whistler wasn't Gleyre's only well-known student; others included Sisley, Monet, and Renoir. His studio closed in 1864.

Continue along the street to:

18. **No. 17 rue Campagne-Première,** in which Eugène Atget had a studio from 1898 to 1927. One of France's most famous photographers, Atget began his life as a seaman and then moved to a career in acting. It wasn't until he was 42 that he became a photographer.

At first he made money selling some of his photographs to painters for use as source material and others to the city of Paris for use as historical records. Not long after he began, his documentary work crossed the line and became artwork, and he started producing his famed poetic images.

Next, continue on the street to:

19. **No. 31 bis rue Campagne-Première,** where Man Ray (1890–1977) lived in July 1922. Model Kiki de Montparnasse (see box above) became his mistress while he was living here, and she stayed with him for six years.

One of the most important photographers of his time, Man Ray was a prominent figure in the dadaist and surrealist movements as well as a friend of Marcel Duchamp. In the 1930s he invented the rayograph (now known as a photogram), made by strategically placing objects on photographic paper and then exposing them to light to create an image. This technique is often utilized today as a first exercise in photography classes.

Cross boulevard Raspail at the end of rue Campagne-Première and go left onto boulevard Edgar-Quinet. Not far along is the main entrance to the:

20. **Cimetière du Montparnasse.** Be sure you go in the main entrance. This will be a brief tour of the cemetery, with directions for the general locations of grave sites you might be interested in visiting.

As you enter, go directly to the graves of **Jean-Paul Sartre** (1905–80) and **Simone de Beauvoir** (1908–86) on the right side of the roadway. Sartre was an existentialist playwright/philosopher/novelist. During World War II he was taken prisoner but escaped and became a Resistance leader. During the Occupation he wrote *Being and Nothingness* (1943) and *No Exit* (1944). He declined the Nobel Prize in 1964. Simone de Beauvoir, Sartre's intimate friend and occasional lover, was also an existentialist novelist and a teacher of philosophy, but she's probably best known for her analysis of women in *The Second Sex* (1950). Toward the end of her life she wrote *The Coming of Age* (1970), about the ways different cultures treat and respond to the elderly.

Continue straight ahead, past the graves, and at avenue de l'Ouest turn left. On your left you'll find the grave of

Chaim Soutine (1894–1943). Born in Lithuania, Soutine arrived in France in 1913 and became one of the greatest contributors to the Ecole de Paris (a loose term combining those artists who participated in the dadaist, cubist, and surrealist movements). He isn't very well known because he suffered from depression and a lack of self-confidence that kept him from showing his work, but many believe Soutine was a man of great genius. It's said that he often destroyed his paintings. He preferred the work of the old masters to that of his contemporaries and particularly admired Rembrandt's *Flayed Ox*. In fact, Soutine's own *Side of Beef* (ca. 1925) was inspired by the old masters. A frequent slaughterhouse visitor, he once brought a carcass home to paint; when his neighbors called the police to complain about the smell, Soutine confronted them with a discourse on the importance of art over sanitation!

After crossing avenue du Nord, you'll find on your left the grave of French symbolist poet/critic **Charles Baudelaire** (1821–67). Only one volume of Baudelaire's major work, *Les Fleurs du mal* (1857), was published in his lifetime, and it was met with great animosity. Once considered obscene, *Les Fleurs du mal* is now regarded a masterpiece.

Cross avenue Transversale and on your left you'll find the grave of **Tristan Tzara** (see Walking Tour 9, stop 17). Farther ahead, on your right across allée Raffet, is the grave of **Emile-Antoine Bourdelle** (see stop 3, above).

Turn around and go right on allée Raffet to avenue Principale. Follow avenue Principale around the circle to the left and straight through to avenue du Nord. Turn right to the grave of French composer **Charles-Camille Saint-Saëns** (1835–1921), who made his debut as a pianist at age 10. Only three years later he entered the Paris Conservatory, and for 20 years he was the organist at the Madeleine (see Walking Tour 7, stop 13, for more about this church). Saint-Saëns disliked modern music, and his most famous work was the romantic opera *Samson et Dalila* (1877).

After viewing the grave of Saint-Saëns, head down rue Emile Richard (crossing avenue du Nord again); on your left is the grave of Romanian sculptor **Constantin Brancusi** (1876–1957). Brancusi decided to come to Paris to work, and soon after his arrival Rodin invited him to work in his studio. Brancusi did the unthinkable—he declined the offer, saying wisely, "Nothing grows well in the shade of a big tree." An abstract sculptor, Brancusi was unafraid of controversy. He believed in the absolute simplification of form and liked working in metal, stone, and wood. His most famous sculpture is *The Kiss* (1908), which you'll see here.

Exit the cemetery by continuing straight ahead. Then make a right and proceed to the Raspail Métro station.

St-Germain-des-Prés Parts I & II

PART I

Start: Musée d'Orsay, intersection of rue de Bellechasse and rue de Lille (Métro: Solférino; walk two blocks up to rue de Lille).

Finish: Carrefour de l'Odéon.

Time: Three hours.

Best Time: About 10am from Wednesday to Saturday.

Worst Time: Monday and Tuesday, when museums are closed.

Originally the site of a large abbey in the 8th century, the Left Bank neighborhood St-Germain-des-Prés is where 18th-century Parisian aristocrats built elegant mansions known as *hôtels particuliers*. It quickly developed into one of Paris's chicest areas, attracting such residents as the queen of the Netherlands, Chateaubriand, and André Gide.

Neighborhood activity centered around the St-Germain-des-Prés church and the cafés (like Café de Flore and Café des

Deux-Magots) in its vicinity. Because of the presence of the Ecole des Beaux-Arts, the neighborhood also attracted a great number of artists, including Picasso.

Presently, St-Germain-des-Prés is home to some of the city's most exclusive antiques shops and boutiques, as well as street markets and bookshops. On this walk you'll have the opportunity to visit the world's greatest collection of impressionist art at the Musée d'Orsay; the food and flower stalls of the Buci Market; and the building where Natalie Barney held her famous salon, which attracted the likes of Marcel Proust. You'll also spend some time viewing part of the Delacroix Museum's enormous collection.

● ● ● ● ● ● ● ● ● ● ● ● ● ● ● ●

Begin your tour in the:

1. **Musée d'Orsay.** Constructed within the old Gare d'Orsay railway station (designed by Victor Laloux), this museum houses one of the greatest art collections from the second half of the 19th century. Your visit could take anywhere from two hours to all day, so plan accordingly if you want to finish this tour—perhaps come back another day if you want to spend more time. You'll easily find your way around, especially if you buy the museum guidebook.

   Glass ceilings and enormous windows flood the display areas with natural light, making the impact of the central sculpture gallery truly inspiring. Although most of the pieces came here from the Louvre, the museum also holds the impressionist works that had been squeezed into the Musée du Jeu de Paume for years (see Walking Tour 7, stop 7). You'll see sculptures by Claudel, Maillol, and Rodin (to name a few), as well as a large collection of Daumier caricatures. The fantastic decorative arts display includes several rooms devoted to art nouveau furnishings. Try not to miss Toulouse-Lautrec's stunning pastel drawings.

   Besides an upper-level restaurant/café, there's a don't-miss bookstore and poster shop.

   Across from the museum on rue de Bellechasse is the:

2. **Palais de la Légion d'Honneur,** built in 1782 as the *hôtel particulier* for the Prince de Salm-Kyrbourg; during

the Reign of Terror this German count met his demise under the guillotine's blade. Napoléon acquired the building in 1804 as the home for the Légion d'Honneur, which was to employ those "who by their talents contribute to the safety and prosperity of the nation." An 1871 fire did much damage, so the classical structure you see today has been heavily restored. Inside you'll learn the history of the Legion of Honor and see medals and insignia from other parts of the world—including the American Purple Heart and the British Victoria Cross. There's even a room dedicated to women.

Walk to the right down rue de Bellechasse to rue de l'Université and turn left, looking for:

3. **No. 50 rue de l'Université,** where Edna St. Vincent Millay crafted her Pulitzer Prize–winning poem, "The Ballad of the Harp Weaver."

When you get to rue du Bac, turn left and walk to the quai Voltaire. Turn right and stop at no. 19, the:

4. **Hôtel du Quai Voltaire,** where American novelist Willa Cather (1876–1947) stayed for two months in 1920. At the age of nine, Cather moved with her family to the Nebraska prairie, where she eventually attended the University of Nebraska. Later, she moved to Pittsburgh and worked as a journalist and teacher. In 1904 she moved to New York City and lived in Greenwich Village while working as an editor for *McClure's* magazine. She left *McClure's* in 1912 (after having been promoted to managing editor) so she could devote herself to her fiction writing. Author of *O Pioneers!* (1913) and *My Antonia* (1918), she won a Pulitzer Prize for her novel *One of Ours* (1922), which she worked on while living here.

Baudelaire spent time working on *Les Fleurs du mal* while he stayed here from 1856 to 1858. Richard Wagner and Oscar Wilde were also guests for a brief period.

Just a bit farther on is:

5. **No. 17 quai Voltaire,** where American composer/organist Virgil Thomson (1896–1989) lived from 1927 to 1940. During his Paris stay he was inspired to write two operas for librettos by Gertrude Stein: *Four Saints in Three Acts*

(1928) and *The Mother of Us All* (1947). He also composed works for organ, piano, and chamber ensembles, and he worked as a music critic for the New York *Herald Tribune* from 1940 to 1954.

Backtrack to rue de Beaune and turn left. In 1872 Henry James met Ralph Waldo Emerson for the first time at no. 7 while on assignment to write letters on Parisian life for the New York *Tribune*. And Ezra Pound lived next door in July 1920. Continue down rue de Beaune to rue de l'Université and turn left. At the corner of rue des Sts-Pères, just before rue de l'Université becomes rue Jacob, are:

6. **Nos. 2–4 rue de l'Université,** on the right. Benjamin Franklin lived here in 1776 while trying to get French support for the American Revolution. Being a devotee of the good life, Franklin loved Paris, and the French returned the affection. In fact, when he was scheduled to return to the United States, the queen sent her personal litter and two mules to take him to the ship.

Turn right and walk down rue des Sts-Pères.

Take a Break   Raise your energy level and indulge your sweet tooth at **Debauve et Gallais,** 30 rue des Sts-Pères; open Tuesday through Saturday. This is a chocolate shop, so don't go in looking for lunch. Many years ago this was a pharmacy that distributed "medicinal chocolate."

When you reach boulevard St-Germain, cross to the other side and go left toward rue du Dragon. Incidentally, rue du Dragon used to be named rue du Sépulchre, but its name was changed in the 18th century because the residents preferred the name Dragon—after the huge gateway of the Cour du Dragon (you can see a copy of the gateway at **no. 44** if you continue walking down after the next stop). Turn right down rue du Dragon (a quaint little shopping street) and proceed to no. 31, the:

7. **Académie Jullian.** Many artists who weren't accepted into the Ecole des Beaux-Arts attended this school, which opened in 1868 but didn't move to this location until 1890. In the French tradition, the academy was conservative and traditional, though considered inferior to the Beaux-Arts. Among the Americans who attended were Maurice Prendergast

(1891–93), Max Weber (1905), and Jacques Lipchitz (1910). George Biddle described the place in 1911 as "a cold, filthy, uninviting firetrap"; when he arrived, he found this scene: "Three nude girls were posing downstairs. The acrid smell of their bodies and the smell of the students mingled with that of turpentine and oil paint in the overheated, tobacco-laden air." He also said that while the artists "worked there was a pandemonium of songs, catcalls, whistling andrecitations of a highly salacious and bawdy nature."

Turn around and head back up rue du Dragon to boulevard St-Germain. At no. 151 is the:

8. **Brasserie Lipp.** Frequented by Hemingway, this brasserie has been a favorite of the literati since the 1920s. The best reason to go inside (the Alsatian food isn't) is to see the painted ceilings and the art nouveau ceramics.

Across the boulevard St-Germain is the:

9. **Café de Flore,** where Pablo Picasso used to hang out after 1945. As Janet Flanner describes, "He always sat at the second table in front of the main door, with Spanish friends. . . . He never did anything except sip his one small bottle of mineral water, speak with his Spanish friends, and look at all the people who were not looking directly at him. When he had finished his libation, he left for home, invariably before eleven." Jean-Paul Sartre and Simone de Beauvoir rendezvoused here in the early 1940s to write.

Cross the street at the place St-Germain-des-Prés; on your left, across from the church, is the:

10. **Café des Deux-Magots,** named after the wooden statues of two Chinese dignitaries *(magots)* sitting atop boxes of money that are attached to a column within the café. Deux-Magots was another of Hemingway's hangouts. Janet Flanner, a close friend of Hemingway and the writer who (under the pen name Genêt) vividly captured Paris's 1920s café and salon scene, described Hemingway's habit of coming here to have "serious talk" and read works aloud. His love for Deux-Magots is apparent in several passages of *The Sun Also Rises,* particularly the one in which Jake Barnes meets Lady Brett.

Head across the place St-Germain-des-Prés to:

11. **St-Germain-des-Prés,** the oldest of the city's large churches, located on the site of a former temple to the Egyptian goddess Isis. In Roman times, this area was an open field (*prés*). The original church was built here in 452 by the Merovingian king Childebert; however, it was continually destroyed by the Normans, rebuilt, destroyed, and rebuilt. In 1163 it was rebuilt for the last time.

In the late 18th century, French revolutionaries took over the abbey here and filled it with titled prisoners. Later they held tribunals (very brief trials) that led to the massacre of more than 200 people, including a few of Louis XVI's ministers and his father confessor, in the abbey's courtyard (at the corner of rue Bonaparte and boulevard St-Germain). After the massacre, while the bodies still lay in piles, there was an auction of the victims' belongings.

On a much less horrifying note, it was also here that a fairground sprang up to host many a dancing bear, juggler, acrobat, and the like. Street performers still entertain in front of the church, especially in warm weather.

In the church's nave are murals by Hippolyte Flandrin (1809–64), one of Ingres's favorite students and winner of the 1830 Prix de Rome. While in Italy, Flandrin was greatly impressed by the "monumental" work being done, and on returning to Paris in 1838 he became the leading muralist of his time. The murals he executed in St-Germain-des-Prés were done from 1856 to 1861.

You'll also find a memorial to 17th-century philosopher/mathematician René Descartes, whose skull is buried here; plus a bust of Jean Mabillon (1623–1707), a French scholar/Benedictine monk who developed a technique for determining the authenticity of documents.

When you come out of St-Germain-des-Prés, turn to the right and walk around it to rue de l'Abbaye, in the rear. Behind the church is the tiny square Laurent-Prâche, a quiet park containing a **Picasso bronze bust of a woman** dedicated to Guillaume Apollinaire. Picasso and Apollinaire were great friends, and the bust was dedicated 41 years after Apollinaire's death.

Continue to the right (if you're facing away from the square Laurent-Prâche) along rue de l'Abbaye. Look for rue de Furstemberg, then turn left, and here you'll find the:

12. **Place de Furstemberg,** named for Cardinal Egon von Furstemberg, abbot of St-Germain-des-Prés in the late 17th century. This is a wonderful out-of-the-way spot—in fact, it was one of Henry Miller's favorites. If you're lucky, you might find a group of musicians giving an impromptu concert.

To your left, diagonally across the center of the square at no. 6 rue de Furstemberg, is the:

13. **Musée Eugène Delacroix,** the home and studio of the French Romantic painter (1798–1863) from December 28, 1857, to August 13, 1863. Here is an entry from his journal the day he moved into this studio:

> *Made a quick change to the new studio today. . . . Decidedly, my new place is charming. After dinner, I felt a bit of melancholy over finding myself transplanted. Little by little I got reconciled and was perfectly happy when I went to bed.*
>
> *Woke up the next morning and saw the most gracious sunlight on the houses opposite my window. The sight of my little garden and the smiling aspect of my studio always cause a feeling of pleasure in me.*

Today, from inside the museum you can look out on the garden he describes.

Among the museum's pieces are Delacroix's portraits of George Sand, his self-portraits, and his animal paintings, plus his collections of sketches and many of his letters. Exhibits rotate, so there's no telling which part of the enormous collection you're going to see.

After exiting the museum, go left up rue de Furstemberg to rue Jacob. (Note that as you approach rue Jacob there are some wonderful **fabric shops** to your left and right.) Go left on rue Jacob to:

14. **No. 20 rue Jacob,** the former residence of Natalie Clifford Barney (1876–1972), who moved here from the United States in 1909 as a student and stayed for just over 60 years. Even though virtually unknown in America, Barney was famous all over Paris for her literary salons. Virgil Thomson, Carl van Vechten, Sherwood Anderson, T. S. Eliot, James Joyce, and Marcel Proust were among the many who visited her Friday-night salon.

A rich, beautiful lesbian, Barney was portrayed in many a novel, including Rémy de Gourmont's *Lettres à l'Amazone* and Radclyffe Hall's *The Well of Loneliness*. Hall described her as receiving her guests "dressed all in white, and a large white fox skin was clasped round her slender and shapely shoulders. For the rest she had masses of thick fair hair, which was busily ridding itself of its hairpins." Mata Hari once arrived at one of Barney's parties on horseback, completely naked. Barney was known to have had an affair with Dorothy Wilde, the niece of Oscar Wilde.

Continue up rue Jacob to rue Bonaparte. Turn right on rue Bonaparte and make a quick right onto:

15. **Rue Visconti.** On your left is the residence where classical playwright Jean Racine (b. 1639) died on April 21, 1699. Educated at the Port-Royal abbey, he was Louis XIV's court dramatist and has been described as the most French of French writers. He is particularly well known for injecting his characters with psychological realism.

    Just a bit farther on, **no. 17** was once the site of Balzac's print shop. Retrace your steps to rue Bonaparte. Turn right to no. 14, the:

16. **Ecole des Beaux-Arts,** the most famous of art schools, housed in a group of buildings from the 17th through the 19th century. The Beaux-Arts opened in 1648 as the Académie Royale de Peintre et de Sculpture, then became an individual institution in 1795. The Prix de Rome was bestowed by the Ecole des Beaux-Arts; its teachings remained traditional until well after World War II, and the entrance exam here was so difficult that even Rodin failed it. Among those who passed were Degas, Matisse, Monet, Renoir, and Max Weber.

    Continue up rue Bonaparte and turn right on rue des Beaux-Arts. Oscar Wilde, broke and in despair, died at **no. 13 rue des Beaux-Arts** (the one with the ram's head— it used to be the Hôtel d'Alsace and is now L'Hôtel, owned by actor Guy-Louis Duboucheron). When you get to rue de Seine, make another right. Look to your left for the art bookstore **Fischbacher Livres d'Art,** no. 33 rue de Seine, stocking a fine selection of books on all genres of art, in both French and English. At the intersection of rue de Buci and rue de Seine begins the:

17. **Buci Market,** one of the liveliest markets in the city. Here you'll find stalls selling fish, flowers, *fromage,* and fruit, as well as shop windows filled with mouth-watering pastries— the profusion of sights and smells will make you giddy. If you're in the neighborhood *just before* lunch on a fine day (except Monday), purchase the makings for a picnic here— what could be better? Be aware that if you arrive *at* lunchtime you won't find a market—it goes to lunch. The best time to arrive is between 9am and 1pm or later in the afternoon and evening.

When you get to the Carrefour de Buci, go left up rue Mazarine to passage Dauphine, on your right. In the passage are three sculptures: Rembrandt Bugatii's ***Lutteur nu Assis*** (1907); Chana Orloff's ***Grande Baigneuse Debout*** (1939); and Robert Couturier's ***La Femme à la Cruche*** (1956). Previously sculptures by Max Ernst were here, so don't be surprised if the ones I've mentioned have been substituted for others. This is a great passageway, and it's an easy way to get from rue Mazarine to rue Dauphine. Cross rue Dauphine and head directly into rue Christine. In 1938, Alice B. Toklas and Gertrude Stein moved into an apartment at:

18. **No. 15 rue Christine.** Janet Flanner reported that this apartment was once the home of Queen Christina of Sweden. In fact, it still held the queen's *boiseries* (wall panels) and reading cabinet when Stein and Toklas moved in. On a visit to deliver a housewarming bouquet, Flanner was asked to take an inventory of Stein's incredible art collection. She found over 130 canvases, 25 of them Picassos.

As you continue along rue Christine, you'll find yourself on rue des Grands-Augustins. Diagonally across the street, to the left (just a few steps up the street in the direction of the river) is:

19. **No. 7 rue des Grands-Augustins,** where Picasso lived from 1936 to 1955, near his good friend Gertrude Stein. It was here he painted the masterpiece *Guernica* in 1937, as is noted on the plaque.

Go right down rue des Grands-Augustins to rue St-André-des-Arts; then turn left to:

20. **No. 28 rue St-André-des-Arts,** which used to be a bar called Le Gentilhomme. In 1962 Jack Kerouac spent some time here when he stopped in Paris on his way to Brittany to do some research into his family history.

    Retrace your steps, crossing rue des Grands-Augustins to **no. 46,** on your right, where e.e. cummings lived in 1923. Continue along, looking for Bar Mazet on your left. Near the bar, go left into the:

21. **Cour du Commerce St-André.** Numerous interesting shops and restaurants are here, and the passageway is associated with odd bits of history. At **no. 9,** Dr. Guillotin perfected his invention on sheep before deciding it was fit to use on humans—much to the regret of Marie Antoinette. People dispute the manner in which Guillotin died—some say it was by his own invention, others say it was of grief at what his invention had perpetrated. This was also the site of the **printing shop** to which Jean-Paul Marat (1743–93), Swiss-born revolutionary, would walk in his bathrobe every day to correct the proofs of *L'Ami du peuple,* the paper he founded.

    Exit the Cour du Commerce St-André onto boulevard St-Germain. Turn right and walk to the corner of rue de l'Ancienne-Comédie, where at no. 1 you'll find:

22. **Le Procope** (formerly Café le Procope), founded by a Sicilian named Procopio, just after the 1689 opening of the Comédie-Française (which used to be across the street). It claims to be the world's oldest café. Indeed, Voltaire and Rousseau spent time here; later patrons included Benjamin Franklin, Victor Hugo, and Balzac. Of course, a Paris café couldn't call itself a café (especially not the oldest one) unless Jean-Paul Sartre and Simone de Beauvoir had, at one time or another, been visitors.

    The little island at the center of the boulevard is the Carrefour de l'Odéon. The first part of the St-Germain-des-Prés tour ends here. If you don't wish to continue on with Part II, the Odéon Métro stop is right here. If you choose to continue, Part II begins where you're now standing.

St-Germain-des-Prés

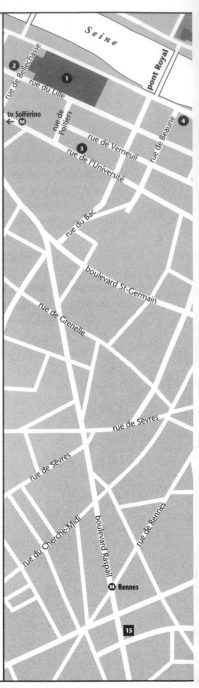

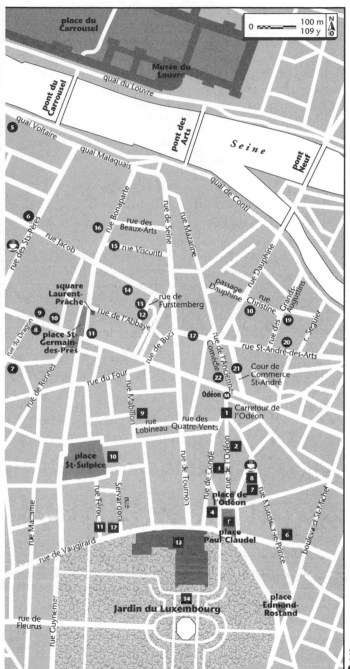

place du
Carrousel

Musée du
Louvre

quai du Louvre

pont du Carrousel

quai Voltaire

5

pont des Arts

Seine

quai Malaquais

quai de Conti

pont
Neuf

6

rue des St-Pères

rue Jacob

rue Bonaparte

rue des Beaux-Arts

16

rue de Seine

rue Mazarine

15 rue Visconti

rue Dauphine

passage
Dauphine

rue
Christine

Grands-Augustins

**square
Laurent-
Prâche**

14

rue de Furstemberg

13

12

18

19

r. Séguier

9 **10**

rue de l'Abbaye

rue St-André-des-Arts

20

rue du Dragon

8

**place St-
Germain-
des-Prés**

11

rue de Buci

17

rue de l'Ancienne Comédie

21

Cour de
Commerce
St-André

7

rue de Rennes

rue du Four

22

Odéon Ⓜ

1 Carrefour de
l'Odéon

rue Mabillon

9

rue
Lobineau

rue des
Quatre-Vents

2

rue de Condé

rue de l'Odéon

3

8

**place
St-Sulpice**

10

rue de Tournon

**place de
l'Odéon**

7

rue Férou

rue Servandoni

rue Madame

11 **12**

rue de Vaugirard

4

13

**place
Paul-Claudel**

rue Monsieur-le-Prince

boulevard St-Michel

6

rue Guynemer

14

Jardin du Luxembourg

**place
Edmond-
Rostand**

rue de Fleurus

Ⓜ Métro

PART II

Start: Carrefour de l'Odéon (Métro: Odéon).
Finish: Boulevard Raspail and rue de Fleurus.
Time: Three hours.
Best Time: Any time during the day.

During Part II of the St-Germain-des-Prés tour you'll visit the site of Sylvia Beach's original Shakespeare & Company; the Marché St-Germain, a marvelous covered marketplace; the St-Sulpice church; the Luxembourg Palace and Gardens; and the former residences of such famous authors as William Faulkner and Richard Wright.

● ● ● ● ● ● ● ● ● ● ● ● ● ● ●

As stated in Part I, the little island in the center of the boulevard St-Germain is the:

1. **Carrefour de l'Odéon.** Take a look at the bronze statue of Georges-Jacques Danton (1759–94), one of the French Revolution's moderate leaders. A lawyer by trade, he became a leader of the Cordeliers and participated in the August 1792 storming of the Tuileries and subsequent overthrow of the king. After the Revolution he served as a member of the National Assembly, but not for long—he was executed by his archrival, Robespierre, during the Reign of Terror.

    Continue across the street into rue de l'Odéon to no. 7, now the:

2. **Galerie Régine Lussan** but formerly Adrienne Monnier's bookstore, La Maison des Amis des Livres, a gathering place for French writers in the 1920s. Guillaume Apollinaire, Paul Claudel, Paul Valéry (whom Monnier actually published), and André Gide were frequent visitors. Sylvia Beach's lover, Monnier, committed suicide in 1955.

    A bit farther along, on the right, is:

3. **No. 12 rue de l'Odéon,** the site of Sylvia Beach's original Shakespeare & Company bookstore (1921–40), which became a favorite stopping place for expatriate Americans. Beach worked hard nurturing James Joyce and was the first to publish *Ulysses* (using her own funds). Later, Bennet Cerf at Random House published the book and is reported to have made at least $1 million. Joyce received a $45,000 advance, yet Beach never saw any money—even though she discovered, edited, and published the original. She claimed not to mind and said she'd do anything for Joyce and his art. Joyce never returned her favors, and when her shop was threatened with closure it was André Gide who came to her rescue.

   Just a couple of doors down, where the Chinese import shop **Heng Seng Heng S.A.** now stands, was the building in which Adrienne Monnier and Sylvia Beach shared an apartment until 1937. Go right at the place de l'Odéon to no. 6, now the:

4. **Hôtel Michelet Odéon.** American poet Allen Tate (1899–1979) stayed here in 1929. He, too, was introduced to Ernest Hemingway by Sylvia Beach.

Sylvia Beach

Born in Baltimore, Maryland, Sylvia Beach (1887–1962) came to Paris with her family as an adolescent. In 1917 she met Adrienne Monnier at her 7 rue de l'Odéon bookshop (see above), where they discussed literature for hours. Monnier encouraged and inspired Beach to open an American bookshop, which she did on November 19, 1919, at 8 rue Dupuytren. The shop was furnished with flea-market bargain items, the walls bare except for two William Blake drawings and, later, some photographs supplied by Man Ray. In 1921 she moved the shop to rue de l'Odéon and went to live nearby with Monnier. During World War II, Beach safely hid from the Nazis in the kitchen of a boulevard St-Michel apartment for two years, but she was later arrested and held for seven months before a high-ranking German officer intervened on her behalf.

Continue right around the place de l'Odéon to the place Paul-Claudel. Here you'll find the:

5. **Théâtre de l'Odéon,** built in 1782 by architects Peyre and de Wailly to house the Comédie-Française. With nearly 2,000 seats, it was the biggest theater in Paris at the time. Beaumarchais's widely praised *Marriage of Figaro* was both created and performed here in 1794.

Cross in front of the theater and walk straight through to rue de Vaugirard. Turn left on rue de Vaugirard to rue Monsieur-le-Prince, then left to:

6. **No. 55 rue Monsieur-le-Prince,** on the right corner. Oliver Wendell Holmes (1809–94) lived here from 1833 to 1835 while studying medicine. A graduate of Harvard University, Holmes was a doctor, an occasional poet, and quite a wit. He came to this city to study because during his lifetime Paris was one of the world's greatest scientific and medical centers. In 1857 he founded the *Atlantic Monthly* magazine with James Russell Lowell. Dr. Holmes was easily flattered, and in his old age he took advantage of his hearing problems and would say to admirers, "I am a trifle deaf, you know. Do you mind repeating that a little louder?"

A bit farther up the street, on the left side, is:

7. **No. 22 rue Monsieur-le-Prince,** the building in which American painter James Abbott McNeill Whistler had a second-floor studio. Many of his contemporaries disliked him because he had such a high opinion of himself. In fact, a wealthy man once visited here (when Whistler was still virtually unknown) and inquired as to the total price of everything in the studio. Whistler quoted him a price of $4 million. As you can imagine, the man could hardly believe his ears. "What?" he exclaimed, to which Whistler replied, "My posthumous prices." This was probably the first time he ever underestimated himself.

Also on the left is:

8. **No. 14 rue Monsieur-le-Prince,** where in March 1959 Martin Luther King, Jr., visited Richard Wright in his third-floor apartment. Sylvia Beach's bookstore was near here, and she and Wright became close friends. She said of him, "Of all writers I have known, he is the most unselfish and

thoughtful. In fact, none of the others . . . were interested in anyone but themselves. Fellas like Hemingway appear uncouth beside Dick Wright."

Take a Break   At no. 12 rue Monsieur-le-Prince is **Chez Maître Paul,** a lovely little restaurant in which to stop for lunch on Tuesday through Saturday from noon to 2:30pm. The chef is best known for his variety of wine sauces. If you miss lunch here, consider coming back for dinner. It's popular then, so call 43-54-74-59 for reservations.

After a pleasant lunch, return to the place where rue de l'Odéon, rue Monsieur-le-Prince, and rue de Condé come together to form the Carrefour de l'Odéon (where the tour started). Look for rue des Quatre-Vents and turn left onto this street, crossing rue de Seine into rue Lobineau. At the corner of rue Lobineau and rue Mabillon is the:

9. **Marché St-Germain.** Inside this covered market you'll find stalls of fresh fruits and vegetables, fish, meats, and cheeses. If you're in a market mood, wander through and perhaps do some shopping; if not, speed through and come out the other side and turn left (if you come out the way you came in, go right, then left at the corner). Head toward:

10. **St-Sulpice,** one of the largest and richest churches in Paris. It also happens to be the most frequented and the liveliest of the parish churches.

Building began in 1646 but wasn't completed until the late 18th century; the south tower is still unfinished. Two of the architects who worked on the church were Louis Le Vau and Jean-Baptiste Servandoni. As you enter St-Sulpice, note the enormous holy water stoups made of natural shells. The intricately carved pedestals were done by J. P. Pigalle. Go right after you enter and you'll come across three of Eugène Delacroix's greatest masterpieces: *Jacob Wrestling with the Angel, Heliodorus Driven from the Temple,* and *St. Michael Vanquishing the Devil,* all completed in 1881. Wander through and view the other spectacular pieces of art.

Another interesting feature is the bronze meridian line running along the north-south transept. Somehow 19th-century scientists were able to determine that during both equinoxes and at the winter solstice (at midday), sunlight would hit the line, run along the floor, climb up the obelisk to the globe on top, and light the cross.

Leave the church and head across the place St-Sulpice to:

11. **Rue Férou.** Man Ray lived at **no. 2** when he came back to Paris in 1951, and Hemingway lived at **no. 6** while working on *A Farewell to Arms.* He'd just left his wife, Hadley, and child and moved in with Pauline Pfeiffer, his mistress. When asked why he did so, he replied, "Because I'm a bastard."

At the end of rue Férou, turn left in front of the palace and proceed to the corner of rue de Vaugirard and rue Servandoni. Stop in front of:

12. **No. 42 rue de Vaugirard,** where William Faulkner stayed for several months in 1925. He particularly enjoyed going across the street to the Jardin du Luxembourg, where he could sit and write in peace. He describes the gardens in his 1931 novel *Sanctuary:*

> *In the Luxembourg Gardens . . . the women sat knitting in shawls and even the men playing croquet played in coats and capes . . . the random shouts of children had that quality of autumn. . . . From beyond the circle with its spurious greek balustrade, clotted with movement, filled with a gray light of the same color and texture as the water which the fountain played into the pool, came a steady crash of music.*

Located across from Faulkner's old place and the Théâtre de l'Odéon is the:

13. **Palais du Luxembourg,** built by Marie de Médicis shortly after she was widowed by Henri IV's murder. She was never a tenant, however, because before it could be finished she was banished by her son, Louis XIII, for opposing Cardinal Richelieu. During the Revolution the palace was

used as a prison. Currently the French Senate sits here. The palace is open only one day a month, and when it is the line is very long.

Beyond the palace is the:

14. **Jardin du Luxembourg.** Some people swear Hemingway used to come here when he was broke to catch pigeons, wring their necks, and take them home for dinner. Other people believe that's absolute nonsense. (I wouldn't have put it past him.)

As you enter the gardens, go straight until you reach the large, impressive **Medici Fountain** (1624), on your left. This is a glorious place to sit and relax away from the crowds that gather around the central ornamental lake. After some leisure time, go around the back side of the bandstand area (near the boulevard St-Michel entrance) to find **Rodin's bust of Stendhal** and **François Sicard's sculpture of George Sand** (1905). As you head for the other side of the gardens, look for the rose garden, the beehives, and the orchard. Also, try not to miss the **miniature Statue of Liberty,** just to the left of the rue Guynemer exit.

Exit at rue Guynemer and cross onto rue de Fleurus. At:

George Sand

A popular romance novelist, George Sand (born Amandine-Aurore-Lucile Dupin, 1804–76) wrote 80 novels in her lifetime. She was married to Baron Casimer Dudevant, had two children by him, then divorced him. Next, she had a series of affairs—with Jules Sandeau (from whom she derived her pseudonym), playwright/novelist Prosper Mérimée, composer Frédéric Chopin, and poet/novelist Alfred de Musset. Known for her unconventionality, George Sand wore men's clothes and championed the cause of women's rights.

15. **No. 27 rue de Fleurus** is the former home of Gertrude Stein and Alice B. Toklas—a plaque marks the spot. You're probably tired of hearing about these two at this point, but this is their most important residence: the apartment in which Stein amassed her incredible modern art collection and held her famous salons. Hemingway and Fitzgerald visited regularly, as did Picasso, Matisse, and Gauguin. Stein helped guide the careers of more than a few of them and took credit for many of their successes. The art dealers and collectors of her time watched what she and her brother Leo bought and then bought that, too. She had the power to make or break almost any modern artist who walked through her door. Although her salons sparkled with brilliance and attracted a varied cast of artists, by the time she'd moved to rue Christine she'd ostracized many of her literary and artistic friends.

Part II of the St-Germain-des-Prés tour ends here. If you turn right at the corner of boulevard Raspail, you'll reach the Rennes Métro station.

THE LATIN QUARTER
PARTS I & II

PART I

Start: Place St-Michel (Métro: St-Michel).
Finish: La Sorbonne.
Time: Three to five hours.
Best Time: Any time during the day.

Since Roman times, the Quartier Latin (Latin Quarter) has been Paris's intellectual center, where for 700 years Latin was the language of its inhabitants. During Part I of this tour you'll see the world-renowned Sorbonne set amid cafés, bookstores, and boutiques. You'll follow in the footsteps of Dante, Descartes, and Sartre and visit one of Paris's oldest medical-supply shops. A highlight of this part is the Musée de Cluny, where you can see the remains of the Roman baths and a spectacular tapestry collection.

• • • • • • • • • • • • • •

Begin your tour at the:

1. **Place St-Michel,** planned by Napoléon III and famous for its fountain—Davioud's 1860 sculpture of St. Michel slaying the dragon. The place St-Michel has been a center of activity for hundreds of years. Traditionally, celebrating students from the Ecole des Beaux-Arts go for a swim in the fountain after their annual ball; a grim association is that of the students killed here by the Nazis during protests in August 1944.

   From here, go down rue de la Huchette (if you're facing the fountain, rue de la Huchette is on your left, between the yellow awnings of **Gibert Jeune,** one of the few remaining truly collegiate bookstores in the Latin Quarter). At no. 28 (on your left) is the:

2. **Hôtel Mont Blanc,** the former residence of American author Eliot Harold Paul (1891–1958), whose *The Last Time I Saw Paris* (1942) chronicled the city in the 1920s. You'll also see a plaque commemorating Jean Albert Vouillard, who was killed here by the Gestapo at 8pm on May 17, 1944. Rue de la Huchette, almost 800 years old, used to be home to diamond cutters and rotisseurs, who set up shop here; these days the only meat sellers you'll find are those who own the Greek restaurants lining the pedestrian alley. You'll be hard-pressed to find a diamond seller.

   As you walk, on your left you'll pass rue du Chat-qui-Pêche ("Street of the Fishing Cat")—see Walking Tour 1, stop 9, for more about this alley. Continue to the end of rue de la Huchette and turn right down rue du Petit-Pont, which turns into rue St-Jacques. Turn right again onto rue St-Séverin. Continue past the Tango du Chat Restaurant, on your right, and on your left will be the church of:

3. **St-Séverin.** Go in the side door, off rue St-Séverin. The original building, an oratory, was built to honor a hermit named Séverin who lived here in the 6th century. Norsemen burned it down in the 11th century, and a new chapel was erected in its place; by the end of the 11th century, it had become the Left Bank's parish church. The flamboyant gothic building you see today was begun in the early 13th century, and the work continued well into the 16th century.

The two ambulatories (one of which is currently filled with chairs) are what really make St-Séverin unique among Paris churches. Unfortunately, the organ obscures your view of the rose window, but note that the organ case was built by Dupré. Saint-Saëns was said to have played on it.

The rest of the stained glass behind the altar looks like an impressionist painting, with great swaths of color. Best viewed at a distance, the windows, designed by Jean Bazaine in 1966, depict the Seven Sacraments. Since you're not expected to know what the sacraments are by just looking at them, underneath each window is a small plaque telling which of the Seven Sacraments is represented. The chapel to the right of the altar (Chapelle de la Communion) contains some beautiful Georges Roualt etchings done between 1922 and 1927 and pulled by Jacquenin, a master Parisian printer. There's a biography of Roualt on the door to the left of the chapel. Also in this room is an extraordinary G. Schneider rendition of the crucifixion (1989).

Exiting the church the way you entered, make a left on rue des Prêtres-St-Séverin to the front of the church, then proceed along this street to rue de la Parcheminerie. At no. 27 is the:

4. **Abbey Bookshop,** a Canadian-based bookstore selling works in both French and English, with an impressive selection of Canadian titles. The store's presence is significant because the street was named after the professional letter writers, booksellers, copyists, and parchment sellers who set up shop here. At one time it was called rue des Ecrivains ("Street of Writers").

After you've finished browsing, retrace your steps along rue de la Parcheminerie. Cross rue Boutebrie and turn right onto rue St-Jacques. Go left on rue Dante at this slightly confusing intersection and look on your right for no. 9:

5. **A L'Imagerie,** a superb print/poster shop. It stocks hoards of art deco and art nouveau posters, as well as any museum poster you could possibly desire. This is supposedly the oldest (not to mention biggest) shop of its kind in the city.

Keep walking to the **Librairie Gourmande,** no. 4 on your left, famous for its selection of cookbooks (all in

French). If you love to cook and your French is up to snuff, this is the place for you.

Eventually rue Dante turns into a small section of street called:

6. **Rue du Fouarre.** This is quite a famous little street: Beginning in the 12th century, students used to sit in the street on piles of straw (hence the name, derived from the word *feure,* meaning "straw") listening to teachers lecture. Dante is believed to have heard some lectures here in 1304. You might want to stop in at the **bookstore** and **salon de thé** (tearoom) on your left.

Backtrack and turn right onto rue Galande (the street you passed before going onto rue du Fouarre). During Roman times rue Galande was the Lyons-Paris road. In the 17th century the street was much more attractive than it is today, for it was lined with aristocratic residences. At no. 42 on your right is the:

7. **Studio Galande,** currently a cinema (not very attractive, unfortunately) famous for its nightly showing of the *Rocky Horror Picture Show.* Nevertheless, it features a charming 14th-century bas-relief of St. Julien le Hospitaller (or le Pauvre) in his boat. The facade of the cinema is currently being restored.

On your left at no. 65 bis is the **Cybele Archaeological** bookstore, with a marvelous collection. At nos. 50–52 on the right is **Le Chat Huant,** an appealing shop specializing in Asian and African merchandise like jewelry, inks, Sumi-e kits, and beautiful wooden sculptures.

Go to the corner of rue Galande and rue St-Julien-le-Pauvre. At no. 1 bis rue St-Julien-le-Pauvre take a detour down the winding staircase of the **Caveau des Oubliettes** for a good look at a true Parisian nightclub. (This 17th-century house was built on the existing medieval foundations.)

Go right on rue St-Julien-le-Pauvre to the church of:

8. **St-Julien-le-Pauvre,** thought to be Paris's oldest church since it was built sometime before the 9th century. It began much the same way St-Séverin did—as an oratory dedicated to a saint.

During the Revolution, the church was used to store fodder. It was so damaged during this period (and by regular wear and tear up until the Revolution) that much of it had to be rebuilt, including the facade you see today. Inside, it retains one of the few rood screens extant. Since 1889 it has belonged to the Greek Orthodox church. Today, religious and chamber music concerts are frequently held here.

When you come out of the church, go right and keep an eye out for no. 14 (on your left), the **mansion of Isaac de Laffemas,** governor of the Petit Châtelet prison. It has a wonderful portal dating from the late 17th century.

Take a Break   Also on your left is the quaint little **Tea Caddy,** at no. 14 rue St-Julien-le-Pauvre, where you can stop for some real English tea and scones. Light lunches are also served.

At the end of rue St-Julien-le-Pauvre is the square René-Viviani, graced with lime trees and lilac bushes. The false acacia held up by supports is thought to be one of the oldest trees in Paris.

Go left at the corner of rue St-Julien-le-Pauvre to no. 37 rue de la Bûcherie. Here you'll find:

9. **Shakespeare & Company.** Not Sylvia Beach's original, this namesake is run by George Bates Whitman (the self-professed grandson of Walt). Whitman purchased part of Sylvia Beach's library, which is housed at the top of a treacherous flight of stairs. You're welcome to browse through Beach's personal collection.

In case you're wondering if the cots located in niches around the shop are for sitting or sleeping, I'll tell you they're most likely for both. I've heard that Whitman once in a while allows poor writers to spend a little time here until they can secure enough money to get a room elsewhere.

Each book you purchase here will be stamped with the official Shakespeare & Company inscription: "Shakespeare and Co., Kilomètre Zéro, Paris." It's open daily from noon to midnight.

Backtrack to the square René-Viviani and pass it. At the corner make a right on rue Lagrange, then a quick left onto the extension of rue de la Bûcherie, which got its name because barges used to load and unload wood shipments there. Cross rue Frédéric-Sauton onto rue des Grands Degrés (which runs directly into rue de la Bûcherie). Continue out to the end and turn right on the quai de la Tournelle, proceeding to rue de Bièvre, where you turn right and go to:

10. **No. 22 rue de Bièvre,** the home of François Mitterrand, former president of France. During his presidency, Mitterrand insisted on residing in his private home rather than in the Palais de l'Elysée, the traditional home for France's presidents. After looking at this quaint house on a quiet street can you blame him? Mitterrand was a prominent figure in the Resistance during World War II, and in 1971 he founded the French Socialist party. He was reelected in 1988 to a second term; however, in May 1995 Jacques Chirac took over as president.

Continue down the street, cross boulevard St-Germain, and make a little jog off to the right onto rue Monge. If you're ready for a picnic, rue Monge is a good street along which to gather supplies. Stop at the charcuterie on the left for pâté or some other delicacies; cross the street to the fromagerie to pick up some cheese; and a bit farther on stop at the boulangerie/pâtisserie for a baguette or two and a couple of fruit tarts. You'll find a perfect picnic spot not far ahead at the square P. Langevin.

On the way to your picnic you'll come to another interesting church, on your left at 30 rue St-Victor:

11. **St-Nicolas-du-Chardonnet.** This site was once a field of thistles *(chardons)*, and the original place of worship was a 13th-century chapel. Construction of the present church began in 1656. It's thought that Charles Le Brun, a former parishioner, designed the left side of the church.

A Catholic parish that still holds masses in Latin, St-Nicolas-du-Chardonnet is a veritable treasure trove of art, much of it the work of Charles Le Brun. Once you get inside, turn to the right to view his *Martyrdom of John the Baptist.* In the first chapel on the left wall as you enter is Corot's *Baptism of Christ.* Continue around behind the altar, and as you come to the other side you'll see the

The Latin Quarter Part I

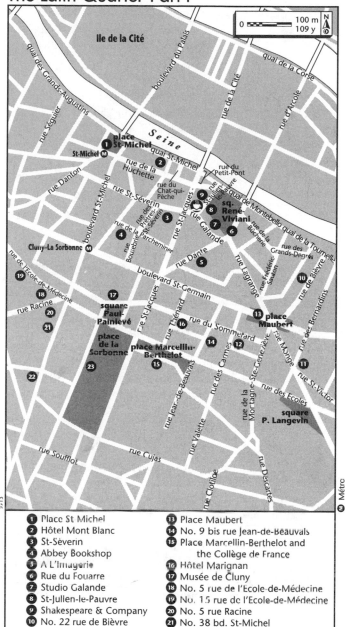

Ile de la Cité

0 ——— 100 m
109 y

quai des Grands-Augustins
quai de la Corse
boulevard du Palais
rue de la Cité
rue d'Arcole
rue Séguier
Seine
place St-Michel
St-Michel M
Quai St-Michel
rue de la Huchette
rue du Petit-Pont
rue Danton
rue St-Séverin
rue du Chat-qui-Pêche
boulevard St-Michel
rue des Prêtres-St-Séverin
rue St-Jacques
rue Galande
rue Saint-Julien-le-Pauvre
sq. René-Viviani
quai de Montebello
quai de la Tournelle
rue de la Bûcherie
rue de la Parcheminerie
rue de la Bouteillerie-St-Séverin
Cluny–La Sorbonne M
rue des Grands-Degrés
rue Dante
rue Lagrange
rue Frédéric-Sauton
rue de Bièvre
rue de l'École-de-Médecine
boulevard St-Germain
rue Racine
square Paul-Painlevé
rue St-Jacques
rue Thénard
rue du Sommerard
place Maubert
rue des Bernardins
rue de la Montagne-Ste-Geneviève
rue de Monge
rue St-Victor
place de la Sorbonne
place Marcellin-Berthelot
rue des Carmes
rue des Écoles
square P. Langevin
rue Jean-de-Beauvais
rue Valette
rue Soufflot
rue Cujas
rue Clotilde
rue Descartes

M Métro

9713

1 Place St Michel
2 Hôtel Mont Blanc
3 St-Séverin
4 Abbey Bookshop
5 A L'Imagerie
6 Rue du Fouarre
7 Studio Galande
8 St-Julien-le-Pauvre
9 Shakespeare & Company
10 No. 22 rue de Bièvre
11 St-Nicolas-du-Chardonnet
12 Musée des Collections
   Historiques de la
   Préfecture de Police
13 Place Maubert
14 No. 9 bis rue Jean-de-Beauvais
15 Place Marcellin-Berthelot and
   the Collège de France
16 Hôtel Marignan
17 Musée de Cluny
18 No. 5 rue de l'École-de-Médecine
19 No. 15 rue de l'École-de-Médecine
20 No. 5 rue Racine
21 No. 38 bd. St-Michel
22 Hôtel Luxembourg
23 La Sorbonne

tomb of Le Brun's mother as well as an Antoine Coysevox memorial to Le Brun and his wife (other works by this artist are pointed out in Walking Tour 7, stop 9, and Walking Tour 8, stop 4). Above the altar and on the ceiling are some fine paintings by Le Brun.

Exit onto rue des Bernardins (which intersects with rue Monge running along the side of the church) and walk to rue des Ecoles. Before you lies the square P. Langevin, where you can enjoy that picnic lunch. Afterward, return to rue des Ecoles and go left as you exit the park. Cross rue de la Montagne-Ste-Geneviève to rue des Carmes, then turn right to no. 1 bis rue des Carmes, where you'll find the:

12. **Musée des Collections Historiques de la Préfecture de Police.** This museum is located in the ugly building on your right, but don't let that deter you—it contains some very interesting exhibits. Created in 1909, the museum documents the Parisian police department's history from the Middle Ages to today. You'll find items of interest like the orders for the arrest of Dr. Guillotin, the bloodstained book from President Paul Doumer's 1932 assassination, weapons used by many infamous outlaws, and a huge collection of memorabilia from World War II's Nazi Occupation.

Continue along rue des Carmes to the:

13. **Place Maubert.** Called Maubert Cesspit by Erasmus (see box below), this square was once a place of execution in which people were hanged and burned at the stake. One such person was scholar/philosopher Etienne Dolet (b. 1509), who was burned here in 1546 after being convicted of heresy. Later, a statue was erected as a tribute to him, but it was taken down during the Nazi Occupation and never seen again. So many Huguenots were killed here that it became a place of pilgrimage. Today the place Maubert is an upscale shopping area with a popular outdoor food market. Not a trace of the cesspit remains. Take some time to poke around through the market, where you'll find innumerable cheeses and a wide variety of meats, as well as lovely fruits and vegetables.

Erasmus

Dutch humanist, theologian, scholar, and writer Desiderius Erasmus (1466–1536) was an ordained priest of the Roman Catholic church even though he was a reformer. He spent time studying at the University of Paris, and one of his greatest achievements was a translation of the Old Testament from its original Greek into Latin.

He disagreed with the ideology of Martin Luther, the father of Protestantism, and actually attacked Luther's ideas regarding predestination with his essay *On the Freedom of the Will.* When once asked why he wasn't observing the Catholic tradition of the Lenten fast, Erasmus said, "I have a Catholic soul, but a Lutheran stomach."

Turn left on boulevard St-Germain and then left again onto rue Jean-de-Beauvais to:

14. **No. 9 bis rue Jean-de-Beauvais,** one of the Sorbonne's first college chapels, built in 1375. Its gothic spire is the only one of its period left in the city of Paris. Since 1882 it's been used as a Romanian Orthodox church.

    Continue along and go up the stairs to rue des Ecoles. Note the interesting sculpture on your left at the top of the stairs. Turn right onto rue des Ecoles and on your left will be the:

15. **Place Marcellin-Berthelot** and the **Collège de France.** Rebelling against the narrow-mindedness of the teachings of the Sorbonne, François I founded the College of France in 1530.

    The professors at the new Collège de France were paid by the king rather than the students, a radical change from the Sorbonne's procedure. The school began as a trilingual institution, teaching Latin, Greek, and Hebrew—another departure from the traditional. Not long after its founding, courses in mathematics, philosophy, surgery, medicine, law, Arabic, and astronomy were also made available; while Louis XV was king, a French literature course was added, the first of its kind. Reflecting a tradition of nondiscriminatory policies, the inscription outside the school reads *Docet omnia*—"All are taught here."

In the place Berthelot is an **Aube bronze of Dante,** as well as a **Eugène Guillaume statue of Claude Bernard,** a famous 19th-century physiologist who worked in the Collège de France's laboratory. Bernard died nearby at no. 40 rue des Ecoles.

Turn right off rue des Ecoles onto rue Thénard. As you walk, look to the right down rue de Latran for a great view of the Romanian Orthodox church you saw earlier. Continue to rue du Sommerard and go right to no. 13, the:

16. **Hôtel Marignan,** where American poet e.e. cummings stayed in 1921. As exhibited by the style of his name, he had a preference for lowercase letters and very little (if any) punctuation. Turn around and go in the other direction on rue du Sommerard. At the square Paul-Painlevé is the:

17. **Musée de Cluny,** 6 place Paul-Painlevé. At the beginning of the 3rd century a Gallo-Roman building, the Palais des Thermes (presumed by archaeologists to be Roman baths), stood here. The baths date from between A.D. 161 and 181 and were thought to have been burned down several times by barbarians. About a thousand years later, Pierre de Chalus, abbot of Cluny-en-Bourgogne, bought the ruins and the neighboring land in order to build a residence for visiting abbots. The building you see today is the work of another abbot, Jacques d'Amboise, who turned it into something of a palace. After the Revolution, the property changed hands several times, until it was finally purchased by Alexandre du Sommerard, a state official and medieval art collector. After his 1842 death, his house and its contents were sold to the state. The museum opened in 1844, with Alexandre's son, Edmond Sommerard, as curator.

Today, thanks to both Sommerards, the museum houses one of the world's greatest collections of medieval art and artifacts. Included are finely wrought jewelry, brilliant stained-glass windows (this is the closest you'll ever get to glass like this), and some amazing tapestries that by themselves make a visit to the museum worthwhile. Be sure not to miss the original Abbot's Chapel, complete with an incredible vaulted ceiling.

Exit the Musée de Cluny, walk to rue du Sommerard, and then turn right and go to boulevard St-Michel. Cross the boulevard to rue de l'Ecole-de-Médecine and look for:

18. **No. 5 rue d l'Ecole-de-Médecine,** the former location of the Brotherhood of Surgeons, founded by St. Louis. Half barbers, half surgeons, they performed surgeries on "minor ailments" until the 17th century. Currently, the building houses the Institute of Modern Languages. Note the plaque commemorating the birth of actress Sarah Bernhardt in this house on October 25, 1844.

Continue along rue de l'Ecole-de-Médecine, passing on your left **Establissements du Docteur Anzoux S. A.,** which has been here since 1822. It's filled with all kinds of medical gadgets—from plastic models of the ear to scalpels and stethoscopes.

On your left at:

19. **No. 15 rue de l'Ecole-de-Médecine** there was once a Franciscan monastery. The first attempt at mapping the city of Paris was undertaken here in 1785 by a geometrician named Verniquet. His maps were used as the basis for all later maps of Paris.

Turn around and go back to boulevard St-Michel. Make a right and walk to rue Racine, then turn right and approach:

20. **No. 5 rue Racine** (on your left), where Henry Wadsworth Longfellow lived while studying at the Sorbonne. When he began his studies in 1826 he lived in a *pension de famille* (boardinghouse) until he began to feel imprisoned by the curfew and mealtime restrictions. He moved here so he could be more independent.

Return to boulevard St-Michel, where at:

21. **No. 38 boulevard St-Michel** you'll find the apartment Richard Wright sublet in 1946 from a professor who was on leave in Australia.

Proceed to rue de Vaugirard. At no. 1 bis is the **Hôtel Trianon Palace,** where Richard Wright took up residence when he first arrived in Paris after a long battle for a passport with the U.S. government.

At no. 4 is the:

22. **Hôtel Luxembourg** (formerly the Hôtel Lisbonne), where author William Shirer lived in September 1925. It was a bargain at $10 per month, but Shirer reported that one had to use the bidet as a bathtub since the owner used the only bathtub as a coal bin. Further, he and other Americans who were accustomed to creature comforts had a lot of trouble learning how to use the hotel's Turkish toilets.

   Again return to boulevard St-Michel. Take a side trip down the boulevard to see the homes of two more expatriates of note. During his first visit to Paris in 1923, American poet Archibald MacLeish lived at **no. 85;** a friend of James Joyce, he originally came to Paris as a lawyer. And at **no. 93,** now the Foyer International des Etudiantes, Sylvia Beach hid out in a top-floor kitchen during the Nazi Occupation from 1942 to 1944.

   If you're not interested in taking the long walk down boulevard St-Michel and back up, cross the boulevard and walk through the place de la Sorbonne (1634), anchored by a statue of Auguste Comte (see Walking Tour 10, stop 11, for more on Comte), to:

23. **La Sorbonne.** In 1253 Robert de Sorbon, confessor of St. Louis, founded the Sorbonne (with the help of the king) for poor students who wished to pursue theological studies. He wanted it to be a place where they could live and go to school without having to worry about money. Since then it has seen such famous teachers as St. Thomas Aquinas and Roger Bacon and such famous students as Dante, Calvin, and Longfellow. In 1469 France's first printing press was set up here; during the Nazi Occupation the Sorbonne became the headquarters for the Resistance. The courtyard and galleries are open to the public, and in the Cour d'Honneur are statues of Victor Hugo and Louis Pasteur.

   This ends Part I of the Latin Quarter tour. If you don't want to continue with Part II, go back up boulevard St-Michel toward the river until you reach the Cluny–La Sorbonne Métro station. If you do wish to continue, Part II begins where the first part ended, in the Sorbonne.

PART II

Start: La Sorbonne (Métro: Cluny–La Sorbonne).

Finish: The intersection of rue Mouffetard and rue Daubenton.

Time: About three hours.

Best Time: Either early morning or late afternoon so you can visit the Mouffetard Market while it's open.

Part II of the Latin Quarter tour will take you to major attractions such as the Panthéon (which contains the tombs of some of France's most notable politicians and scholars). You'll also visit France's oldest zoo, a mosque bedecked with spectacular mosaics, and a fabulous food market.

• • • • • • • • • • • • • • •

Exit the Sorbonne (see Part I for details), turn left on rue de la Sorbonne (which turns into rue Victor-Cousin), then turn left again onto rue Cujas. On your left you'll pass the **Lycée Louis-Le-Grand** (founded 1550), the alma mater of a long list of notables—Robespierre, Hugo, Baudelaire, Voltaire, and Pompidou are but a few. Continuing along rue Cujas, you'll arrive at the place du Panthéon, where to your right, at the top of the Montagne Ste-Geneviève, is the:

1. **Panthéon,** one of Paris's best-known monuments. There's an interesting story behind its foundation: In 1744 Louis XV fell seriously ill. He vowed that if he recovered he'd rebuild the Ste-Geneviève abbey in the patron saint's honor. Upon recovering, he entrusted the job to the marquis de Marigny, Madame de Pompadour's brother, who passed on the responsibility to architect Jacques-Germain Soufflot. The original plans called for a church, but construction stopped due to financial difficulties and Soufflot's death. After the death of an important Revolution-era politician by the name of Mirabeau, the French parliament decided the Ste-Geneviève church should be changed into a "Temple of Fame" to hold the remains of all the great men of France, the first of whom would be Mirabeau.

Shortly after Mirabeau's burial, Voltaire's remains were exhumed and moved to the Panthéon, which became a "temple dedicated to all the gods." Among its denizens are Jean-Jacques Rousseau, Victor Hugo, Paul Painlevé, Louis Braille (inventor of the Braille system for the blind), Emile Zola (see Walking Tour 9, stop 20), Jean Moulin (a Resistance fighter who was tortured to death by the Nazis), and Marcelin Berthelot and his wife—the only woman entombed here.

Across rue Cujas stands the **Bibliothèque Ste-Geneviève** (1824), which houses more than two million volumes. Walk around to the right of the Panthéon (if you're facing away from the building) to:

2. **St-Etienne-du-Mont,** a beautiful example of gothic architecture. Completed and consecrated in the 17th century, the church holds a shrine to Ste. Geneviève, as well as the remains of Racine and Pascal. Walk to the right. Notice the spiral staircases leading up to the 16th- and 17th-century rood screen. Not far beyond are the epitaphs of Pascal and Racine, then the relics of Ste. Geneviève. Continuing your way around, you'll see stained-glass windows, some from the 16th and 17th centuries, plus busts of Pascal and Racine.

Come out of St-Etienne-du-Mont, turn left onto rue Clovis, and walk to the:

3. **Lycée Henri IV,** on your right. One of the city's best-known high schools, Lycée Henri IV is housed in one of the Ste-Geneviève abbey's former buildings. Sartre was among the teachers here. Within the walls is Clovis tower, named for King Clovis of the Franks; he was responsible for building the original abbey, of which only this tower remains. Physicists Ampère and Arago used the tower for their experiments in the 19th century.

Proceed along rue Clovis, turn right on rue Descartes, and note on the left:

4. **No. 39 rue Descartes,** where poet Paul Verlaine (1844–96) died. He became a major figure in the bohemian literary world with the 1869 publication of *Fêtes galantes*. His *Romances sans paroles* distinguished him as the first symbolist poet.

Ste. Geneviève

Born in Nanterre, Ste. Geneviève (420–500) was still a small child when she told Bishop St-Germanus d'Auxerre that she wanted to devote herself to God. When she turned 15 the bishop gave her a veil symbolic of a virgin dedicated to God, and shortly thereafter, it's said, she performed her first miracle—she cured her mother's blindness.

Ste. Geneviève later moved to Paris. She's credited with sparing the city in 451 from an attack by Atilla the Hun. Virtually everyone had fled at the mere thought that the Huns might arrive, but Geneviève stayed and literally prayed the attackers away. The city was delivered.

Some of her other alleged miracles included curing the sick and actually stopping a rainstorm. People began to worship her even while she was alive. After her death, her relics were paraded through the streets during a terrible epidemic, and the disease stopped spreading. To this day, as a consequence, her relics are paraded through the streets every year, and Ste. Geneviève is recognized as the patron saint of Paris.

When you come to the end of rue Descartes, turn left onto rue Thouin. Follow this street to rue du Cardinal-Lemoine, where you should turn right. At no. 74 is the:

5. **Salon de Thé Under Hemingway,** Hemingway's first home in Paris. In 1922 he was visited here by Gertrude Stein and Alice B. Toklas, who told him he needed to rewrite, from beginning to end, his first attempt at a novel.

Now turn around and recross rue Thouin, proceeding to:

6. **No. 71 rue du Cardinal-Lemoine,** where Irish novelist James Joyce lived in 1921, a year before Sylvia Beach (see Walking Tour 4, Part II, stop 3) published his masterpiece, *Ulysses.* Other publishers considered the book obscene and unpublishable.

Continue along the street to:

7. **No. 67 rue du Cardinal-Lemoine,** where mathematician/philosopher Blaise Pascal (1623–62) died. A child genius, Pascal invented a calculating machine at age 19 and was also the founder of the modern theory of probability. However, most people know Pascal for his *Pensées,* which outline a mystical faith.

   A little farther down the road, across rue Monge, you'll find at no. 49 the:

8. **Hôtel le Brun,** at which painter Jean-Antoine Watteau (1684–1721) spent the last few years of his life. One of the leading figures of rococo art, he's famous for creating the *fête galante* (paintings of a pastoral, dreamy nature).

   Return to rue Monge and turn left to rue de Navarre. Follow the signs to the:

9. **Arènes de Lutèce,** a Roman amphitheater. With its 36 rows of stone seats, it had a seating capacity of 15,000; some seats actually had the names of their owners chiseled into them. Archaeologists believe the amphitheater was built in about the late 1st century. At the end of the 3rd century, when the barbarians invaded, it fell into disuse; by the 4th century, it was being used as a cemetery. It was buried when a moat was dug around Philippe III's city wall in the late 12th century. Then in 1869 it was rediscovered and restored, and today the Arènes de Lutèce is a public garden featuring the square Capitan, named for a sponsor of the restoration. You'll always find lots of children playing here, watched over by their nannies or parents; you might even find a full-fledged soccer match in progress.

   Retrace your steps to rue de Navarre, turn left and go to the corner, then turn right along the extension of rue de Navarre. When you come to rue Lacépède, turn left and follow the street to its end. Across rue Linné and straight ahead into the rue Cuvier is the entrance to the:

10. **Jardin des Plantes.** In 1626 Louis XIII began to execute a plan for a medicinal botanical garden that Henri IV and his minister, Sully, had conceived. When Louis XIV became king, his doctor, named Fagon, traveled around the world collecting specimens and set the groundwork for the curator, Buffon, who was later able to finish Henri IV's

The Latin Quarter Part II

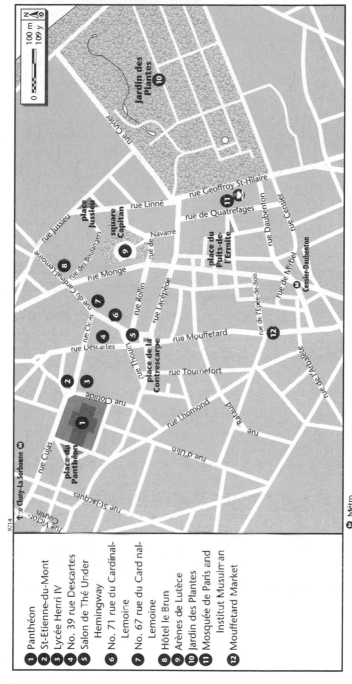

1. Panthéon
2. St-Etienne-du-Mont
3. Lycée Henri IV
4. No. 39 rue Descartes
5. Salon de Thé Under Hemingway
6. No. 71 rue du Cardinal-Lemoine
7. No. 67 rue du Card nal-Lemoine
8. Hôtel le Brun
9. Arènes de Lutèce
10. Jardin des Plantes
11. Mosquée de Paris and Institut Musulman
12. Mouffetard Market

plans. Some of France's great naturalists have worked in the gardens, including Jussieu, St-Hilaire, Daubenton, Lacépède, and Lamarck (who many argue was the originator of the theory of evolution).

Today the gardens, which include greenhouses and a maze, cover 74 acres that from April to October are a riot of colors and scents.

The **Ménagerie** (zoo), the oldest in France, began as a sort of holding area for animals from Versailles that had managed to survive the Revolution. The first inhabitants weren't too thrilling, just your average zebra, hartebeest, and rhino. Elephants were brought here in 1795, and by 1827 (with some bears and giraffes) it started looking more like a real zoo. Unfortunately, the Ménagerie's period of growth didn't last long—many of the animals were killed and eaten by starving Parisians during the Franco-Prussian War (1870–71), when the city was under siege. The zoo hasn't been quite the same since, but that doesn't matter to most of the children (or adults) who visit here.

The park also contains the **Museum of Natural History,** which possesses a major collection of minerals and insects.

Exit the Jardin des Plantes from the entrance and re-trace your steps to rue Lacépède. Go right on rue Lacépède and then left to rue de Quatrefages. Continue along to the place du Puits-de-l'Ermite. On your left, at no. 1, will be the:

11. **Mosquée de Paris** and **Institut Musulman,** constructed between 1922 and 1926. As you enter these buildings, notice the grand patio with its cedar woodwork, eucalyptus plants, and gurgling fountain. On the walls of the mosque are some lovely mosaic friezes with quotations from the Koran, and the prayer rooms house an incredible collection of handwoven carpets, some from the 17th century. The Institut Musulman teaches Arabic and Islamic culture.

Take a Break If you're hungry for lunch or just a snack, try the **Moorish café** or the **Arabic restaurant** on the mosque grounds. Recommended are the delicious pastries and strong, sweet Turkish coffee.

Take a Steam   If after eating (or instead of) you feel like indulging yourself, not far from the mosque is a **Turkish bathhouse.** Exit the way you entered and (facing away from the mosque) turn left to rue Daubenton. Make a left on rue Daubenton, go to rue Geoffroy St-Hilaire, then make another left. At nos. 29–31 is the bathhouse entrance. There are three steam rooms—available to men and women on different days—plus an Islamic art gallery.

If you don't wish to enjoy some steam (see above), exit the mosque, go through the place du Puits-de-l'Ermite (take the roadway on the left side), and continue on rue du Puits-de-l'Ermite to rue Monge. Turn left on rue Monge to rue de l'Epée-de-Bois, then turn right. Follow this street all the way to rue Mouffetard. Go left on rue Mouffetard to the:

12. **Mouffetard Market,** another of Paris's colorful outdoor food markets. This narrow street overflows with people and is lined with displays of fruits, vegetables, cheeses, and meats—sensual overstimulation indeed. Savor this true Paris experience; it may become one of your fondest memories of the city.

If you turn left at the corner of rue Daubenton and rue Mouffetard you'll find the Censier-Daubenton Métro station.

THE MARAIS

Start: Place de la Bastille (Métro: Bastille).

Finish: Centre Pompidou.

Time: Three to eight hours, depending on how much time you spend in the museums—try to decide ahead of time which of them you'd most like to visit.

Best Time: Wednesday through Sunday, beginning at 10am.

Worst Time: The Musée Picasso and Centre Pompidou are closed on Tuesday; the Musée Carnavalet is closed on Monday. Also, if you start late in the day you'll never make it to more than one museum.

The Marais district, in the 3rd and 4th arrondissements on the Right Bank, was originally a swampland outside the city walls set aside for grazing animals. By the 17th century, it had developed into the seat of Parisian aristocracy, where nobles built opulent *hôtels particuliers* (mansions). However, the fashionable set eventually moved elsewhere, and many of these houses were abandoned and neglected until the 1960s, when the Minister of Cultural Affairs took an interest in restoring them. You'll get to see some of these mansions while walking this tour.

Today, the Marais is home to Paris's Asian and Jewish communities. This tour will take you into the bustling heart of the Jewish district, where homey delicatessens, pâtisseries, and takeout falafel shops share the streets with ultrachic boutiques. You'll also have the opportunity to visit several museums—one is the Musée Picasso, where you'll be able to see pieces you've never seen before.

• • • • • • • • • • • • • • • •

Begin your tour at the:

1. **Place de la Bastille.** The original Bastille fortress was built as a palace for Charles V. Later, Cardinal Richelieu used it as a political prison for those who opposed royal power; Voltaire was twice imprisoned here. On July 14, 1789, 633 people stormed the Bastille, lynched the governor, freed the seven prisoners, and destroyed the fortress. You can follow the paving stones tracing the walls and towers of the original fortress from no. 5 to no. 49 bd. Henri-IV.

   The **Colonne de Juillet** (July Column) at the square's center is not, however, associated with the storming of the Bastille. Instead, it commemorates the 615 people who died in the July Revolution of 1830, which overthrew the Bourbon king Charles X and replaced him with Louis-Philippe, duc d'Orléans. The new king requested that this monument be erected in memory of those who had died here for him. In 1840 the victims' bodies were moved here to the underground vaults. The dead from the 1848 revolution were entombed here as well.

   The hollow bronze column weighs 174 tons and is 170 feet tall, topped by the *Génie de la Liberté* (Genius of Liberty) statue. If you want to reach the upper gallery, you'll have to climb approximately 240 steps. The names of the victims who are entombed within are inscribed on the column's sides.

   From here, you can see the controversial:

2. **Opéra de la Bastille,** designed by Canadian-Uruguayan architect Carlos Ott and opened on July 14, 1989, to mark the bicentennial of the Bastille's fall. A venue for popular

opera, it was intended to be the biggest opera house in the world, and it boasts a 2,700-seat main auditorium that's the largest in France, as well as five movable stages. The all-glass curved building is certainly one of the world's most unusual opera houses.

Exit the place de la Bastille and make a left on rue St-Antoine, following it to rue de Birague. Turn right at this street and walk to the:

3. **Place des Vosges.** Inaugurated on April 5, 6, and 7 in 1609, this was the first public square built by Henri IV and was originally called the place Royal. Henri intended it to be the scene of both commercial business and social festivities. During the Revolution, the square became the place de l'Invisibilité when its statue of Louis XIII was stolen (and probably melted down); at this time it was also used as a military site. Today, at the center of the square stands a replacement statue of Louis XIII.

The square enjoyed happier days after it was renamed place des Vosges (in the entire city of Paris, the Vosges department was the first to pay its taxes) on September 23, 1800. When it became the center of industrialized Paris, however, it suffered. The grand buildings around the square were divided into small rooms and apartments, and the area went into a decline. Only recently has it recovered, when it was declared a historic monument.

Thirty-six pavilions surround the square, and the two tall buildings flanking it are the **Pavillon de Roi** (King) and **Pavillon de la Reine** (Queen)—you entered through the King's Pavilion. Most of the pavilions house antiques shops, bookstores, art galleries, and cafés. While walking through, you're likely to come across a parade of musicians playing for their dinner—especially on weekends.

As you enter the square, go right to no. 6, which is the:

4. **Musée Victor Hugo,** housed in the Hôtel de Rohan-Guéménée, where Hugo lived from 1832 to 1848. (In 1848 he went into exile because he opposed Napoléon III, who'd just come to power.) Inside are hundreds of books and drawings donated to the city in 1902 by Paul Meurice, Hugo's friend and the executor of his will. This museum owns more than 500 of his "spontaneous drawings," so they're rotated

regularly. The museum also possesses a collection of all the editions of Hugo's works.

Continue along the square to:

5. **No. 8 place des Vosges,** the former residence of authors Théophile Gautier (see Walking Tour 9, stop 20) and Alphonse Daudet. Daudet (1840–97) began his career as an adolescent: Forced into a position as a "study master" at 16 because of his father's financial problems, he came to Paris to pursue his writing career at 17. He's most famous for his naturalistic stories and novels on the lives of the French, from both a Parisian and a provincial point of view. His best-known works include *Le petit chose* (1868) and *L'Evangeliste* (1883).

As you continue around the square, note that **no. 12** is where Henri IV's topographer, Claude de Chastillon, lived. He was, at that time, responsible for making official maps and reproductions of famous Paris monuments. Also note the historic **Pavillon de la Reine** at no. 28 (now one of the most fashionable hotels in this area).

Still farther along the square is:

6. **No. 21 place des Vosges,** another of Alphonse Daudet's addresses, but this is more notable as the home of Armand-Jean du Plessis, duc de Richelieu, best known as Cardinal Richelieu (1585–1642). Richelieu became secretary of state in 1616 with the help of Louis XIII's mother, Marie de Médicis, who acted as regent until her son reached maturity. In 1622 he became a cardinal of the Roman Catholic Church, and in 1624 Louis XIII appointed him prime minister. Six years later, jealous of Richelieu's power, Marie de Médicis turned against him —however, she lacked the king's support and was banished. Soon afterward, Richelieu secured complete control over the French government.

Head back to rue de Birague (coming from the opposite direction in which you began) and on your right will be the:

7. **Hôtel de Sully,** one of Paris's most exquisite mansions. It was built in 1624 by Mesme-Gallet (an affluent banker), but it was Henri IV's minister, the duc de Sully, who beautified it throughout with painted ceilings and painted and

gilded pilasters. The building is now home to the Caisse Nationale des Monuments Historiques et des Sites (National Historical Monuments and Sites Commission), and temporary exhibitions are occasionally held here. An interesting historical footnote: Voltaire was beaten by the servants of a nobleman under the portal here. The building is open Monday through Saturday from 9am to 6pm.

Come back out of the Hôtel de Sully. Now go to:

8. **No. 1 place des Vosges,** where the marquise de Sévigné, famous in French literature for the series of letters she wrote her daughter, was born on February 6, 1626.

Exit the place des Vosges the way you entered (via rue de Birague) and turn right onto rue St-Antoine. At rue de Sévigné, look on your left for no. 99, which is the church of:

9. **St-Paul–St-Louis,** constructed between 1627 (Louis XIII laid the first stone) and 1641 by the Jesuits. It seems that this was the parish church for many of those who resided in the place des Vosges at one time or another. On May 9, 1641, Cardinal Richelieu said the first mass here. Note that the holy water stoups on each side of the entrance were donated by Victor Hugo. It's said that for many years the hearts of Louis XIII and Louis XIV were kept here. Though most of the art originally housed here was taken during the Revolution, Delacroix's *Christ in the Garden of Olives* remains and can be viewed.

When you exit the church, cross the street, and turn left on rue St-Antoine (which becomes rue de Rivoli). Here you'll find **Pottier,** a pâtisserie where you can pick up some goodies to sustain you on the rest of the tour. Continue walking along rue de Rivoli to rue Pavée (on your right). Turn right onto the city's first paved road and go to the:

10. **Synagogue de Guimard,** the only synagogue (1913) designed by Hector Guimard, the master of art nouveau.

At no. 24 rue Pavée is the:

11. **Hôtel Lamoignon/Bibliothèque Historique.** Commissioned in 1584, it was designed by Baptiste du Cerceau in 1611. Diane de France, the illegitimate daughter of Henri II (made legitimate at age seven by an adoption that granted

The Marais

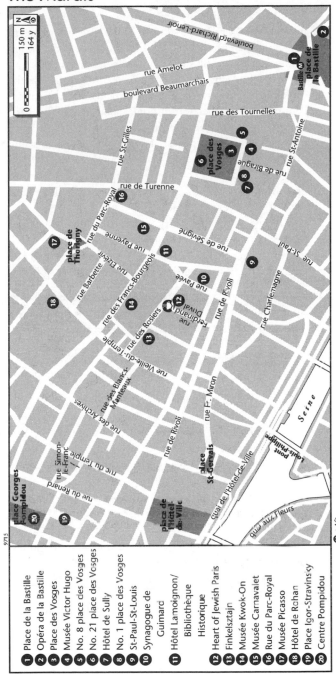

1. Place de la Bastille
2. Opéra de la Bastille
3. Place des Vosges
4. Musée Victor Hugo
5. No. 8 place des Vosges
6. No. 21 place des Vosges
7. Hôtel de Sully
8. No. 1 place des Vosges
9. St-Paul-St-Louis
10. Synagogue de Guimard
11. Hôtel Lamoignon/ Bibliothèque Historique
12. Heart of Jewish Paris
13. Finkelsztajn
14. Musée Kwok-On
15. Musée Carnavalet
16. Rue du Parc-Royal
17. Musée Picasso
18. Hôtel de Rohan
19. Place Igor-Stravinsky
20. Centre Pompidou

Ⓜ Métro

0   150 m
    164 y

9715

her all noble rights), lived here from the time it was built until her death. From 1658 to 1677 the hotel was rented to Guillaume de Lamoignon, the first president of the Parliament of Paris. In 1688 Lamoignon's son bought it.

A new building was added in the 1960s to house the Bibliothèque Historique de la Ville de Paris. There's no more comprehensive collection of books about the city of Paris anywhere. Unfortunately, it's open only to those with specific research purposes. If you're interested in using the library, there's an information booth to the right of the street entrance. The library is open from 9:30am to 6pm Monday through Saturday. It's closed holidays and the first two weeks of August.

Coming out of the library, go left to rue des Rosiers and turn right. At no. 4 is the **Hammam,** or Jewish Public Baths. As you approach the corner of rue des Rosiers and rue Ferdinand-Duval, you'll find yourself in the:

12. **Heart of Jewish Paris.** Rue des Rosiers was named after the rosebushes that used to grow within medieval Paris's walls, though that name hardly describes what you'll find here today. Lined with falafel shops and delis, the street is your best bet for a quick bite. Rue des Rosiers is always packed with people, making it difficult to get around, but take your time in this area—there's a lot to absorb.

Take a Break At no. 7 rue des Rosiers is **Jo Goldenberg,** founded by Albert Goldenberg. You can't miss it since its window displays (mainly of hanging sausages) are unusual for Paris. Here you can lunch on some chopped liver, pastrami, or gefilte fish. The place can get so crowded you sometimes need to make a reservation, but there's no harm in trying to get in without one. If unsuccessful, you can stop for falafel at **Le Roi du Falaffel-Rosiers Alimentation,** 34 rue des Rosiers (or any similar place along the way).

Not far beyond Jo Goldenberg is:

13. **Finkelsztajn,** 27 rue des Rosiers. Established in 1851, this is one of the city's finest Jewish pastry shops. You'll probably have to fight the crowds to get in, but the pastries are worth the effort.

Turn right when you get to rue Vieille-du-Temple. On your left, at no. 47, will be the **Hôtel des Ambassadeurs de Hollande,** where Beaumarchais wrote *The Marriage of Figaro.* This is one of the most beautiful mansions in the Marais (though it's not open to the public). Note that despite its name this was never occupied by anyone in the Dutch embassy. Turn right at rue des Francs-Bourgeois and continue until you reach the:

14. **Musée Kwok-On,** on your right at no. 41, just past the trendy **Café les Enfants Gâtés**. The museum's entrance is virtually unmarked—there's only a small plaque near the door—so pay close attention to the numbers.

    This Asian museum is unique and worth a quick visit. The temporary exhibitions from the works donated by Chinese collector Kwok-On might include costumes from Chinese opera, masks from Indian theater, costumes from Japan's Kabuki and No theaters, or an incredible collection of string and shadow puppets.

    If you're interested in the history of Paris, continue along to rue de Sévigné. Turn left and walk to no. 23, the:

15. **Musée Carnavalet,** housed in the Hôtel Carnavalet (a 16th-century mansion occupied by Madame de Sévigné—see stop 8, above—during the last 19 years of her life) and the Hôtel Le-Peletier-de-St-Fargeau (whose namesake was considered responsible for Louis XVI's death sentence). Its exhibits of paintings, sculptures, decorative arts, and period costumes take you from the Middle Ages through the Renaissance and up to the present. Try not to miss the portrait of Madame Récamier, one of Paris's most beautiful "ladies of the evening." The painting conveys an absolutely luminous quality, and you can stare at her for hours and never grow weary of her image. The museum has a good bookshop as well.

    Leave the museum, turn left, and walk to the end of rue de Sévigné. As you go left onto:

16. **Rue du Parc-Royal,** note the mansions on the right side of the street, the most interesting of which are nos. 4 and 10. At no. 4 (if you make a right for a few steps) you'll find the 17th-century **Hôtel de Canillac.** It now houses a

popular tearoom, Dattes et Noix, where you can order ice cream, tarts, and light lunches. Backtrack and cross rue de Sévigné. At no. 10 is the **Hôtel de Vigny.** Once scheduled to be demolished, this building is now registered as a historic monument, saved primarily because of its beautiful painted ceilings and beams.

Continue along rue du Parc-Royal to place de Thorigny, where at no. 5 is the fantastic:

17. **Musée Picasso.** This museum is housed in the Hôtel Salé, built between 1656 and 1660 for salt-tax collector Pierre Aubert de Fontenay (hence the building's name—*salé* means "salted"). Ironically, Fontenay couldn't pay his own bills, and the house was confiscated. It has changed hands many times since and has even housed the Ecole des Arts et Métiers (which left it considerably damaged). The building was eventually restored and became the Musée Picasso.

Opened in September 1985, the museum holds works from Picasso's personal collection. When he died intestate in 1973, he left behind a huge amount of his work. At one time he decided that every year he'd keep for himself a certain number of his paintings, and what you see here is a large part of this collection. Picasso so liked his own work that he often even bought back his pieces from art auctions or dealers.

The state chose 203 paintings, 158 sculptures, and over 3,000 prints and drawings (not to mention reliefs, ceramics, and sketchbooks)—together they track the artist's career from beginning to end. As you wander through the museum, you'll see Picassos you never even knew existed as well as canvases you'd never guess were painted by Picasso. You'll gain a new appreciation for the genius of this man who experimented with all types of art, including traditional, cubist, surrealist, and comic. The curators have done a commendable job arranging the pieces so visitors get a good overview of Picasso's life and work.

In addition, the museum has a great bookstore—you won't believe how many books have been published about Picasso.

When you exit the museum, note that Balzac once lived down the block at **no. 9** (to your left). Head to the right, back to the place de Thorigny. Proceed straight through the place to rue Elzévir and then to rue Barbette. Turn right on rue Barbette (note at no. 17 **L'Eléphant Dans la Porcelaine,** a little antiquities shop selling interesting knickknacks). At the end of rue Barbette, turn right onto the rue Vieille-du-Temple and go to the:

18. **Hôtel de Rohan.** The mansion's first occupant, François de Rohan, was reputed to have been Louis XIV's son. Inside, the main attraction is the amusing 18th-century Salon des Singes (Monkey Room)—however, the interior is open to the public only during exhibitions. In the courtyard (open from 9am to 6pm on Monday through Friday), you can see a stunning bas-relief, *The Watering of the Horses of the Sun,* which includes a nude Apollo and four horses against a background of exploding sunbursts.

    Exit the Hôtel de Rohan and make a right and proceed on rue Vieille-du-Temple, crossing its intersections with rues Barbette, des Francs-Bourgeois, and des Rosiers. Turn right at rue des Blancs-Manteaux. Note that after it crosses rue du Temple, this street becomes rue Simon-le-Franc. As you cross rue du Renard, in front of you will be the colorful Centre Pompidou. Head along into the:

19. **Place Igor-Stravinsky,** where you'll find the whimsical kinetic fountain *Rites of Spring,* designed by Niki de Saint-Phalle and Jean Tinguely. Its giant lips, musical notes, and all sorts of animals delight children and adults alike. This is a great place for a few minutes' pause before finishing the tour.

    When ready, head into the place Georges Pompidou (also known as plateau Beaubourg), the huge square on your right, and check out the variety of street performers—jugglers, fire eaters, mimes, dancers, and acrobats—who gather in front of the:

20. **Centre Pompidou,** officially named the Centre National d'Art et de Culture Georges-Pompidou but known by everyone as the Centre Pompidou or the Beaubourg. Opened in 1977, this museum boasts an avant-garde exoskeletal architecture that features brightly painted exposed pipes and ducts and infrastructure—the effect

either attracts or repulses people. Most seem to have been attracted, however, since more than 6 million people visited during its first year. The museum's main goal is to make modern art accessible to as many people as possible by providing an "interactive" display space with no permanent walls. After the first time I visited (when I was too young to appreciate it) I didn't remember any of the artwork I'd seen, only the incredibly long escalators that allow riders to look outside and inside at all the museum's "inner architecture." In some way, even though I hadn't been impressed enough with the paintings and sculptures to recall them, I'd interacted with the building, a work of art in and of itself.

The entire first floor houses a library open to the public, and the upper levels house the **Musée National d'Art Moderne,** with displays from the turn of the century to the present. The collection includes works by Cézanne, Braque, Matisse, Léger, Kandinsky, Klee, Dubuffet, and Rauschenberg, among others. There's also space allocated for changing exhibitions of contemporary work.

Turn left after exiting the museum's front entrance and walk to rue A. le Boucher, where you should turn right. Turn right again at boulevard de Sébastopol, then turn left on rue de la Cossonnerie. The Châtelet–Les Halles Métro station will be directly in front of you.

The Champs-Elysées & St-Honoré

Start: Place du Carrousel (Métro: Palais-Royal).

Finish: Arc de Triomphe.

Time: Three or more hours.

Best Time: If you don't mind missing a visit to the museum at the Arc de Triomphe, I'd suggest scheduling this tour so you walk the first half during the day and the second half after dark— you can see the shops and the Champs-Elysées lit up and can witness the magical effect of the Arc de Triomphe's Eternal Flame at night.

This neighborhood, boasting the Arc de Triomphe, the Jardin des Tuileries, the place de la Concorde, and the Madeleine church, is one of the city's most opulent. In fact, the avenue des Champs-Elysées has been called the "highway of French grandeur." You'll walk through the gardens along to the Madeleine, through a flower market, past prestigious art galleries and exclusive boutiques (Chanel,

Hermés, Gucci), and along avenue Montaigne. In addition, you'll have the opportunity to rub elbows with Paris's wealthiest in the upscale "grocery store" Fauchon.

Other discoveries will include Ben Franklin's haunts and the presidential palace, as well as the theater where Josephine Baker and Sidney Bechet made their debut in *La Revue nègre*. When in the place de la Concorde, you'll be standing where the Revolution was its bloodiest, for here the guillotine disposed of the likes of Louis XVI and Marie Antoinette, Robespierre, and Danton. This walk on the second half of the Champs-Elysées ends at the magnificent Arc de Triomphe.

• • • • • • • • • • • • • • • •

Begin your tour at the:

1. **Place du Carrousel,** on the Louvre's west side, between the wings of the new palace. From August 22, 1792, to May 10, 1793, during the Revolution this was the location of Dr. Guillotin's invention (see Walking Tour 4, Part I, stop 21). It was moved only once during that time, to the place de la Révolution (now place de la Concorde) for the execution of Louis XVI on January 21, 1793. After May 10, the guillotine was permanently moved to the place de la Révolution.

When you're facing the Tuileries, behind you will be the Musée du Louvre and its I. M. Pei glass pyramid entrance (you'll get to explore part of the museum in Walking Tour 11). The Louvre has a past that's been interesting and often sordid. Though most people think of it as the museum it's been since 1793, this building now holding some of the world's greatest art treasures was built as a palace, with Napoléon I and his nephew, Napoléon III, responsible for most of the grandeur. It's been many other things in be-tween, including a prison, a publishing house, a shopping mall, and an institute for advanced studies.

In the palace courtyard hundreds of Protestants were massacred on St. Bartholomew's Day in 1572. On a very much lighter note, Henri IV, the "Gay Blade," turned the Louvre into a sort of fairgrounds with his singing, danc-ing, and carrying on. At that time, various commercial enterprises occupied the Grande Galerie, like a gold-smith, a tapestry factory, and a clock maker, all of whom reported frequent sightings of the dauphin and his pet camel strolling the length of the gallery. After Henri's murder, the Louvre was transformed several times over.

Under Louis XIV, certain talented artists and scholars were given the right to live rent free in the Grande Galerie. Later, these privileges were abused and the Louvre was taken over by an assortment of riffraff who looted paintings and paneling, operated a black market, cooked in the halls, and generally dragged the whole place down into debauchery and disrepute. By 1773 the Louvre was in a shambles.

Rebuilding began in the wake of the Revolution, but it wasn't until Napoléon came to power and assigned architects Charles Percier and Pierre-François-Léonard Fontaine the task of restoring the palace that it began to resemble its former (and present) condition. Napoléon and Joséphine were actually married here after a procession along the Grande Galerie. And it was Napoléon who set about turning the place into a museum—the Musée Napoléon was founded to house the artwork he'd brought back from conquered Europe, chosen and organized by Baron Denon (see box).

Baron Dominique-Vivant Denon

Baron Denon (1747–1825) was numerous things: an en-graver, a diplomat, a writer, a museum official—a sort of jack-of-all-trades. In 1798 he followed Napoléon on his Egyptian campaign and wrote a book called *Voyage dans la basse et la haute Égypte* four years later. Appointed director-general of the national museums in 1804, Denon held the position for 11 years. Among other things, he played a major role in helping Napoléon assemble the collections at the Louvre (where an entire wing is named for him—see Walking Tour 11, Part II). He was also responsible for commissioning the statues of the Arc de Triomphe du Carrousel.

Head out of the place du Carrousel into the Jardin du Carrousel, walking straight ahead to the:

2. **Arc de Triomphe du Carrousel,** built from 1806 to 1808 by Percier and Fontaine. Leaders of the Empire style in France, they restored and redecorated the Tuileries Palace as well as the Louvre, but the Arc de Triomphe du Carrousel is their most notable work.

Standing 48 feet high and 64 feet wide, this Empire-style arch was meant to serve as a "triumphal" entrance into the Tuileries Palace. Eight rose marble Corinthian columns flanking the arch support statues commissioned by Denon to celebrate Napoléon's victories; the sculptures you see today are reproductions, though, not originals. The bas-reliefs on the sides also celebrate Napoléon's conquests—among them are *The Capitulation of Ulm, The Battle of Austerlitz, The Meeting of Napoléon and Alexander at Tilsit, The Entry into Munich, The Entry into Vienna,* and *The Peace of Pressburg.*

The view from under the Arc de Triomphe du Carrousel is probably one of Paris's best known because from here you can see all the way through the Tuileries Gardens to the obelisk in the place de la Concorde and even beyond, up the Champs-Elysées to the Arc de Triomphe.

Walk straight out of the Arc de Triomphe du Carrousel and turn right along one of the garden pathways (this will be before you cross avenue du Général-Lemonnier, so if you cross it, go back). You are now standing in front of the:

3. **Musée des Arts Décoratifs.** Founded in 1887, this museum houses one of the world's most interesting collections of decorative arts, with works dating from the Middle Ages to the present. If you'd like to tour the museum, go around to the right to rue de Rivoli for the entrance and plan to spend an hour or more going through the exhibits.

The museum was established to encourage new designs in the field of decorative arts. It was thought that if people could see what decorations had been used in the past, as compared to what existed in the present, they might demand more creative interior design elements, china patterns, and furnishings, thus forcing the birth of new ideas.

Current displays include carpets, tapestries, jewelry, paintings, furniture, porcelain, toys, and more. One room is dedicated to the king of art nouveau, Hector Guimard (who designed those wonderful Métro entrances—see Walking Tour 2, stop 5). The collection's highlights are gorgeous Lalique glass pieces, stunning 15th- and 16th-century tapestries, and a few Gauguin paintings. Try not to miss the 17th- and 18th-century furnishings or the Restoration wallpapers.

Housed next door at no. 109 rue de Rivoli is the:

4. **Musée des Arts de la Mode.** Exploring the Museum of Fashion could take an hour, so plan accordingly—you've still got a long walk ahead. This museum holds an immense collection of costumes from the 16th century to the present, as well as spectacular material samples. Since the materials are so easily discolored or destroyed by light and exposure, they're rotated frequently, meaning there's no way you can know what'll be on display when you arrive. However, rest assured that you won't be disappointed.

Head back to avenue du Général-Lemonnier. Retrace your steps until you're facing the place de la Concorde. As you proceed to the place, be aware that you're walking through the area once occupied by the:

5. **Tuileries Palace,** which was built in 1564 on the site of some *tuile* (tile) kilns and factories. Designed by Philibert Delorme for Catherine de Médicis, the palace ran between the Louvre's two wings and joined with the Pavillon de Flore (on your left) and the Pavillon Marsan (on your right).

On August 10, 1792, a revolutionary mob attacked the palace, causing Louis XVI and his family to flee. The Swiss guards who were also here at the time attempted to run, but two-thirds of them were slaughtered. In 1830, when Charles X was in residence, the Tuileries was again attacked by a mob and he, too, fled. In 1871 the Communards set fire to the palace and destroyed it.

Continuing on, you'll soon arrive at the beginning of the:

6. **Jardin des Tuileries.** The 63 acres now occupied by the gardens originally had two uses: The clay soil was utilized

at the tile factory, and other parts of the land were used as a garbage dump. François I built stables here in 1525, and in 1564 Catherine de Médicis bought some of the land to build an Italian-style garden.

Soon after, the Tuileries developed into a fashionable promenade. In 1649 the gardens were redesigned by André Le Nôtre, Louis XIV's gardener. Dotted with fine sculptures and beautifully manicured gardens, they became the aristocracy's favorite meeting place—they're still a rendezvous point, though now open to everyone, and still contain some of the world's greatest sculptures.

The first of these will be directly to your right and left after you cross avenue du Général-Lemonnier. On your immediate right is a statue of Pierre de Wissant. Across from it is *Great Shadow.* To your right a bit farther on is *Jean de Frennes,* and to your left is *Meditation.* Just ahead is a pond both visitors and Parisians find to be a wonderful place to sit and relax; if you sit long enough you're likely to see a fish jump. Continue to walk through and just past the place where they give pony rides to children you'll find a wooded area on your right. Wander around in there and have a look at the 18 bronze nudes by Aristide Maillol.

You might be interested to know that a $50-million cleanup and restoration project of the gardens has been scheduled for the near future.

Continue on. Just before reaching the Octagonal Pond, note to the left and right the four statues representing the seasons. On the left you'll see *Spring* and *Autumn* (the one closer to you), both by François Barois (1656–1726). On the right are *Summer* by Guillaume Coustou (1677–1746) and *Winter* (closer to you) by Jean Raon (1631–1707). Walk around the pond to the garden's entrance (or exit, depending on how you look at it). The four statues flanking it depict six rivers: *The Tiber,* by Pierre Bourdict (?–1711), is on your right, closest to you. On your left, the first one is *The Nile* by Lorenzo Ottoni (1648–1736). Just beyond on the right is *The Seine and the Marne* by Guillaume Coustou; to the left is *The Loire and the Loiret* by Corneille Van Cleve (1645–1732).

On your right in the distance is the:

The Champs-Elysées & St-Honoré

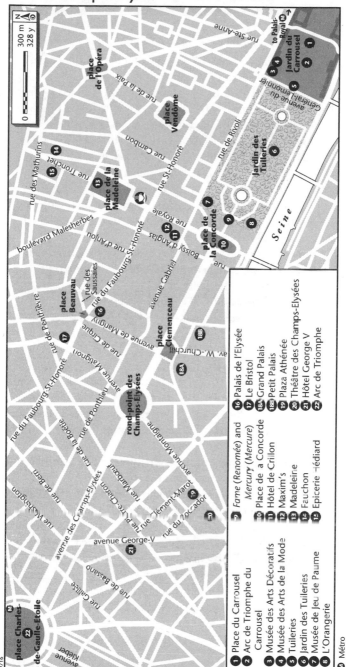

place de l'Opéra

place Vendôme

place de la Madeleine

place Beauvau

place Clemenceau

place de la Concorde

rond-point des Champs-Elysées

place Charles-de-Gaulle-Etoile

Jardin des Tuileries

Jardin du Carrousel

Seine

300 m
328 y

rue Ste-Anne

rue de la paix

rue Cambon

rue St-Honoré

rue de Rivoli

rue Royale

boulevard Malesherbes

rue d'Anjou

rue des Mathurins

rue Tronchet

rue de Penthièvre

rue du Faubourg-St-Honoré

rue des Saussaies

avenue Gabriel

avenue de Marigny

av. W.-Churchill

avenue de Matignon

rue de Ponthieu

rue de Berri

rue Washington

avenue des Champs-Elysées

avenue Montaigne

avenue George-V

rue de Bassano

rue Galilée

avenue Kléber

rue du Colisée

rue Clément-Marot

rue Jean-Goujon

rue François-1er

rue Marbeuf

rue de la Boétie

rue Boissy d'Anglas

avenue du Général-Lemonnier

1. Place du Carrousel
2. Arc de Triomphe du Carrousel
3. Musée des Arts Décoratifs
4. Musée des Arts de la Mode
5. Tuileries
6. Jardin des Tuileries
7. Musée de Jeu de Paume
8. L'Orangerie
9. Fame (Renomée) and Mercury (Mercure)
10. Place de a Concorde
11. Hôtel de Crillon
12. Maxim's
13. Madeleine
14. Fauchon
15. Epicerie Hédiard
16. Palais de l'Elysée
17. Le Bristol
18A. Grand Palais
18B. Petit Palais
20. Théâtre des Champs-Elysées
21. Hôtel George V
22. Arc de Triomphe

Ⓜ Métro

Aristide Maillol

Though known primarily for his sculpture, Aristide Maillol (1861–1944) was a tapestry artist and painter early in his career. It wasn't until 1900, at 39, that he decided to devote himself entirely to sculpture. In 1902 Rodin praised Maillol's first one-man exhibition. Actually, for Rodin and his contemporaries Maillol was a sort of bridge from classic Greek and Roman style to modern-style sculpture. He was more interested in the philosophy of expressing form, but in a way that broke from the traditional: He began to look for a simpler way to express it, without mythological or literary allusion or in connection to an architectural form. Maillol simply celebrated the form being sculpted, rather than a particular event or idea. Since he especially loved the nude female form, you'll be hard-pressed to find other subjects in his body of work.

Rodin went on to take Maillol's idea one step further by adding a psychological element to his sculpture.

7. **Musée du Jeu de Paume.** *Jeu de paume,* meaning literally "game of the palm," was invented in the 1400s by monks who for amusement used to bat around a knot of rags with their hands. By the 1800s the rags had changed to balls, the hands to rackets. The jeu de paume became France's national game and evolved into a highly explosive and dangerous sport. In fact, several nobles and kings are said to have dropped dead from the strain.

This building originally housed the Royal Tennis Courts and was constructed under Napoléon III for the recreation of the Prince Imperial. Not long after lawn tennis (the next logical step from jeu de paume) was invented, the building was used to display impressionist paintings.

From 1947 to 1986 the Jeu de Paume hosted a permanent exhibition of impressionist works—they've since moved to the Musée d'Orsay (see Walking Tour 4, Part I, stop 1). Presently, the building is used as an exhibition space for changing shows of contemporary art and design.

To your left around the fountain is:

8. **L'Orangerie,** formerly the Tuileries Garden's orange nursery. The small building now permanently houses, and is the official museum for, the Walter-Guillaume collection. Art dealer/collector Paul Guillaume was extremely interested in the work of new and unknown artists, and in 1914, at age 23, he opened a rue de la Boetie gallery specializing in the work of then-contemporary artists like Picasso, Modigliani, and Renoir. The collection's Walter part was the extension of Guillaume's collection by his widow and her new husband, Jean Walter. All of the 144 masterpieces, ranging from the impressionist period through the 1930s, were donated to the Louvre in 1977.

   Well worth a visit, L'Orangerie can be easily managed in an hour or less. Within you'll find Monet's *Water Lilies;* several Chaim Soutine pieces (see Walking Tour 3, stop 20); an entire room devoted to Cézanne, including the still life *Fruit, Napkin, and Milk Can* (1880); many Renoirs, including *Young Girls at the Piano* (1890); works by Henri Rousseau and Maurice Utrillo; Picasso's *The Bathers* (1921); and, finally, Modigliani's *The Young Apprentice* (1917).

   Just as you emerge from the Jardin des Tuileries are two statues:

9. **Fame** *(Renomée)* and **Mercury** *(Mercure),* on your left and right, respectively. Both are by Antoine Coysevox, the most successful French sculptor of Louis XIV's reign. Note that these are replicas of the originals, which are now housed in the Louvre (see Walking Tour 11, Part I, stops 2A and 2B). In addition to these two, he did a number of statues for the gardens and interior of Versailles.

   Passing between the two statues, you'll find yourself in the:

10. **Place de la Concorde.** The building of this square was begun in 1755 to honor Louis XV, and it took 20 years to complete. A statue of Louis on his horse was placed in the center, but in 1792 it was overturned, and the square was renamed place de la Révolution. On January 21, 1793, the guillotine was moved here from the place du Carrousel for Louis XVI's execution. Just before the blade dropped, he

said, "Frenchmen, I die innocent." The executioner displayed the king's head to the crowd, causing them to roar "Vive la République!" The councillors dipped their handkerchiefs and pikes in his blood, and the executioner took the liberty of selling locks of Louis' hair. Though the guillotine was then returned to the place du Carrousel, a few months later it moved here permanently, and 1,234 others were guillotined on this spot, including Marie Antoinette and Charlotte Corday (Marat's murderer). In July 1794, Robespierre's execution here ended the Reign of Terror.

It wasn't until Louis-Philippe's reign that the obelisk from the temple at Luxor was chosen as the square's centerpiece. A gift from Muhammad Ali, the pasha of Egypt, the solid pink granite obelisk weighs over 230 tons, stands 75 feet tall, and is more than 3,300 years old. The hieroglyphs on its sides represent the "epic deeds" of Ramses II. A box of medallions bearing Louis-Philippe's likeness was placed in the ground before the obelisk was erected—and it still rests there today.

Built between 1836 and 1846, the fountains flanking the obelisk are copies of those in St. Peter's Square in Rome. Around the square are statues representing the eight great towns of France, erected during the reign of Louis-Philippe: Caillonette's *Bordeaux* and *Nantes* (diagonally to the left and in front of the obelisk, facing the Champs-Elysées); Petitot's *Lyons* and *Marseille* (diagonally to the left and behind the obelisk); Cortot's *Rouen* and *Brest* (diagonally to the right and in front of the obelisk); and Pradier's *Lille* and *Strasbourg* (to the right and behind the obelisk).

As you head out of the square toward the avenue des Champs-Elysées, you'll see the Marly horses, sculpted by Guillaume Coustou for a drinking trough in Marly, Louis XIV's castle near Versailles. The statues you see today are replicas—the originals were removed in 1984 and are now housed in the Louvre (see Walking Tour 11, Part I, stops 2A and 2B).

Instead of heading straight down the Champs-Elysées, go out between the *Brest* and *Rouen* statues, diagonally to the right in front of the obelisk. Cross avenue Gabriel (which can be hazardous at this intersection—watch your step) and you'll be in front of the:

11. **Hôtel de Crillon.** In 1758 the comte de Crillon asked architect Jacques-Ange Gabriel (1698–1782) to design this residence, which has become one of Paris's most prestigious hotels. It was here that the Treaty of Friendship and Trade between France and the infant United States was signed on February 6, 1778; both Benjamin Franklin and Louis XVI were in attendance. This treaty was significant because it meant France officially recognized the United States as a free and independent nation.

Benjamin Franklin only begins the extensive list of Americans who've stayed at the hotel. Others include Mary Pickford and Douglas Fairbanks, said to have honeymooned here in 1920; Fred and Adele Astaire, who vacationed here in 1924; and William Randolph Hearst and his mistress, Marion Davies, who were guests in 1928.

Turn right in front of the Hôtel de Crillon and make a left onto rue Royale. On the left side of the street, affixed to the hotel's side, is a plaque commemorating the afore-mentioned treaty signing. A bit farther on this street are some of the city's most renowned shops and restaurants; first, on the left side of the street, is:

12. **Maxim's.** Need I say more? Probably not, but I'm going to anyway. Some of the most interesting incidents at the restaurant have involved Americans, among them a Californian known only as Mr. L; his real name has never been disclosed. Mr. L used to perform a strange ritual, since dubbed the Liturgy of the Golden Calf: It began with the gathering and lining up of all the Maxim's staff, whereupon Mr. L would walk down the line carrying a plate with stacks of gold coins. As he passed each person he'd place on his or her tongue one coin. Before he moved to the next person he'd make the sign of the cross.

One Mr. Todd (a New Yorker) proceeded in a much less ceremonial manner: He'd simply throw piles of *louis d'or* around the restaurant and amuse himself watching the staff and resident courtesans falling all over one another to get their hands on the money.

After you pass Maxim's you'll come to **Christofle,** one of the most exclusive silverware manufacturers in the world; next is **Cristal Lalique,** with its art nouveau frosted glass. Once you cross rue St-Honoré, **Gucci** will be on your left.

Take a Break   If you'd like to pause for a snack with some of Paris's richest citizens and devour some of the city's best croissants, stop at **Ladurée** (diagonally to the right, across from Gucci at no. 16 rue Royale), an elegant turn-of-the-century café/salon du thé. Try the chocolate macaroons or almond cakes *(financiers)*. You won't be disappointed.

Even if you decide not to go into Ladurée, cross the street and continue walking up rue Royale into the place de la Madeleine. Here you won't be able to miss the:

13. **Madeleine,** with its 52 Corinthian columns. The building was used as a bank, a theater, a banquet hall, a monument to Napoléon's Grande Armée, and the national library before it became a church (with absolutely no windows and no crosses) dedicated to St. Mary Magdalene. Built to look like a Greek temple, the 355-foot-long, 141-foot-wide, 60-foot-tall structure was begun in 1764 but not completed until nearly 100 years later. Inside are some beautiful rose marble and a Lemaire bronze door depicting the Ten Commandments.

    In 1975 the funeral for Josephine Baker, the first woman ever to receive a 21-gun salute, was held here. Other major events were the occasion when Saint-Saëns played the organ and the premiere of Chopin's *Funeral March*—at the composer's own funeral!

Josephine Baker

In 1925 Josephine Baker (1906–75) debuted at the Théâtre des Champs-Elysées in *La Revue nègre* and was an immediate success—Parisians adored her. She made her entrance nude except for a pink flamingo feather placed between her legs. Janet Flanner described her as "an unforgettable female ebony statue." During a performance some time later, she appeared wearing her now-famous banana skirt and was hailed as the biggest American star in Europe. She maintained a loyal following throughout her career in Paris.

Continue around the place de la Madeleine, wander through the **flower market,** and head to no. 26, which is:

14. **Fauchon.** Founded in 1886 by Auguste Fauchon, this is probably Paris's most elite "grocery store." An adult's trip inside can rightly be compared to a child's trip through a candy factory. You can look but not touch. You place your order, then wait for someone to bring it to you—there's no squeezing of produce here. Everything is beautifully displayed, and you're sure to find just about anything you could possibly want in their selection of 4,500 spices and over 20,000 other products.

    If you're not interested in entering or are afraid you might faint from overstimulation (or might be tempted to buy and buy), do at least take a peek at the impressive window display. However, you may have to squeeze through the large crowd that's usually outside.

    The two extensions of Fauchon are directly ahead at the end of the square. The one on the right is the cake shop; at the one on the left you can purchase a bottle of fine olive oil or even madeleines like those Proust so lusciously described in his masterwork, *A la recherche du temps perdu (Remembrance of Things Past).*

    When you're finished here, proceed past **La Maison de la Truffe,** a truffle specialty store, to no. 21:

15. **Epicerie Hédiard,** another elite grocery store. Hédiard, a lot less commercial than Fauchon, seems to me to be the store where French "old money" shops. You're likely to find produce to rival Fauchon's, but will also find less haughty service here. Pop in and judge for yourself.

    Pass **Baccarat** and **Lucas Carton.** Go to the other side of the Madeleine and back onto rue Royale to the Gucci store you passed earlier. Turn right on rue du Faubourg St-Honoré and cross rue Boissy d'Anglas. Here you'll see **Hermès** at no. 24 (in case you're interested, there's a small Hermès museum on the top floor of this building). Ahead on the right side are **Givenchy** and **Guy Laroche.** On the right just after rue d'Anjou is the **Cour aux Antiquaires.** It's well worth taking a detour down this little passageway, the home of 18 fine antiques shops.

    Come back out of the Cour aux Antiquaires and go right

on rue du Faubourg-St-Honoré, passing, on the right, **Ungaro, Chloé,** and **Gianni Versace.** Across the street from rue des Saussaies (on the left side) is the:

16. **Palais de l'Elysée.** Built in 1718 by Mollet as the home of the comte d'Evreux, this has been the official residence of the French president since 1873. During the Revolution it housed the national printing press and at one time was home to Napoléon's sister Caroline and her husband, Joachim Murat. You can't go inside, but you should know that France's former president, François Mitterrand, didn't call the Elysée Palace home—he lived in his private rue de Bièvre residence (see Walking Tour 5, Part I, stop 10). At press time, Jacques Chirac had just been elected president; it's uncertain whether he will take up residence at the palace.

Proceed past the palace and cross avenue de Marigny. (As you do, be sure to check out the hats in the window of **Pierre Cardin.** Also, if you need to sit down for a minute or two, there are benches off to the left.) Continue along rue du Faubourg-St-Honoré, noting some of the galleries of fine art—this is probably the only place in the world where you might find a Utrillo or something similar displayed in a shop window. Soon you'll come to no. 112 rue du Faubourg-St-Honoré, which is:

17. **Le Bristol.** Because it's so close to the Palais de l'Elysée, this very classy hotel has played host to a long line of VIPs, among them Ulysses S. Grant, who stayed here for almost a month in 1887. Sinclair Lewis lived here in 1925, during which time his book *Arrowsmith* was selected for the Pulitzer Prize (which he refused). In addition, this was where Josephine Baker celebrated her 50th anniversary in show business.

Turn left on avenue Matignon. Walk past the offices of the newspaper *Le Figaro* and some expensive art galleries to the Champs-Elysées, where you should turn left and cross the street at the place Clemenceau. Cross the place Clemenceau to avenue Winston-Churchill. As you head down this avenue, you'll find yourself between the:

18A. **Grand Palais** (on your right) and 18B. **Petit Palais** (on your left). Both palaces were constructed for the 1900

Universal Exhibition (as was the Eiffel Tower) and are exceptional examples of art nouveau architecture. The 54,000-square-foot Grand Palais, designed by three architects, often features major exhibitions and retrospectives. The Petit Palais, built to hold a French art retrospective for the Exhibition, now holds collections from various museums all around the city and is called the Musée des Beaux-Arts.

The exteriors of both buildings are covered with bas-reliefs and sculptures in a classical style that's entirely contrary to the art nouveau iron-and-glass interiors.

Retrace your steps to the avenue des Champs-Elysées. Go left, then make a left onto avenue Montaigne, staying on the right side of the street. On the left side will be **Chanel** and **Christian Dior,** on the right **Nina Ricci.** No doubt you've already realized you're walking down Paris's equivalent of New York City's Fifth and Madison avenues combined. Cross rue Clément-Marot. Eventually you'll come to no. 25 avenue Montaigne, the:

19. **Plaza Athénée.** George Patton lived here in December 1918, during which time he gave a series of talks regarding the importance of tanks to the infantry. Only one French officer—Charles de Gaulle—believed him; the rest thought him a bit mad. In the bar of this hotel the infamous Mata Hari was arrested for her work as a spy.

A bit farther on, across rue du Boccador, is no. 15, the:

20. **Théâtre des Champs-Elysées,** built in 1913. The Isadora Duncan bas-reliefs on the exterior were sculpted by Emile-Antoine Bourdelle (see Walking Tour 3, stop 3). This is the theater where *La Revue nègre* with Sidney Bechet and Josephine Baker opened. It was Baker's first performance in Paris and, as mentioned earlier, was a complete success.

Adrienne Monnier wrote this after seeing Baker: "With her get ups, her grimaces, her contortions, she kicks up a shindy that swarms with mocking enticements—she's a Queen of Sheba who turns into a frog, into a mischievous chicken with its feathers plucked; she passes from an enamored expression to a frightful squint, she even succeeds in a squinting with her behind."

On June 19, 1926, George Antheil's *Ballet mécanique* was performed here. The orchestra included six electric player pianos, six electrically run airplane propellers, car horns, whistles, and a multitude of other modern noise-makers. Janet Flanner commented that it was "good but awful."

When you get to avenue George-V, turn right and walk along until you reach no. 31, the:

21. **Hôtel George V,** where Duke Ellington stayed in July 1933. The hotel opened in 1928, and between then and 1968 the owner amassed a huge art collection (about $7 million worth). If for no other reason, enter and have a look at the portions of the collection hanging in the public rooms.

Continue up avenue George-V to the Champs-Elysées. Turn left on the avenue and head for your final destination, the underground passageway leading to the:

22. **Arc de Triomphe.** I must warn you: Do not try to cross the street aboveground to get to the arch—if you do, you're likely to end up in the hospital.

It took 30 years to create this massive Second Empire arch at the center of the place Charles-de-Gaulle-Etoile, where Baron Haussmann's 12 radiating avenues intersect (see "Paris: City of Light" for more information); conceived in Napoléon's mind in 1806, the arch wasn't completed until 1836. The entire structure measures 163 feet high and 147 feet wide. The arch itself is 48 feet wide—wide enough for one Sergeant Godefroy to fly his plane through in 1919. Beneath the arch is the Tomb of the Unknown Soldier and the Eternal Flame, over which it's been reported that a jokester once cooked himself an omelet. The inscription reads, "Ici repose un soldat français mort pour la patrie, 1914–1918" ("Here lies a French soldier who died for his fatherland"). The Eternal Flame is relit around 6 o'clock every evening.

Inside the arch is a museum documenting the stages of its construction (open Monday and Wednesday to Saturday from 10am to 6pm). If you're not interested in how the arch was built, at least go up and enjoy the magnificent view.

The Charles-de-Gaulle-Etoile Métro station is at this same location.

The Palais-Royal & the Grands Boulevards

Start: Place du Palais-Royal (Métro: Palais-Royal).

Finish: Jardin du Palais-Royal.

Time: Three to four hours.

Best Time: Monday through Saturday during business hours.

Worst Time: Sunday and Monday through Saturday after 5pm.

This walk will take you through landmarks of Second Empire and Belle Epoque Paris and bring you back to the cloistered gardens of the Palais-Royal.

Today it may be hard for visitors to imagine the scenes associated with the Palais-Royal, particularly during Louis XV's regency, when it was notorious for debauchery and orgies of all sorts. Crowds were drawn to the entertainments offered in the galleries—shadow theaters, waxworks, and optical illusions—as well as to the cafés, like the Café de Foy, where Camille Desmoulins stirred up an angry mob into a bloody Revolution. A statue of him stands in the gardens there.

The Grands Boulevards, stretching from the Madeleine to the place de la Bastille, were originally laid out by Louis XIV; however, the boulevards you'll walk along today were created by Baron Haussmann under the direction of Napoléon III. These broad thoroughfares provided access to the 19th century's railroad stations, and Parisians and those from the rest of France flocked to them to enjoy their cafés, theaters, and restaurants, especially on the boulevard des Italiens between rue de Richelieu and rue de la Chaussée d'Antin. The most famous were Café Tortoni, Café Anglais, Café de Paris, and Café Riche, to which *tout* fashionable Paris went during the Second Empire and the Belle Epoque.

The place de l'Opéra was nearby, on the site Haussmann had laid out and where Charles Garnier built his huge rococo masterpiece, which opened in 1875. Today cafés and cinemas remain, but fashionable society has departed, except around the place de la Madeleine (see Walking Tour 7, stop 13). While walking along, try to imagine what the scene must've been like here in those *très* elegant years before World War I—a visit to the Opéra (renamed the Opéra Garnier with the opening of the Opéra de la Bastille—see Walking Tour 6, stop 2) should help you recapture some of the spirit of the area in its heyday.

• • • • • • • • • • • • • • • •

Emerge from the Métro station at the place du Palais-Royal and turn left (as you're facing the Conseil d'Etat). Go right on rue de Richelieu (the first intersection after you pass the Conseil d'Etat) and walk to the first building on your right, the current location of the:

1. **Comédie-Française,** which moved here in 1799. In 1673, Molière, actor unto the very end, died onstage at 51 while performing in his play *La Malade imaginaire,* leaving his troupe of actors leaderless. Seven years later, Louis XI established the Comédie-Française with Molière's old troupe, and ever since this has been Paris's most renowned theater group.

One of its greatest talents was Sarah Bernhardt. During her debut at age 17 in the title role of Racine's *Iphigénie,* Bernhardt suffered severe stage fright. The audience heckled her, jeering that Achilles might "impale [himself] on her toothpicks," a reference to her skinny arms—nevertheless, she persevered and eventually developed into one of Paris's most loved and respected actresses. Indeed, backstage before the curtain rose, she was often told, "Madame, it will be eight o'clock when it suits you." It should not surprise you that Oscar Wilde deemed her the "divine Sarah."

Retrace your steps to rue St-Honoré. Turn right and proceed along the street to rue de l'Echelle. To your left is the showroom of:

2. **Sèvres,** the national porcelain factory, which made Europe's premier porcelain from about 1760 to 1815. The factory has a long, august history: Founded in 1738 at the Château de Vincennes, Sèvres was granted a 20-year monopoly in 1745 for "porcelain in the style of the Saxon . . . painted and gilded with human figures." Seven years later Louis XV became the principal shareholder, and in 1753 porcelain and white pottery could not be manufactured anywhere but this factory. Three years later the factory moved to Sèvres; and within another three years it was being run entirely by the king—all sales of porcelain were held right in his dining room at Versailles.

Sèvres figurines are world famous, and many of the models were supplied by Pigalle and Houdon. Other pieces ranged in size from plates to enormous urns, and Napoléon commissioned such large and complex pieces that architects Percier and Fontaine had to be consulted as designers.

On your right, at no. 7 rue de l'Echelle, is the:

3. **Hôtel Normandy,** where Mark Twain lived from April to July 1879. He was most annoyed because it rained the entire time he was here, and all he could do was read, sleep, and write—*quel désastre!*

Continue along rue St-Honoré to rue St-Roch. At no. 398 rue St-Honoré, on the corner, is:

4. **St-Roch,** one of the city's largest and most prestigious churches, designed by Lemercier (architect of the Louvre).

The foundation stone of this immense church was laid by Louis XIV in 1653. On October 5, 1795, a battle took place here between Le Pelletier's rabble and Napoléon (you can still see the bullet holes in the facade). The church marks one of the most significant events in the history of Paris, for it is here Bonaparte came to power.

St-Roch holds a spectacular collection of religious art (in spite of the Revolution). As you enter, go to the right, where you'll come to Coysevox's *Bust of Fr. de Crequi*. A bit farther on is a Coustou statue of Cardinal Dubois. Make your way around the church, in the direction of the Communion Chapel (in a half circle). On your right will be *Jarius's Daughter* by Delormé. Head back toward the entrance, passing the Coysevox bust of Le Nôtre (on your right) and the Girardon *Monument to Mignard*. Exit through the center door, but pause to note the memorial to Pierre Corneille on your way.

When you leave the church, turn right along rue St-Honoré and go to rue St-Roch, then turn left and walk to rue de Rivoli. Go right to:

5. **No. 206 rue de Rivoli** (you'll know it by the green tile pattern outside the door), formerly the Hôtel du Jardin des Tuileries. Writer Henry Adams (1838–1918, grandson of John Quincy Adams) spent six weeks here from December 1879 to February 1880. He claimed to despise everything about Paris; however, one of his best works as a historian was a medieval study, *Mont-St-Michel and Chartres* (1904). You'll also see the plaque commemorating Leo Tolstoy's stay here.

   Continue on rue de Rivoli to rue du 29 Juillet, then turn right. Continue to the corner of rue St. Honoré. Turn right and proceed to:

6. **No. 211 rue St-Honoré,** on the right side of the street. Sinclair Lewis (1885–1951) and his wife and son stayed here at the Hôtel St-James d'Albany in October 1921. Lewis is considered the greatest satirist of his era. His book *Arrowsmith* won him a Pulitzer in 1925, and in 1930 he became the first American to win the Nobel Prize for literature. While he was at the Hôtel St-James d'Albany he worked on *Babbitt,* his novel ridiculing the values, lifestyles, and

mannerisms of the money-grubbing members of society. Most consider it his chef d'oeuvre. When he wasn't writing, he spent a bit too much time imbibing at various bars and cafés.

Turn around and walk in the other direction on rue St-Honoré. Eventually you'll come to:

7. **No. 239 rue St-Honoré,** the hotel in which Franklin and Eleanor Roosevelt spent their 1905 honeymoon. He was staying here when he visited a psychic who predicted that one day he'd become president of the United States. In December 1946 American author Carson McCullers (1917–67), famous for *The Heart Is a Lonely Hunter* (1940), stayed here for about a year. Even though she didn't speak a word of French, she communicated well, primarily because she and her French friends had two loves in common— whisky and wine. Alas, it was drink that forced her to return to the United States in 1947—she had drunk so much on two occasions that she had to be hospitalized. The second time, she and her husband decided it would be best if they went home.

Continue along to rue Cambon, turn left, and proceed to rue de Rivoli. Go left again. The **Hôtel Brighton,** at no. 218, was one of Mark Twain's favorite Paris hotels. Later, at no. 228 rue de Rivoli, you'll come to the·

8. **Hôtel Meurice,** said to be the only early 19th-century hotel in Paris that provided guests with soap. Because of this singular creature comfort the Meurice hosted a lot of Americans—including Herman Melville, Wilbur Wright (on a trip to sell his airplane to the French government), Henry Wadsworth Longfellow (in the summer of 1836), and Walter Lippmann (who in 1967 stayed here while awaiting the completion of his new home, which turned out to be a veritable money pit).

Go left up rue Castiglione. As you walk, note rue Mont Thabor (on your right), the street where the brassiere was supposedly invented. As you head into the place Vendôme, note that Fred Astaire and his wife, Adele, stayed at the **Hôtel Vendôme** (no. 1) in 1936. At no. 3 you'll find the:

9. **IBM Building,** formerly the Hôtel Bristol. John Pierpont Morgan (1837–1913), American financier/investment

banker, spent every spring here from 1890 to 1910. During the Franco-Prussian War Morgan loaned $50 million to the French government. In addition, he set up the United States Steel Corporation in 1901 and International Harvester in 1902; he also played a vital role in stabilizing the U.S. economy in 1907. Morgan was an avid art collector, and it's said that whenever he was in Paris, art dealers deluged the Bristol, hoping to make a sale.

As you continue on, you'll enter the sprawling:

10. **Place Vendôme,** one of the city's most imposing architectural designs. Window shop to the right around the square. Around 1670, Jules Hardouin-Mansart purchased the palace of the duc de Vendôme, including the land stretching north of rue St-Honoré, which was meant to be subdivided. Instead, a minister to Louis XIV decided to build a square, at the center of which would be an enormous statue of the king; unfortunately, work stopped when the minister died. About 18 years later the land was turned over to the city and Mansart, the original owner, was asked to finish the square. A statue of Louis XIV was placed in the center, as originally planned, and the square was called place Louis-le-Grand.

The houses surrounding the octagonal square were built in the early 18th century. When Napoléon came to power, the Louis XIV statue was torn down and replaced with the column you see today, which celebrates Napoléon's victory at Austerlitz. The 144-foot-high column is covered with bronze taken from the 1,200 cannons captured at Austerlitz, and on it is a series of bas-reliefs showing battle scenes. The statue at the top is a reproduction of the original one of Napoléon; however, in the French tradition, several sculptures were placed there (then torn down) over the years, including a giant fleur-de-lis, the royal family's emblem.

These mansions were purchased by immensely wealthy financiers (including John Law, a Scotsman who became Controleur Général des Finances and bought several of them), and the place Vendôme quickly became the most prestigious address in the city. If you walk around the square to the right, you'll come to **no. 12,** where Chopin died in 1849. The comtesse de Castiglione lived at **no. 26.** Apparently she was dubbed the Madwoman of the place Vendôme, because as she got older she refused to go outside during the day, fearing she would been seen and thought ugly with age.

After you cross rue de la Paix, head around the other side of the square to the:

11. **Hôtel Ritz,** founded in 1898 by César Ritz. Tales about colorful Ritz guests are legion. Hemingway frequented the place—indeed, one of the hotel's bars is named after him. The small bar off rue Cambon used to be the women's bar in the days when women weren't allowed to drink, but now it's been decorated to look like a jolly old English pub.

    Legend has it that Hemingway left his luggage here for nearly 30 years. When he finally did remove it, inside he found notes for the beginnings of *A Moveable Feast,* the novel that soon made him one of the most hated men in all Paris. Of course, some say this story is apocryphal. What's your opinion?

    Other Americans who enjoyed spending time at the Ritz (if not for a room, then for a drink or two) included F. Scott Fitzgerald (who was seen stumbling out on more than a few occasions), Fred Astaire, J. P. Morgan, and Theodore Roosevelt. Cole Porter and his wife, Linda Lee Thomas, took an apartment here in 1919. They drove a Rolls-Royce, owned about a dozen dachshunds, and partied with the likes of Tallulah Bankhead, Irving Berlin, George Gershwin, and the Barrymores.

    Return to rue de la Paix and look to your left for no. 13, which is the:

12. **Hôtel Westminster,** where a preteen Henry James stayed with his parents while they looked for an apartment in 1856.

    When you get to rue Daunou, keep an eye out for:

13. **No. 6 rue Daunou,** where Oliver Wendell Holmes stayed during his August 1886 visit to chemist/microbiologist Louis Pasteur (it was the Hôtel d'Orient back then). Holmes wanted to shake the hand of the inventor of the rabies vaccine, the discovery of which led to the 1888 creation of the Institut Pasteur. Pasteur is also renowned for pasteurization, the process that rids dairy products of tuberculosis bacteria.

The Palais-Royal & the Grands Boulevards

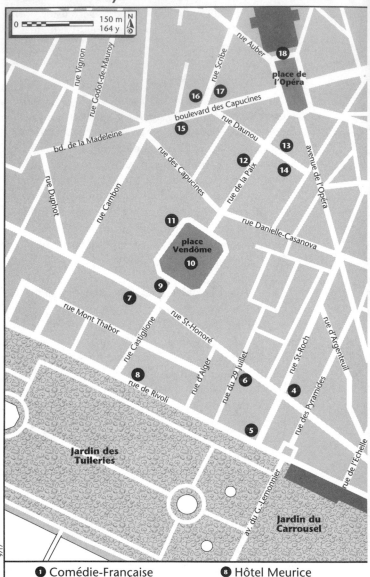

1. Comédie-Française
2. Sèvres
3. Hôtel Normandy
4. St-Roch
5. No. 206 rue de Rivoli
6. No. 211 rue St-Honoré
7. No. 239 rue St-Honoré
8. Hôtel Meurice
9. IBM Building
10. Place Vendôme
11. Hôtel Ritz
12. Hôtel Westminster
13. No. 6 rue Daunou
14. Harry's New York Bar

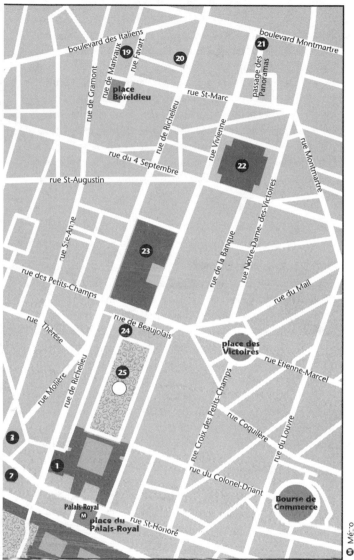

Méːo

Across the street is:

14. **Harry's New York Bar,** no. 5 rue Daunou. This bar opened in 1911, though it wasn't until a bit later that the place started jumping. Of course, wherever alcohol was served those crazy American expatriates could be found. Hemingway was unable to resist a mahogany bar tended by an American jockey called Harry, and neither could F. Scott Fitzgerald. Even Sinclair Lewis couldn't resist "Sank Roo Doe Noo," as Harry's sign translates into franglais. The Bloody Mary and Sidecar were born at Harry's, and it was here that many Parisians discovered the only American-born alcoholic beverage—bourbon.

Head back in the direction from which you came, cross rue de la Paix, and walk along rue Daunou until reaching boulevard des Capucines. Turn left and look for:

15. **No. 35 bd. des Capucines,** on your left. At today's Les Impressionistes restaurant is the former studio of Nadar (see Walking Tour 10, stop 13). On May 15, 1874, Nadar donated his studio to the impressionists for their first exhibit, which was almost universally panned; many thought it made a mockery of true art. Renoir was disappointed with the reviews and said, "The only thing we got out of it was the label 'Impressionism'—a name I loathe."

Across the street at **no. 14** the Lumière brothers held a public showing of the first movie in 1895. A bit farther down, at **no. 43,** the first shot that sparked the revolution of 1848 was fired. Retrace your steps back to rue Daunou. Directly across from this street is the entrance to rue Scribe. At no. 1 rue Scribe is the:

16. **Hôtel Scribe,** the press headquarters for Allied forces from August 1944 until the fall of 1945. John Dos Passos was one of the lucky newsmen who were able to secure jobs here.

On your right is the **Olympia music hall** (entrance at 28 bd. des Capucines), a prerequisite performance hall for all pop singers who aspire to stardom. Edith Piaf, the Beatles, Lou Reed, and Elvis Costello are among those who have played here.

Proceed to no. 2, the:

17. **Grand Hôtel,** which has been one of Paris's grandest since its 1860 opening; it's also one of the oldest five-star hotels in the city. Charles Garnier (also the architect of the Opéra, see below) designed the hotel, which was built for visitors to the 1867 International Exhibition. Fifteen years later, Henry James was a guest after he returned from a whirlwind tour of the country, during which time he took notes for his book *A Little Tour in France* (1885).

    Continue along rue Scribe to rue Auber. Turning right will bring you almost immediately to the:

18. **Place de l'Opéra** and the **Opéra Garnier,** at one of the busiest intersections in Paris. The Opéra Garnier, decked out in Second Empire style, is wildly embellished (with what was probably originally considered too much of everything). When Charles Garnier (1825–98) built the Opéra, he introduced Paris and the world to Napoléon III's style. Construction began in 1862 and continued until 1875. The result is a truly stunning building. Inside, you'll find a sweeping marble staircase with an onyx balustrade and the incredibly ornamented Grand Foyer, about 177 feet long. The Grand Foyer's walls are bejeweled with mirrors, mosaics, paintings, and pieces of marble that hail from the Italian island of Murano (where the famous glassblowing factory is located).

    The auditorium boasts the famous 6-*ton* chandelier, as well as a series of paintings done by Marc Chagall in 1964.

    Note: The Grand Foyer and the Auditorium are open daily but only between 1 and 2pm.

    After you come out of the Opéra Garnier, turn left (facing away from the Opéra) on boulevard des Capucines, which turns into boulevard des Italiens shortly afterward. (The composer Offenbach died at **no. 8**.) Turn right on rue de Marivaux; on your left as you approach the place Boïeldieu you'll see the:

19. **Opéra Comique,** still referred to as the Salle Favart (after 18th-century playwright Charles-Simon Favart). This building opened in 1898 (two preceded it, including one by Claude Charpentier), and its back faces the boulevard, which is no accident—the actors didn't want to be confused with the mountebanks who worked the streets. American soprano

Mary Garden gave a dazzling performance here when called on to finish the final act of *Louise,* for which she was an understudy. The audience loved her, so she sang the next hundred performances.

Playwright/novelist Alexandre Dumas *fils* was born in 1824 at **no. 1 place Boïeldieu.** Go left around the front of the Opéra Comique onto rue St-Marc, following it to rue de Richelieu. Turn left to see:

20. **No. 95 rue de Richelieu,** formerly the Hôtel des Patriotes Etrangers. Gouverneur Morris arrived here in 1789, prepared to serve as American ambassador to France. He was a redoubtable character sporting a wooden leg and a withered arm. During the Reign of Terror his carriage was stopped by a mob who wanted to kill him; he stuck his wooden leg out the door and yelled, "Goddamn you—*me,* an aristocrat! Who lost his leg in the cause of American liberty!" The mob cheered and allowed him to continue on his way. Though other ambassadors fled Paris, he remained, and while in this very hotel he amassed a 12-volume diary of what it was like to be in this city during the Revolution. Morris even allowed royal treasures to be stored in the American embassy until they could be smuggled to England.

Walk up rue de Richelieu and turn right onto boulevard Montmartre. Shortly after you cross rue Vivienne on your right will be the:

21. **Passage des Panoramas.** At first two huge towers flanked this passageway. Under the direction of American inventor Robert Fulton, who'd received a patent for panorama painting from the French government, Pierre Prévost painted 18 panoramas in the towers. Parisians would pay just to look at the paintings. With the money he made, Fulton was able to work on his submarine (he'd come to Paris to sell the idea to Napoléon) and his steamboat. The first steamboat he tried out—on the Seine—was 66 feet long, with a flat bottom. Unfortunately, when the engine and boiler were put on board the boat split in two. His second boat ran at an amazing clip of about 4.5 miles per hour.

Regrettably, the towers were destroyed (the paintings with them) in 1831, but this wonderful little passageway remains.

When you come out of the passageway, turn right and go to rue Vivienne, then turn left. Just before you get to rue du 4 Septembre you'll find yourself alongside the:

22. **Bourse des Valeurs** (Paris Stock Exchange). The creation of a stock exchange began in 1720, when it was forbidden for anyone not a broker to engage in financial deals in a public building. Four years later, the French government required all brokers to work in a stock exchange, and during the next 80 or so years the Bourse moved to several different sites. Finally, Napoléon commissioned Aléxandre-Théodore Brongniart to design this building as its permanent home, begun in 1808 and finished (64 Corinthian columns and all) in 1826. You can watch the traders in action from the spectators' gallery (entrance is on the rue du 4 Septembre).

Continue down rue Vivienne to the:

23. **Bibliothèque Nationale,** on your right. The story of the French national library dates back to the royal collections, which became official libraries when the copyright law of 1537 went into effect. The law required one copy of every book ever printed in France to be "deposited" in what would eventually become the library you see today.

Every year approximately 40,000 volumes are added to the already immense collection. More than 12 million works are housed in the Department of Printed Books alone. In addition, the library boasts one of the largest collections of maps in the world; the Department of Manuscripts holds original manuscripts by Victor Hugo, Marcel Proust, and Marie Curie; and the Music and Record Library contains an enormous collection of original musical scores, records, and tapes.

Unfortunately, you can't enter the great Reading Room, designed by Labrouste (1801–75), but do try to look in through the windows at the cast-iron columns and the nine square-vaulted bays. In the Salle d'Honneur is a wonderful Houdon statue of Voltaire (his heart is in the pedestal).

When you come out of the library, turn right on rue Vivienne, walk to rue des Petits-Champs, then go right and walk to rue de Richelieu. Turn left and go to no. 52 and the entrance to rue (or passage) de Beaujolais. If you walk straight out of the passageway, continuing on rue de Beaujolais, you'll find the entrance to the Palais-Royal gardens (which you'll visit in a few minutes). At no. 15 rue de Beaujolais is the:

24. **Hôtel Beaujolais,** where Margaret Anderson lived in 1923. She was fined and fingerprinted for publishing a review with reprints of portions of James Joyce's *Ulysses,* which was considered obscene at the time.

    Sylvia Beach and her sister had rooms here in 1917, but the street's most famous resident was writer Colette, who lived at **no. 9** and spent a great deal of time sitting in the Palais-Royal gardens, enjoying the beauty of the lime grove (see Walking Tour 10, stop 1, for more on Colette). She also enjoyed dining at **Le Grand Véfour** (no. 17), once frequented by Napoléon and Joséphine, Hugo, and Cocteau, among others. Today it's been restored by the Taittinger family (of Champagne fame), complete with carved *boiserie* ceilings and black-and-gold Directoire chairs that will make you think of the Palais-Royal in its glory.

    From here, head into the:

25. **Jardin du Palais-Royal.** Louis XIII's Cardinal Richelieu was responsible for building the Palais-Royal, designed by architect Jacques Lemercier in 1642. When Richelieu died, he left the palace to Louis, who died shortly afterward; Louis' wife, Anne of Austria, then took up residence here, and at that time the Palais-Royal received its name. In 1781 Louis XIV gave the palace to the Orléans family, and following the Revolution Napoléon established the Tribune here. It housed the Bourse for a brief time, then, not long after, gambling houses that remained popular until they closed in 1838. The palace was burnt down during the Commune and rebuilt. It's become progressively quieter as the cafés, restaurants, and jewelers that once occupied the galleries have moved out.

    The gardens and square were designed after 1781 by Victor Louis under the direction of Philippe, duc d'Orléans, who had the idea of creating the pavilions and allotting space for apartments and shops. The streets surrounding the gardens were named after the duke's sons—Beaujolais, Montpensier, and Valois.

It was here, in the Café de Foy, that on July 12, 1789, Camille Desmoulins (whose statue is in the gardens) gave a speech sparking the Revolution: "Citizens . . . the time for talking has gone, the time for action has come. The people must take up arms, they must show by their cockades to which party they are pledged." And the people certainly did.

Exit from the gardens, cross cal d'Orléans, turn left and walk to rue de Valois, then turn right. Follow along this street to the Palais-Royal Métro station.

MONTMARTRE

Start: Place Pigalle (Métro: Pigalle).

Finish: Place Blanche.

Time: Four to six hours, depending on how long you spend in the churches, museums, and cemetery.

Best Time: Get an early start because you don't want to end up at the cemetery after dark.

Worst Time: Monday, when the Musée du Vieux Montmartre is closed.

The history of Montmartre stretches all the way back to the 3rd century, when its name was still Mont de Mercure. St. Denis and two of his prelates were tortured and taken to the top of Mont de Mercure, where they were beheaded. A miracle then happened—St. Denis is said to have picked up his own head and carried it to a nearby fountain, washed the blood from his face, and then walked 4 miles before he collapsed. Not long after this incident the hill was renamed Mont des Martyrs. Over time, it has become known to all as Montmartre.

Much later the hill was used for its quarries, from which gypsum was mined (when you heat gypsum you get plaster of paris). The mining continued until well into the 19th century, at which time a colony of artists began to settle here.

Today, the hill is known for the Moulin Rouge nightclub and the great white Basilique du Sacré-Coeur, which seems to swallow the "mountain" whole. Along this tour you'll walk through the place du Tertre, where Utrillo and his mother, Suzanne Valadon, lived and worked. In Montmartre you won't find good restaurants and glamorous shops but quiet streets, old cafés, the last remaining windmills on the hill, and the haunts of artists like Toulouse-Lautrec.

• • • • • • • • • • • • • • •

Begin your tour in the:

1. **Place Pigalle.** Aside from being the center of a famous writers'/artists' colony, place Pigalle was built on the site of an old Montmartre tollgate by Jean-Baptiste Pigalle in the 19th century. Pigalle was a sculptor/painter whose special subject was the Virgin Mary. However, he wasn't completely pious—he sculpted Voltaire in the buff (see Walking Tour 11, Part I, stop 17).

Before she gained fame, the "little sparrow," Edith Piaf, used to sing in the alleys off the place Pigalle, hoping to earn enough money for a hot meal.

As you come out of the place Pigalle, go up boulevard de Clichy in the direction opposite the Hôtel Timhotel. Head away from the confusing intersection and proceed to:

2. **No. 10 bd. de Clichy,** where composer Darius Milhaud (1892–1974) lived. He began his studies at the Paris Conservatory but also spent time in Brazil working with Paul Claudel, French minister to Brazil and brother of artist Camille Claudel (see Walking Tour 2, stop 23); this experience had a profound influence on his music.

In 1940 Milhaud became a professor of music at the all-women's Mills College in California. Ultimately he became a professor of composition at Paris's National Conservatoire. Among his most famous operas are *Le Pauvre Matelot* (1926) and *Christophe Colomb* (1928), which features a libretto by Paul Claudel.

Continue along. On the other side of the street are **nos. 11** and **13,** two of Picasso's former residences. A bit farther on, at **no. 6,** is the building in which Degas died. Keep walking until you reach boulevard de Rochechouart, named after Marguerite de Rochechouart, abbess of Montmartre from 1717 to 1727. The intersection of boulevard de Rochechouart, boulevard de Clichy, and rue des Martyrs is where the famous:

3. **Cirque Montmartre** was established. In 1873 a man named Fernando began a circus here (Cirque Fernando) featuring high-wire acts, jugglers, trapeze artists, and clowns. In 1897, one of Fernando's star clowns, Medrano (known to his admirers as Boum Boum), took over management, and the circus changed names. Parisians loved Cirque Medrano, which became an inspiration to many artists, including Toulouse-Lautrec, Picasso, Degas, Renoir, and Seurat, who painted the trapeze artists and Boum Boum himself.

   One of the most famous high-wire acts of the 1920s was Barbette, who was partial to Chanel gowns, ostrich-feather hats, and leotards. Not too unusual for a woman, right? However, Barbette was a man—an American named Vander Clyde who hailed from Austin, Texas. So brilliant was his artistry that Paul Valéry described him as "Heracles transformed into a swallow." Barbette was toasted by the rest of Paris and was a fixture of café society. Sadly, he took a nasty fall at the Moulin Rouge one night and was forced to stop performing. He returned to America and died in obscurity.

   Turn left onto rue Dancourt to place Charles-Dullin, where you'll find the:

4. **Théâtre de l'Atelier,** set up in 1921 by Charles Dullin (1885–1949) in the old Théâtre de Montmartre (renamed in 1957 for Dullin). Dullin was an actor/director/producer who was famous for his "experimental" dramas and introduced the works of Pirandello to French audiences.

   Continue past the place Charles-Dullin onto rue des Trois-Frères to rue Yves-le-Tac. Turn left into the:

5. **Place des Abbesses,** built on the site of Montmartre's old town hall. Verlaine was married here on August 11, 1870 (before having an affair with his protégé, Arthur Rimbaud). On your left is **St-Jean-l'Evangéliste** (1904),

the first church to be built entirely of reinforced concrete. Also to your right is one of the art nouveau **Métro stations** designed by Hector Guimard (see Walking Tour 2, stop 5).

Exit the church and go to the right, crossing the street to the passage des Abbesses. Turn right. When you get to rue des Trois-Frères, go left. Soon you'll come to the:

6. **Place Emile-Goudeau** and the **Bateau-Lavoir,** on your right. Before you go into the square, look down the hill to your left—there's a great view. At no. 13 is the Bateau-Lavoir, a small building many artists have called home, including Picasso from 1904 to 1912 (it was here he painted his famous portrait of Gertrude Stein, *The Third Rose,* as well as *Les Demoiselles d'Avignon*); Juan Gris from 1906 to 1922; Modigliani in 1908; Max Jacob in 1911; and Charpentier in 1912. Look at the photographs, including one of a very young Picasso. The original building burned in 1970 but was rebuilt in 1978; the studios now house 25 artists and sculptors.

Go up the hill, turning right out of the place Emile-Goudeau onto rue Berthe. As you walk along this street (it turns into rue André-Barsacq) note the window treatments at **nos. 11** and **13.** When you reach rue Chappe you can choose one of three ways to get to the Sacré-Coeur. You can head up the rue Chappe stairs; this is a strenuous climb for anyone not in good physical shape, but it's the quickest way. (There's a soda machine at the top of the stairs on the right if you need an incentive to go this way.) Your second option is to continue to the stairs at the end of rue André-Barsacq and go down to the Funiculaire (Paris's shortest Métro line), which will carry you to the top of the hill for the price of a Métro ride. Third, you can go down the stairs as if you were headed for the Funiculaire, but instead go around it, check out the Carousel, take a breather, and then head straight up the hill; this route affords a magnificent view of the great white basilica.

Note: On your way into the church, don't get bamboozled by the nice women who will put cards and pendants in your hand—they're not giving you presents, they're gathering alms.

Whichever route you choose, you'll end up at the:

7. **Basilique du Sacré-Coeur,** certainly one of Paris's most spectacular churches. During the Franco-Prussian War, Alexandre Legentil and Rohault de Fleury made a pact to build at the top of this hill a church dedicated to the Sacré-Coeur (Sacred Heart) as a symbol of hope for the city's Catholics. Construction began in 1876, and it was consecrated on October 16, 1919. Sacré-Coeur's dome is the second-highest peak in Paris (the highest is the Eiffel Tower).

Unfortunately, most of the stained-glass windows were shattered during a World War II air attack on Gare de la Chapelle, but there are some wonderful mosaics throughout the church, including Luc Olivier Meron's *Great Mosaic of Christ* (1912–22). In the ambulatory are two Renaissance-style silver statues of the Virgin Mary by P. Brunet. You can tour the dome with a guard stationed on the first terrace.

When you come out of the church, make one right and then another onto rue du Cardinal-Guibert. Take your first left on rue du Chevalier-de-la-Barre and walk to the corner of rue du Mont-Cenis. Turn left and approach the entrance of:

8. **St-Pierre de Montmartre.** Consecrated in 1147, this church also claims (along with St-Julien-le-Pauvre) to be the oldest in Paris, and it is, in fact, the last trace of the original abbey that stood here. Among its parishioners have been St. Thomas Beckett, St. Ignatius of Loyola, and Dante. Jean-Baptiste Pigalle is buried in its tiny cemetery. The stained-glass windows date from 1954; earlier ones were destroyed by a bomb during World War II.

Leave Sacré-Coeur and turn left, proceeding to the:

9. **Restaurant La Bohème du Tertre,** where from 1919 to 1935 Suzanne Valadon and her son, Utrillo, used to eat. Valadon, a famous painter in her own right, began her career as a circus acrobat, then modeled for such artists as Renoir, Toulouse-Lautrec, and Degas. Degas encouraged her to take up painting. Her favorite subjects were nudes and still lifes and her work is easily identified by the bold use of color punctuated with heavy black outlines. Degas once commented that she and Mary Cassatt were the only two female painters who had any talent (and he didn't

Montmartre

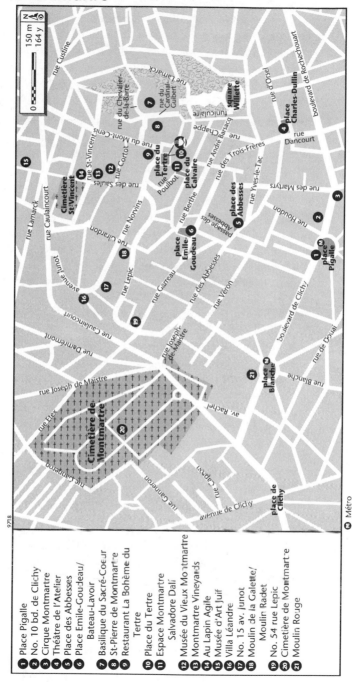

1. Place Pigalle
2. No. 10 bd. de Clichy
3. Cirque Montmartre
4. Théâtre de l'Atelier
5. Place des Abbesses
6. Place Emile-Goudeau/
   Bateau-Lavoir
7. Basilique du Sacré-Coeur
8. St-Pierre de Montmartre
9. Restaurant La Bohème du
   Tertre
10. Place du Tertre
11. Espace Montmartre
    Salvadore Dalí
12. Musée du Vieux Montmartre
13. Montmartre Vineyards
14. Au Lapin Agile
15. Musée d'Art Juif
16. Villa Léandre
17. No. 15 av. Junot
18. Moulin de la Galette/
    Moulin Radet
19. No. 54 rue Lepic
20. Cimetière de Montmartre
21. Moulin Rouge

Ⓜ Métro

really believe in women painters). She helped start her son's career by giving him a set of paints, in the hope that painting would curb his drinking problem. Utrillo did begin painting—but didn't stop drinking.

Go right at the end of rue du Mont-Cenis and you'll find yourself in the:

10. **Place du Tertre,** one of the most-frequented tourist spots in the city. Many artists scrape together a living here by doing tourist portraits or scenes of Montmartre. In earlier times, the abbey gallows and stocks stood here.

Utrillo used to hang out in the place du Tertre, and this might well have been where he first met Modigliani (see Walking Tour 10, stop 15, for more on Modigliani). Their mutual admiration did not create a harmonious union but led to a fight that started with one of them announcing, "You are the world's greatest painter."

"No, you are the world's greatest painter," contradicted the other.

"I forbid you to contradict me."

"I forbid *you* to forbid *me*."

"If you say that again, I'll hit you."

"You are the world's great—," and the fight began.

Afterward, they decided to be friends and went to a nearby restaurant to down several bottles of wine. When they finally walked back out into the street, one said, "You are the world's greatest painter."

"No, *you* are," contradicted the other. And the fists flew again.

They beat each other until falling in the gutter, where they fell asleep; they woke in the morning (probably the afternoon) to find their pockets had been emptied.

☕ **Take a Break**   It's possible that Utrillo and Modigliani drank away those hours at **La Mère Catherine,** 6 place du Tertre. Founded in 1793, this is the oldest restaurant in the place du Tertre. Dine on the terrace or on one of the red velvet benches inside and enjoy a leisurely lunch.

Continue around the place du Tertre and go through to the place du Calvaire, where there's a spectacular view. As you come out of the place du Calvaire, on your right you'll see the interesting:

11. **Espace Montmartre Salvadore Dalí,** housing a permanent display of 330 works by the Spanish artist. The exhibit's darkness is punctuated by lights that move from one painting to another as Dalí's voice moves through the exhibit along with visitors. The experience, like the artist's works, is somewhat surreal. Also here are an art gallery and a library.

After coming out of the museum, continue around to the right, head down the steps onto rue Poulbot, and cross rue Norvins onto rue des Saules. When you get to rue Cortot, go right to nos. 12–14, the:

12. **Musée du Vieux Montmartre,** whose wide collection of mementos of old Montmartre you can visit in about half an hour. This building was once occupied by van Gogh, Renoir, Suzanne Valadon, and Utrillo. Besides charting Montmartre's history, the museum features a re-creation of the workroom of Gustave Charpentier (composer of the opera *Louise*); a reconstruction of Café de l'Aubrevoir, another of Utrillo's favorite spots; and an entire room devoted to Emile Bernard of the Pont-Aven group. Also of note are some caricatures by Steinlen (1853–1923) and an extensive collection of china from the Clignancourt Pottery.

Exit the museum and go left to rue du Mont-Cenis. Turn left on rue du Mont-Cenis and go down the stairs to rue St-Vincent. Turn left. A little way down the road is the:

13. **Montmartre Vineyards,** one of two remaining vineyards in Paris. The vineyard produces approximately 500 bottles of Clos Montmartre red annually, and every year on the first or second Saturday of October there's a celebration called the "harvest fête." If you're lucky enough to be in Paris at harvest time, you'll find it's quite a party—there's even a parade.

Cartoonist Francisque Poulbot (1899–1946), known for his caricatures of children and Montmartre street scenes, so loved the vineyards he helped save them from destruction by developers in the 1930s.

On your right is:

14. **Au Lapin Agile,** the original Cabaret des Assassins. Legend has it that the cabaret got its name because a band of assassins broke in and killed the owner's son. It was renamed

in 1880 because of a sign featuring a rabbit in a bow tie, painted by André Gill. People began saying it was the "Cabaret à Gill," which eventually became "Agile."

The building originally belonged to a famous Parisian singer named Aristide Bruant, who gave it to a man named Father Fred, who used to entertain his clientele by singing and playing the guitar. Since Montmartre was the heart of artistic Paris at the time, there was much discussion here about the "meaning of art," and Roland Dorgeles (a popular writer at that time) took it upon himself to make a mockery of the debate by dipping the tail of Father Fred's donkey into some paint, smearing it on a canvas, and exhibiting the result, called *Le Coucher du soleil sur l'Adriatique (Sunset over the Adriatic)*. Much to Dorgeles's amusement, the critics actually liked it. Of course, he did eventually tell them (to the further amusement of many Parisians) it was merely a joke.

The Cabaret des Assassins was often captured on canvas by Utrillo, and today this corner is one of the most visited and photographed in all Paris.

Turn right on rue des Saules and on your left will be the **Cimetière St-Vincent,** where Emile Goudeau, Utrillo, composer Arthur Honegger, and conductor D.-H. Inghelbrecht are buried. To get into the cemetery, continue down the stairs to rue Caulaincourt. Make a left on rue Caulaincourt and walk to the entrance. When you come out of the cemetery, backtrack to rue des Saules, make a left, and descend the stairs to no. 42, the:

15. **Musée d'Art Juif** (Jewish Art Museum), on the third floor. This museum was founded in 1948 to promote Jewish art. Contributions have included architectural models, drawings, engravings, and paintings by Marc Chagall, Max Lieberman, and Chaim Soutine.

When you're finished at the museum, go back up the stairs to rue Caulaincourt. Turn left and walk to the fork at rue Caulaincourt and avenue Junot. Continue along avenue Junot to the:

16. **Villa Léandre,** 25 av. Junot, a short cul-de-sac that seems an oasis in this fairly busy area of the city. It probably won't

Marc Chagall

Russian-born painter Marc Chagall (1887–1985) originally studied in St. Petersburg. In 1910 he came to Paris
and joined the avant-garde set. Chagall's work reflects an
element of fantasy bordering on surrealism; however, in
his biography he claims that his work was inspired directly by memories of his early childhood. Many of those
memories were filled with Jewish tradition and Russian
folklore. Besides painting, he created a great deal of stained
glass, and his costume designs included those used in a
1945 production of Igor Stravinsky's *Firebird*.

come as a surprise as you walk along that many artists have
called this little alley home.

Continue along the street to:

17. **No. 15 av. Junot,** the former home of Romanian-born
French poet Tristan Tzara (1896–1963). He is best known
as the founder of the dadaist movement. Tzara and André
Breton (1896–1966) collaborated briefly before Breton
broke with the dadaists to found the surrealist movement.
Adolf Loos, architect of Tzara's house, had a modernist's
disdain for architectural ornamentation. This appealed to
Tzara's dadaist sensibilities, and he brought Loos to Paris
from Vienna and commissioned him to build this house.

Continue along avenue Junot to rue Girardon. Turn right
and proceed to rue Lepic, where you should make another
right. Look back across the street to the:

18. **Moulin de la Galette** and **Moulin Radet,** two windmills built in 1622. The former is the one you see before
you, the latter is just a bit farther down rue Lepic (to your
left as you face Moulin de la Galette). In the 19th century,
they were owned by the Debray brothers, who were killed
while defending them from the Prussians. Some say the
brothers were tied to the sails of their windmills and killed.
Their graves are located in the small St-Pierre de Montmartre
cemetery.

The only survivors of the 30 windmills that once dotted the hill, these have been the subject of many paintings, the most famous of which is Renoir's *Moulin de la Galette* (1876). The windmill featured in Renoir's painting was originally named Moulin Blute-Fin, but the name was changed when it became a dance hall that served *galettes*—cakes were made with the flour ground inside the windmills. In the 1860s it became a favorite venue of the impressionists, including Toulouse-Lautrec, van Gogh, Renoir, and Utrillo.

Facing Moulin de la Galette, turn left and walk to:

19. **No. 54 rue Lepic.** Currently in a state of disrepair, this is the building in which Vincent van Gogh and his brother, Théo, lived from 1886 to 1888. Vincent and Théo had an extraordinarily strong relationship; Théo helped support Vincent, both financially and emotionally, throughout his life, particularly during his art career. Théo ran an art gallery, which at the time exhibited very traditional art, but he believed in his brother's talents. When Vincent shot himself to death, Théo was so destroyed that many think he died of grief.

Continue along rue Lepic to rue Joseph-de-Maistre and go right to rue Caulaincourt. Make a left on this street and go to no. 20 av. Rachel, which is the entrance of the:

20. **Cimetière de Montmartre,** founded in 1798. As you enter stop at the main office to pick up a map (not a great one, but it'll give you a general idea of where to find graves not covered here).

Begin by going around the circle to the left and up the stairs, where you'll find the grave of **Emile Zola** (1840–1902), the French novelist who earned his living in journalism. As a novelist, he took a very scientific approach to his writing, describing everything in minute detail. He didn't always make a living as a journalist; at one time he was so poor he had to sell his raincoat and pants and stay home working in only his shirt. His remains have been moved to the Panthéon.

Continue around the circle and make a right on avenue Dubuisson, taking it to avenue Berlioz. Turn left on avenue Berlioz and approach the grave of **Louis-Hector Berlioz** (1803–69), just beyond Chemin Artot on the left side of the street. Berlioz was a French composer who started out in medicine but gave that up to go to the Paris Conservatory. His music was composed in a loose form and has a highly emotional style. He won the Prix de Rome in 1830 and over the next decade composed *Romeo and Juliet.*

Cross avenue Berlioz and go left on avenue Cordier to the grave of French painter **Jean-Honoré Fragonard** (1732–1806), on the left. (If you get to the next intersection, you've gone too far. It's located fairly close to the intersection of avenue Berlioz and avenue Cordier, about four rows back. You might have to ask for help in finding the plain gravestone.) Fragonard won the Prix de Rome and studied in Italy from 1756 to 1761. Much of his painting consists of scenes of erotic love, though after he married his works lost their sensual quality. A sad commentary!

Continue along avenue Cordier to the grave of **Théophile Gautier,** on the right. Gautier (1811–72), a poet/novelist who sidelined as a critic, was a member of the group that believed in "art for art's sake." In his writing he adhered to a theory of "plasticity," by which he meant that a writer should create art by manipulating words in the same way a painter manipulates paint or a sculptor manipulates whatever medium he or she uses. His best-known works include *Le Capitaine Fracasse* (1863) and *Emaux et camées* (1852).

Proceed to avenue du Montebello. Turn right and ascend a flight of stairs to the grave of impressionist painter **Hilaire-Germain-Edgar Degas** (1834–1917). He's buried in his family tomb; as you'll see, the original family name was de Gas. Degas was first a student of law, then a student of Ingres; his artistic career began at the Ecole des Beaux-Arts. Later, he broke from traditional style and joined the impressionists. His favorite subjects were ballet dancers and women at their toilette. As his eyesight failed and made painting in oils difficult (because of the detail required), he began using pastels and charcoal. Degas had a profound influence on Toulouse-Lautrec and Picasso and aided in Mary Cassatt's career.

When Degas was present at an auction where one of his paintings was being sold for an astonishing amount, someone asked him how he felt (supposing that he'd think it a great honor)—he said, "I feel as a horse must feel when the beautiful cup is given to the jockey."

Descend the stairs and go around to avenue du Tunnel. Turn right on avenue des Carrières. When you get to avenue des Anglais, go left to the grave of composer **Léo Delibes** (1836–91). Delibes attended the Paris Conservatory. Once an accompanist at the Paris Opéra, he went on to enjoy success with the ballets *Coppélia* (1870) and *Sylvia* (1876) and the opera *Lakmé* (1883), from which the Flower Duet is the most famous.

Continue down avenue des Anglais to the grave of **Jacques Offenbach** (Jacob Eberst, 1819–80). Offenbach was a darling of the Second Empire. He was conductor at the Théâtre Française in 1849 and particularly successful as a composer of operettas. During his lifetime he composed over a hundred of them, including *La Belle Hélène* (1864) and *La Vie parisienne* (1866). He spent every waking moment with his music, as is evidenced by the following anecdote.

Offenbach once fired a personal servant; shortly after, he gave a glowing reference to a friend who was considering hiring the servant. The friend, confused, asked him why he would give such a good reference to a man whom he had just fired. Offenbach's explanation was, "Oh, he's a good fellow, but he won't do for a composer. He beats my clothes outside my door every morning and his tempo is nonexistent."

Continue down avenue des Anglais to avenue Samson, then turn right and cross avenue du Tunnel. Avenue Samson turns into avenue Travot. Follow along avenue Travot and cross avenue de Montmorency. Just across avenue de Montmorency is the grave of **Stendhal** (Marie-Henri Beyle, 1783–1842). He traveled to Italy as a dragoon in Napoléon's army, and it was in Milan in 1814 that he launched his literary career by writing one of his two great novels: *Le Rouge et le noir* (*The Red and the Black,* 1831). Stendhal wrote the other, *The Charterhouse of Parma* (1839), while traveling around France during a leave of absence from his work as a consul.

Follow avenue de la Croix (which you walked onto when you crossed avenue de Montmorency) straight out to the circle at the cemetery entrance. Go right around the circle, back to avenue Rachel. Follow this avenue out of the cemetery and walk to boulevard de Clichy, where you turn left. At no. 82 bd. de Clichy is the:

21. **Moulin Rouge,** founded in 1889 but still claiming to have the best show in town. Once one of the favorite spots of artists who'd settled in Montmartre—thanks to its low cost of living and mix of pleasure and vice—these days it's most popular with tourists.

   The Moulin Rouge is, of course, famous for the cancan; the "chahut," a high-kicking dance that was a forerunner of the numbers performed by today's Rockettes at New York's Radio City Music Hall; and appearances by La Goulue (the stage name of Louise Weber), whose performances in the late 1880s were talked about all over Paris. She's featured in many of Toulouse-Lautrec's paintings.

Toulouse-Lautrec's Women

Jane Avril (1868–1943). Born to an Italian emigrant and a French mother, Jane Avril performed at the Moulin Rouge at age 20 and was called "the dance incarnate" by her admirers. She died in relative obscurity, even though Toulouse-Lautrec immortalized her in several posters.

Marie-Louise Fuller (1862–1928). Hailing from Illinois, Marie-Louise Fuller abandoned vaudeville and opera to become a dancer, making her Paris debut at the Folies-Bergère. Fuller was known for her performances on a glass platform floodlit from beneath. The mirrors she had set up behind and around her reflected only a silhouette so, as one critic wrote, she looked like a "genie who dances." During her time in Paris she is said to have had an affair with Rodin.

Yvette Guilbert (1867–1944). Appearing at the Moulin Rouge, she became famous for her silhouette of green satin and her long black gloves. Toulouse-Lautrec enjoyed painting her, and when she wasn't available but her gloves were, he painted just her gloves.

Today, the Moulin Rouge's show still features world-famous bare-breasted cancan dancers, provocatively draped with ostrich feathers and covered in rhinestones—but you probably won't find it nearly as racy or interesting as you expected. The dinner and show are quite expensive: $100 to $200.

The place Blanche Métro station is located nearby.

THE PÈRE-LACHAISE CEMETERY

Start: Boulevard de Ménilmontant and avenue Principale (Métro: Père-Lachaise).

Finish: Boulevard de Ménilmontant and avenue Principale.

Time: Two to three hours, depending on how many detours you take.

Best Time: Anytime during the day.

The property comprising the Cimetière du Père-Lachaise was originally the country retreat of Père François de la Chaise d'Aix, confessor to Louis XIV. Nicolas Frochot purchased the land almost 200 years ago from Jacques Baron (who owned it after Père François) and promoted it as a cemetery for the famous or wealthy. You can imagine he was not pleased when his first customer turned out to be an errand boy.

Frochot puzzled over his dilemma and eventually pounced on an opportunity to purchase the supposed bones of Molière and Jean La Fontaine. He buried them side by side, hoping their presence would help attract a more prestigious crowd. These celebrities did generate some interest, but business didn't really pick up until he acquired the bones of the famous lovers Héloïse and Abélard. Then plots began selling like hotcakes.

Now you have the opportunity to visit the resting place of all the famous people who've since been interred here. In this tour I've tried to include all the major luminaries, but there are a few who had to be left out because of where they were located. Using the map you can get at the cemetery entrance, you might find others you'll want to visit. This is a wonderful place.

(In case you're wondering—Père de la Chaise is not buried here.)

• • • • • • • • • • • • • • • •

Go straight up avenue Principale to the sign that says *Chapelle.* Turn left onto avenue Circulaire. The third stone on the right, black with gold lettering, marks the grave of:

1. **Sidonie-Gabrielle-Claudine Colette** (1873–1954). Known simply as Colette, this writer was the first woman president of the Goncourt Academy and the second woman to be made a grand officer of the French Legion of Honor. Most of her writing is for and about women, the best of which are *Gigi* (1945), *The Cat* (1933), and *Chéri* (1920). Colette attributed her success as a writer (and her powers of observation) to her mother, whose oft-repeated advice to "Look, look!" taught her daughter to watch for life's wonders. On her deathbed in 1954, during Paris's worst thunderstorm in almost three-quarters of a century, Colette pointed at the lightning-streaked sky and said, "Look, look!" for the very last time.

Go back to avenue Principale, turn left, and walk to the grave of Italian operatic composer:

2. **Gioacchino Antonio Rossini** (1792–1868), on the left side of the path just before the 6th tree (counting from the intersection of avenue Circulaire and avenue Principale). During his lifetime his operas were a big box-office draw because, like *The Barber of Seville,* they featured the common person. He was indeed a commoner, a wealthy man. When he was elderly, a group of students tried to raise money to have a statue dedicated to him. He told them, "Give me the twenty thousand and I'll stand on the pedestal myself."

Just beyond the next tree, also on the left, is the grave of French romantic playwright/fiction writer/and poet:

3. **Louis-Charles-Alfred de Musset** (1810–57), who was infatuated with George Sand. (Note that his sister is buried behind him.)

Go back in the direction from which you came and turn left on avenue du Puits. Take your second right, then your first left (a dirt pathway), which is avenue Rachel. Just after the 8th tree in the front row of the cemetery's old Jewish section is the:

4. **Rothschild family plot.** A German-Jewish family whose history began with Mayer Anselm (1743–1812), the Rothschilds were one of Europe's great financial powers. Mayer Anselm, a Frankfurt moneylender, lent large sums to various governments and princes. His five sons expanded the business to Vienna, London, Naples, and Paris. The youngest, Jacob (1792–1868), started the Paris branch, and his capital was used to build the French railroad. He was also a great patron of the arts; the Louvre owns many pieces donated by the Rothschilds. But the most successful branch of the business was opened by Sir Nathan Mayer, who not only lent money to Wellington and the British government during wars with Napoléon but also was the first Jewish man to be admitted to England's House of Lords.

Continue five trees down from the Rothschild plot and when you get to the second row, head to the gravesite of painter/graphic artist:

5. **Camille Pissaro** (1830–1903). Born in the West Indies to a Jewish father and a Créole mother, he moved to Paris in 1855. Four years later he met Monet and became a member of the impressionist group. Of the impressionists, Pissaro was the oldest (by about 10 years) and thus became a sort of father figure to Monet, Renoir, and Cézanne. He experimented briefly with pointillism (a technique Georges Seurat would make famous), and though he is not the best known of the group, he was the only one who exhibited in all eight impressionist exhibitions. After 1895 Pissaro was forced to stay indoors because of failing health, but during this time he painted some of his finest works, including his series depicting the avenue de l'Opéra.

Return to avenue du Puits and go right to the fifth tree from the corner. You'll see a gothic structure with a fence around it, which is the grave of:

6. **Héloïse** and **Abélard,** two of the world's most famous lovers. Pierre Abélard was born near Nantes and attended the school of Notre-Dame, where he had a falling out with his master and was expelled. Abélard crossed the river to the Ste-Geneviève school, where he eventually became a master. By the time he was 36 he was recognized as a great scholar and, ironically, became canon and master of Notre-Dame in 1115. His presence attracted to Notre-Dame students from all over medieval Europe.

A bit later, while Abélard was working as the assistant to the canon Fulbert, Héloïse's uncle, he and Héloïse fell in love and were secretly married. When their secret was discovered, Héloïse was sent to the convent of Argenteuil, and her uncle had Abélard castrated. Abélard went to a monastery and not long afterward opened a school of theology in which he challenged ecclesiastical authorities. Although he remained popular with his students, his enemies charged him with heresy and persecuted him constantly.

During the time he and Héloïse were separated, they maintained their romance through letters. Abélard died in 1142, Héloïse 24 years later. Finally, after countless separations, their remains were reunited in Père-Lachaise.

Back out on avenue du Puits, turn right and proceed to chemin Mehul (an unpaved road on your left). Make a left on chemin Mehul, then take your second left (not chemin du Coq, the next one). Note that there's no name marker for this cobbled road. On the right is the grave of Polish composer:

7. **Frédéric François Chopin** (1810–49). As a child, Chopin was asked to play in the salons of Warsaw's wealthiest. When he was 21 he gave his first Paris concert, and by the time he was 29 he'd completed 24 preludes, one in each major and minor key and not one lasting more than five minutes. He gained notoriety for introducing the piano as a solo instrument rather than an accompanying one. It's interesting that Chopin preferred teaching to performing onstage. Like many before and after him, Chopin had a turbulent affair

with George Sand. You might be interested to know that Chopin's heart is buried in a Warsaw church.

About four stones down on the right you'll find another child prodigy, Italian composer:

8. **Maria Luigi Cherubini** (1760–1842), who particularly enjoyed religious, or sacred, music. By 16 he'd already written several masses and other sacred choral pieces. His work profoundly affected Beethoven's vocal works. At 60, after four years as a professor of composition at the Paris Conservatory, Cherubini became its director. Incidentally, Cherubini hated the flute and was heard to say he believed the only thing worse than one flute was two flutes.

Turn right at avenue Laterale du Sud. Ascend two staircases and take a right on avenue de la Chapelle. On the right, just beyond the bench behind the bush, is the grave of Romantic painter:

9. **Théodore Géricault** (1791–1824). On the grave marker is a statue of an artist with his palette, and around the side is a bronze bas-relief of one of his paintings, *Mounted Officer of the Imperial Guard* (1812). Géricault studied in Paris with Carle Vernet and Pierre Guérin. His most famous work, *The Raft of the Medusa,* was one of the first paintings of its size to reflect a contemporary newsworthy event: the 1816 shipwreck of the *Medusa.* He was also one of the first to break traditional form in technique and is thought to have influenced Eugène Delacroix (see below).

Return to the road and continue along to Carrefour du Grand-Rond. Go left around the circle. On your left is the grave of French mathematician/physicist/public official:

10. **Gaspard Monge, comte de Péluse** (1746–1818). A friend of Napoléon, he is best known for his geometrical research and was instrumental in the 1794 founding of Paris's Ecole Polytechnique. Monge's research helped lay the foundations of modern geometry, which is essential to the mechanical drawings produced by today's architects.

Follow the road around the circle to the second left. Walk to the second tree on the left after the first possible right. On the left you'll see a black statue in the posture of a Madonna and Child. In front of that headstone is the grave of French philosopher:

The Père-Lachaise Cemetery

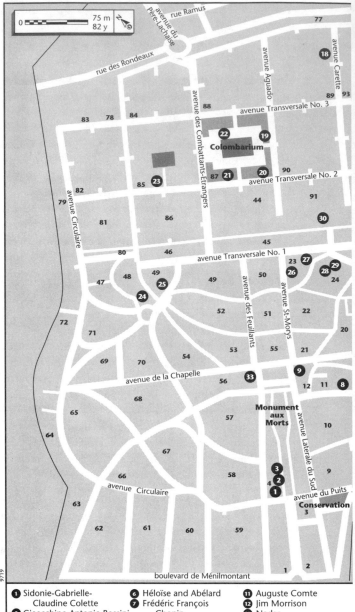

1. Sidonie-Gabrielle-Claudine Colette
2. Gioacchino Antonio Rossini
3. Louis-Charles-Alfred de Musset
4. Rothschild family plot
5. Camille Pissaro
6. Héloïse and Abélard
7. Frédéric François Chopin
8. Maria Luigi Cherubini
9. Théodore Géricault
10. Gaspard Monge
11. Auguste Comte
12. Jim Morrison
13. Nadar
14. Edith Piaf
15. Amedeo Modigliani
16. Gertrude Stein
17. Alice B. Toklas

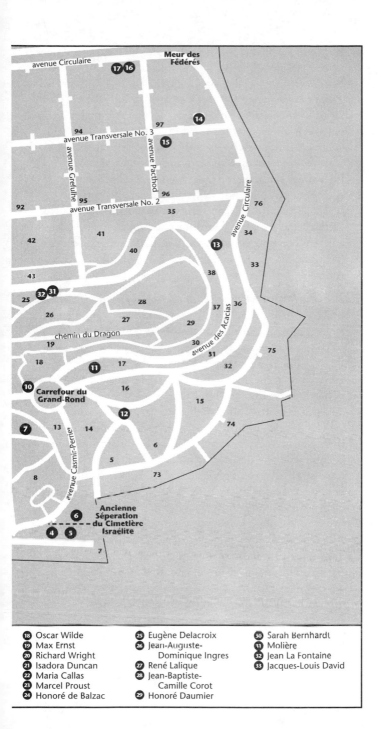

avenue Circulaire

Meur des Fédérés

17 16

94

avenue Transversale No. 3

97

avenue Gretulhe

avenue Pacthod

14

15

95

avenue Transversale No. 2

96

92

35

avenue Circulaire

76

42

41

40

13

34

43

38

33

25 32 31

28

37 36

26

27

29

avenue des Acacias

chemin du Dragon

30

19

31

75

18

17

11

32

10 **Carrefour du Grand-Rond**

16

15

7

13

avenue Casmir-Perrier

14

12

6

74

5

8

73

6 **Ancienne Séperation du Cimetière Israélite**

4 5

7

18	Oscar Wilde	25	Eugène Delacroix	30	Sarah Bernhardt
19	Max Ernst	26	Jean-Auguste-	31	Molière
20	Richard Wright		Dominique Ingres	32	Jean La Fontaine
21	Isadora Duncan	27	René Lalique	33	Jacques-Louis David
22	Maria Callas	28	Jean-Baptiste-		
23	Marcel Proust		Camille Corot		
24	Honoré de Balzac	29	Honoré Daumier		

11. **Auguste Comte** (1798–1857), the founder of positivism, whose goal was to create a peaceful and harmonic society. His system for social reform is described in *The Course of Positive Philosophy* (1830–42), and his *System of Positive Polity* (1851–54) describes his belief in a society that makes a religion out of worshiping humanity. Comte is credited with coining the term *sociology*, and his research contributed to what is now known as modern sociology. Confronting his impending death in 1857, the modest and humble Comte is reported to have said, "What an irreparable loss!"

    Head back to the right turn you passed on your way to Comte's grave: chemin Lauriston (now on your left). Make a left. When you get to the fork in the road, take the left fork (chemin de Lesseps) to the grave of the illustrious American rock singer and 1960s icon:

12. **Jim Morrison** (1943–71). This one is a little tricky to find because it's a small grave site, tucked away amid many larger tombs. The first thing you should look for is the crowd of people always gathered here. Then look for two large trees (on the right), one of which has "God Bless America" carved into it; the other, a bit closer to the road, says, "Elvis is king." Note that the headstone you see today is a new one—the original had a marble bust of Morrison on it.

    The inclusion of the former Doors lead vocalist in this prestigious cemetery is controversial: Because of the number and type of visitors Morrison's grave attracts, the area is heavily trafficked and grafittied. Morrison was buried here because he fit one of the three requirements—you have to be born in Paris, die in Paris, or live in Paris. Morrison died of a drug overdose here while vacationing.

    Go back the way you came to Carrefour du Grand-Rond. Take your first right off the circle, which is avenue des Acacias. This is a bit of a walk, but follow this road up and around. Not far after the sign for section 38 you'll see a cement bench on your right. Just behind the cement bench is the grave of photographer:

13. **Nadar** (Gaspard Félix Tournachon, 1820–1910). Nadar was one of the greatest, if not *the* greatest, photographers of the 19th century. He's remembered for his stunning photographs of Hugo, Sand, Baudelaire, Delacroix, and Bernhardt.

He preferred not to make portraits of women (with a few exceptions) since the result was "too true to nature to please the sitter, even the most beautiful." Eventually Nadar gave up photography and took up hot-air ballooning. It was during a balloon ride that he took the first bird's-eye view photograph of Paris.

Make your first right after Nadar's grave onto chemin Abadie. Go right on avenue Transversale No. 2 to avenue Circulaire. Turn left and walk to avenue Transversale No. 3, then turn left again. Before you get to the next grave, you should note the two **monuments to the victims of Nazi concentration camps** on your right—one from Manthausen, the other from Flossenberg. .

Walk down the first dirt pathway off the right side of avenue Transversale No. 3, then take your first right (another dirt pathway) almost immediately after you get off the main road. Look for the grave of the Famille Gassion-Piaf in the second row back from the street. This is the resting place of world-famous cabaret singer:

14. **Edith Piaf** (1915–63), who was loved for her powerful, emotional voice. Dubbed the "little sparrow," she began singing in cafés and on the streets of Paris at the tender age of 15; she was so loved by her fans that Jean Cocteau even wrote a play for her.

Return to the road and continue in the direction you were headed. Make a left on the pathway before reaching the intersection of avenue Transversale No. 3 and avenue Patchod. Just after you take the dirt pathway, go left again down to the seventh row. The second grave on the left has a very plain stone to mark the resting place of Italian painter/sculptor:

15. **Amedeo Modigliani** (1884–1920), famous for his elongated forms. Wonderfully individualistic, he became passionate about sculpture as a medium after he met Brancusi in 1909; however, the most notable influence on him was African sculpture. In spite of (probably because of) his unique style he remained unknown until well after his death from tuberculosis—a condition aggravated by his abuse of drugs and alcohol.

Back out on avenue Transversale No. 3, turn left and go to avenue Patchod. Turn right and head to avenue Circulaire. First detour to the right to see other **monuments to Nazi concentration-camp victims.** These immense sculptures speak much louder than any inscriptions that could be placed on the monuments themselves.

Now head back in the other direction, crossing avenue Patchod. Just after the fourth tree on the left you'll find the grave of:

16. **Gertrude Stein** (1874–1946), who's perhaps best known for her line, "Rose is a rose is a rose is a rose." Friends with Ernest Hemingway, Sherwood Anderson, Pablo Picasso, Sylvia Beach, and many others, Stein hosted one of the most famous weekly literary salons. She and her brother Leo were trendsetters in the art world, and she had one of the best private collections in Paris at the time. Stein claimed to have discovered Picasso; she used to say of the two Picassos that hung on her wall that if her apartment were on fire and she "could take only one picture, it would be those two." Working alongside Picasso, she attempted to create the written equivalent of cubism, but many people find her writing unintelligible.

Although *The Autobiography of Alice B. Toklas* (1933) brought her the fame she'd been trying to gain entertaining famous and talented people, it was not taken seriously. Leo said it was "a ferrago of rather clever anecdote, stupid brag, and general bosh. . . . I simply cannot take Gertrude seriously as a literary phenomenon." Some acquaintances (including Matisse, Braque, and Tzara) followed Leo's lead by pointing out the book's many lies and/or mistakes. Braque said, "Miss Stein understood nothing of what went on around her. But no superegoist does. . . . She has entirely misunderstood cubism . . . which she saw simply in terms of personalities."

Next to Stein's grave is what looks like an empty plot, or a plot without a stone—this is the resting place of the ever-present, ever-silent:

17. **Alice B. Toklas** (1877–1966), Stein's famous-by-association lover. As always, Toklas has second billing, for

she's noted on the backside of Stein's headstone. Even in death Toklas stands behind Stein—a melancholic ending.

Continue along avenue Circulaire and take your second left onto avenue Carette, following it to the grave of bitingly witty writer:

18. **Oscar Fingal O'Flahertie Wills Wilde** (1854–1900). You can't miss his headstone—a massive art deco Egyptian-like sphinx that looks as if it might take flight. First and foremost a dandy and an aesthete (plus a comedian), Wilde was once quoted as saying, "I put my genius into my life and my talent into my work." Some of his most famous works are *The Picture of Dorian Gray* (1891), *A Woman of No Importance* (1893), *The Importance of Being Earnest* (1895), and his fairy-tale collections. In the late 1890s Wilde was charged with homosexual practices by the marquess of Queensbury (father of Wilde's paramour, Lord Alfred Douglas) and was sentenced to two years' hard labor. One day, while standing handcuffed in the cold rain, he declared, "If this is the way Queen Victoria treats her prisoners, then she doesn't deserve to have any."

At one time, his aesthetic sense made him the central figure of a group that believed in beauty for its own sake, including Whistler and actress Lillie Langtry. His fixation with aesthetics followed him all the way to his deathbed, where he quipped, "Either that wallpaper goes, or I do." He died in Paris of cerebral meningitis (see Walking Tour 4, Part I, the paragraph preceding stop 17). I assume the wallpaper stayed.

Continue to the next intersection and turn right on avenue Transversale No. 3. At the next intersection, go left on avenue Aguado (there's no name marker here). Turn right into the Columbarium and then make your first right under the covered walkway. Just before the second staircase, in the first row of the second section, fourth row from the bottom, is the marker for German-born dadaist/surrealist painter:

19. **Max Ernst** (1891–1976). Originally a psychology student at Bonn University, the man who called himself Dadamax took up painting because of his interest in the painting

of psychotics. Ernst came to Paris in 1922 and joined the surrealist movement two years later. He lived in the United States from 1941 to 1949 and was briefly married to the famous art patron Peggy Guggenheim; however, he returned to France in 1949 and remained until his death.

Turn around and cross the entry road you came in on to the other side (as if you had gone left rather than right on entering the Colombarium). Proceed to the end and make a right when you can't go any farther. Behind the third stair on your left is the marker of African-American writer:

20. **Richard Wright** (1908–60). Wright was born on a Mississippi plantation and joined the Federal Writers' Project in the 1930s. His many books include *Uncle Tom's Children* (1938) and *Native Son* (1940).

In December 1945 the French government invited Wright to come to Paris as its guest. He had a difficult time getting a passport from the U.S. State Department. When he and his wife finally arrived in Paris by ship, they were met by the American ambassador and none other than Gertrude Stein. Stein had, in her usual way, already managed to get in Wright's good graces by sending him a letter that read, "Dear Richard: It is obvious that you and I are the only two geniuses of this era." Wright died at 52 in Paris and was cremated with a copy of his novel *Black Boy*.

Proceed around to the next block. Just before the first staircase, the second row up, the last stone on the right, is the marker of dancer:

21. **Isadora Duncan** (Dora Gray Duncan, 1878–1927). San Francisco–born Duncan achieved fame with her flamboyant expressionism as a dancer. Wearing a scant Greek tunic and draped in a multitude of flowing scarves, she performed barefoot to music not written to be danced to. Though not received warmly in the United States, she was adored in Paris from the time of her 1922 arrival; that adoration soon spread all over Europe. Her final performance was held in Paris.

She spent a good deal of time in the Louvre studying the vases as examples of grace. She was complimented by Rodin when he said, "she has attained sculpture and emotion effortlessly . . . has properly unified Life and The Dance."

Duncan died in a way most fitting to her persona—she was accidentally strangled when her favorite long red scarf became entangled in the wheel of her brand-new Bugatti race car. Her last words as she began driving off were, "Je vais à la gloire!" ("I go to glory!"). Five thousand people attended her funeral.

Walk through the courtyard and around to the stairs between the two structures on the other side (those facing the one with Isadora Duncan's marker). Descend the stairs and make a right. At the end of the hallway, go left to the stone numbered 6258, on your right. This is the grave of Greek-American soprano:

22. **Maria Callas** (1923–77). Born in New York City, she moved to Greece at age 13 and studied at Athens' Royal Conservatory. Loved for her versatility and her dramatic intensity, she debuted in 1947 at Verona and made her first Metropolitan Opera appearance in 1956. Callas's fairly short career ended with her retirement at 42. Several recent biographies have noted her obsession with Aristotle Onassis.

From Callas's stone, continue straight ahead and go up the main stairs, to your right. Make a left at avenue Combattants-Etrangers (the one directly ahead of you). When you get to avenue Transversale No. 2 make a right. Make another right at the first dirt pathway and walk to the fourth grave on the left, which is that of novelist:

23. **Marcel Proust** (1871–1922). The sickly son of wealthy parents, Proust is considered a truly great modern writer because of his ability to communicate the link between a person's external and internal consciousness. His writing culminated in his multivolumed masterpiece, *A la recherche du temps perdu (Remembrance of Things Past)*, which he began in his bed, shortly after his mother's death in 1906. Proust wanted to be buried with his friend/lover, composer Maurice Ravel, though their families wouldn't allow it.

Go back out to avenue Transversale No. 2 and turn right (in the direction you were headed before you detoured), then at the first intersection go left onto avenue des Thuyas. Continue along, crossing avenue Transversale No. 1 and then going straight. On the right, just before the next corner, is the grave of novelist:

24. **Honoré de Balzac** (1799–1850), who studied law at the Sorbonne but decided he'd rather write. He spent all day and most of the night writing, sleeping in the late afternoon for only a few hours. Like many writers throughout history, he spent much time attempting to avoid starvation—so, to support himself, he wrote pulp novels under a pseudonym.

During the time of his greatest poverty Balzac lived in a stark, unheated room. However, he kept a sense of humor, writing on the walls things like, "Rosewood paneling with commode," "Gobelin tapestry with Venetian mirror," and "Picture by Raphael" above the fireplace. His greatest wish was to "be so well-known, so popular, so celebrated, so famous, that it would permit [him] . . . to break wind in society, and society would think it a most natural thing."

Only a few months before his death, he married Polish countess Evelina Hanska, with whom he'd been exchanging love letters for an incredible 18 years.

Turn left at the next intersection onto avenue Eugène-Delacroix and go to the grave of painter:

25. **Eugène Delacroix** (1798–1863), one of the masters of the Romantic movement. He spent a great deal of time copying old masters at the Louvre and was an admirer of Rubens. He once announced that "if you are not skillful enough to sketch a man falling out of a window during the time it takes him to get from the fifth story to the ground, then you will never produce a monumental work." Well, Delacroix produced many monumental works, among them *The Bark of Dante* (1922) and *The Massacre at Scios* (1824). His body of work topped more than 9,000 paintings, drawings, and pastels. He was an inspiration to many of the impressionists, including van Gogh, Seurat, and Renoir. Delacroix's old studio on rue de Furstemberg has been turned into a museum of his work (see Walking Tour 4, stop 13).

Directly on your right is chemin de la Cave. Follow it, crossing avenue Feuillant. Chemin de la Cave turns into chemin Cabail. Follow it to avenue St-Morys. Make a right on the path just past the second tree and you'll find a white stone, about three rows back, facing away from avenue St-Morys. This is the grave of painter:

26. **Jean-Auguste-Dominique Ingres** (1780–1867). Ingres entered David's studio (see below) at 17 and won the Prix de Rome only four years later. His work has a fluid, sinuous, rhythmical quality that broke with traditional classical form. In 1806, because he distorted the human figure (in his portrait of Madame Rivière) in favor of the linear rhythm of his painting, he was alienated from the Académie. That same year, in frustration, he returned to Rome, where he remained until 1820.

Ironically, when Ingres returned to Paris in 1824 (after a brief period in Florence), he was named president of the Ecole des Beaux-Arts. Delacroix didn't like that very much, and he criticized Ingres again, saying that he taught "beauty as one teaches arithmetic." There was so much animosity between the two that Ingres refused Delacroix's handshake until well into his old age.

He left again for Rome in 1834 when yet another of his pictures was rejected for not following classical rules. He returned to Paris in 1841 and lived out his life here. Some of his greatest works include *Bather of Valpincon* (1808) and *Odalisque with the Slave* (1842).

Return to avenue St-Morys and turn left. Take the first left onto chemin Adonson (the left fork) and follow it to the grave of jeweler/glassmaker:

27. **René Lalique** (1860–1945), an exceedingly talented art nouveau artisan. Most know him for his clear crystal glass engraved with frosted flowers, figures, or animals, which he began designing in 1902. However, the jewelry he made after establishing his Paris workshop in 1885 focused not on the stone but on the design. Lalique particularly enjoyed using semiprecious stones—most notably opals—bringing them back into fashion. His pieces often contained the art nouveau motifs of dragonflies, peacocks, and female nudes.

Continue on. The pathway veers right, and from the path you can see the tops of the heads of two sculpted busts. The black one is of landscape painter:

28. **Jean-Baptiste-Camille Corot** (1796–1875). Born the son of a Paris shopkeeper, Corot worked in textile shops until around 1822 and didn't begin to study painting until

he was 30. Only five years later he started exhibiting regularly at the Salon of the Barbizon School, a group of artists who focused primarily on landscape painting.

Corot, greatly respected by his contemporaries, influenced many younger artists, but he didn't receive great acclaim until he was well into his fifties. If he was broke and had to sell one of his treasured paintings, he'd exclaim in despair, "Alas, my collection has been so long complete, and now it is broken!"

Three rows behind Corot, directly in front of the big tree, is the grave of sculptor/painter/lithographer:

29. **Honoré Daumier** (1808–79). It's appropriate Daumier is buried so near Corot, for Corot gave Daumier a house at Valmondois-sur-Seine-et-Oise when he was old, poor, nearly blind, and threatened with eviction. Most famous for his spontaneous caricature sculptures of political figures, Daumier was even imprisoned for six months because of his 1832 Gargantua cartoon showing Louis-Philippe swallowing bags of gold that had been extracted from his people.

Daumier produced approximately a hundred lithographs per year in addition to his sculpture and painting. A member of the realist school, he was admired by Delacroix, Balzac, Baudelaire, and Degas. In fact, Balzac was once heard to say of Daumier, "this boy has some Michelangelo under his skin."

Return to the main path and cross avenue Transversale No. 1. To the left of the back of the big tomb in front of you is the grave of Paris-born actress:

30. **Sarah Bernhardt** (Henriette-Rosine Bernard, 1844–1923), who was raised in a convent for the first 13 years of her life. A graduate of the Paris Conservatory, she made her debut at 17 and was badly received. However, she persevered and eventually became one of Paris's best-loved actresses. Following her funeral, Janet Flanner said that "for days after what seemed like Bernhardt's last public performance, mourners stood in line in the cemetery to get a view of where she lay dead, just as they had made the box-office queue to see her alive on the stage."

She's especially well known for her performances in Victorien Sardou's *Fédora, Théodora,* and *La Tosca;* in 1912 she even became a silent-film star.

Back on avenue Transversale No. 1, turn left and go to the dirt pathway on the right, just before the sign marking the 39th division. This will be chemin Molière et La Fontaine. Turn right and walk to the grave of writer/actor:

31. **Molière** (Jean-Baptiste Poquelin, 1622–73). Born in Paris, Molière was the king of French high comedy in the 17th century. His satirical plays, including *Le Tartuffe* (1664) and *Le Misanthrope* (1666), pointed out society's hypocrisies and often attacked the church. Not surprisingly, there were many problems when it came to the issue of his burial. Church officials decided he couldn't be buried in consecrated ground, which was said to run 14 feet deep. Louis XIV therefore ordered the grave be dug to 16 feet. Unfortunately, no one knows where the great dramatist was really buried—legend has it that he disappeared before he could be buried in that 16-foot-deep grave, so M. Frochot (who started the cemetery) was most likely taken for a ride when he bought Molière's bones.

Right next to Molière is the grave of French poet:

32. **Jean La Fontaine** (1621–95). He and Molière are side by side, surrounded by a wrought-iron fence. La Fontaine was famous mainly for his books of fables (12 in all) featuring animals behaving like humans. The fables, modeled after Aesop's, were so successful that 137 editions were printed in his lifetime. It's probably safe to assume that if Frochot was duped in regard to Molière's bones, he was probably duped about La Fontaine's as well.

Keep going to the end, taking the left fork and following it all the way back down to avenue de la Chapelle. Turn right and pass Géricault's grave (on your left). Go left on the other side of the park and proceed to the fifth grave on the right, that of neoclassicist French painter:

33. **Jacques-Louis David** (1748–1825), known to most people as just David. His first attempt at the Prix de Rome failed and led to a suicide attempt. Fortunately, he was saved

by some fellow Académie students who found him in his room at the Louvre before it was too late.

In 1774, he did win the Prix de Rome and left to study in Italy, returning to Paris in 1780. He then became very involved in politics and even voted for the execution of Louis XVI in 1793.

David revolutionized art with his huge paintings that were allegories or commentaries on current events. From the terrace outside the Café de la Régence, he liked to sketch prisoners on their way to the guillotine—among them Marie Antoinette. Napoléon recognized David's potential as a propagandist and appointed him official painter. Between 1802 and 1805 he did a series for Napoléon, including the *Coronation of Napoléon* (1805–7, at the Louvre). When Napoléon fell, David went into exile in Brussels. His influence can be seen in the work of Ingres, Gérard, and Gros.

Continue down the steps to avenue du Puits. Make a left to avenue Principale, then make a right on avenue Principale and continue to the exit. For the Métro, go to the Père-Lachaise station at which you arrived here.

The Louvre
Parts I & II

I've made every attempt possible to be sure the layouts of the rooms you'll be visiting in the Louvre wouldn't change in the near future.

This enormous museum has been undergoing renovations for the last several years, and most of the collections have been moved to temporary quarters at one time or another. As of late 1994, the painting and sculpture collections seemed to be staying in their present locations, while the Egyptian and Oriental antiquities were scheduled to be moved in early 1995; consequently, I haven't included those collections on the tour. Also note that it's not unusual for pieces to be moved for cleaning or taken to other museums or other rooms in the Louvre for special exhibitions, so if you can't find a piece I've listed, ask if it's been moved. Otherwise, just skip that work and continue with the rest of the tour.

In other words, don't assume all the pieces have moved if one is not where I said it would be. Likewise, if a major artist, like Jacques-Louis David or Nicolas Poussin, is not mentioned it's because his or her works weren't on display when I wrote the tour. Finally, to make identifying pieces easier, I've listed their names first in French (as they're labeled throughout the museum) and then in English.

Note: These Louvre tours are accompanied by a general map of the Hall Napoléon and the wings rather than detailed maps of the rooms in each wing you'll visit. The Louvre does not supply comprehensive maps of all its rooms, so I decided not to confuse you with pieced-together approximations. Upon entering, request one of the museum brochures, in which you'll find small maps covering groups of rooms. If you follow my written directions you should have no trouble navigating the wings, but if you need help, consult the large maps you'll find on the walls along the way.

PART I: SCULPTURE

Start: Cour Marly in the Richelieu Wing.

Finish: Ground floor in the Denon Wing.

Time: Two to four hours, depending on how much time you spend admiring each piece.

Best Time: In the morning on Monday and Wednesday through Friday, just after the museum opens, or in the evening on Wednesday, when the museum closes at 10pm.

Worst Time: Tuesday, when the museum's closed, or weekends, when it's too crowded.

Part I of the Louvre tour will take you through the museum's Richelieu Wing, where you'll see everything from Romanesque French sculpture, to early 19th-century French sculpture, to Italian sculpture, including Michelangelo's famous *Slaves*. You'll view both the monumental and the small: from pieces retrieved from palace gardens through-

The Louvre

The Pyramid

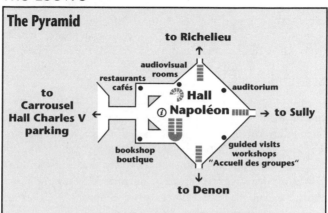

to Richelieu ↑

audiovisual rooms

restaurants cafés

auditorium

i **Hall Napoléon**

to Carrousel Hall Charles V parking ←

→ to Sully

bookshop boutique

guided visits workshops "Accueil des groupes"

to Denon ↓

The Levels

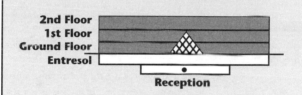

2nd Floor
1st Floor
Ground Floor
Entresol

Reception

The Wings

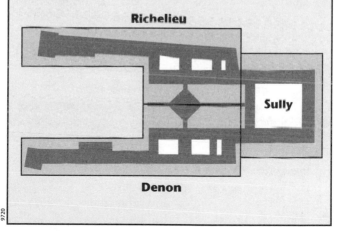

Richelieu

Sully

Denon

9720

out France to beautiful white marble admission pieces from the Académie Française, documenting the changes in sculpture from Louis XIV's time to the Revolution. Other artists represented on the tour are Jean-Baptiste Pigalle, Jean-Antoine Houdon, Pierre Biard, and François Rude.

Enter the Louvre through I. M. Pei's enormous glass pyramid. In the central area inside are several places to buy tickets. Then follow the signs into the Richelieu Wing, continuing past the *caisse* (which will be marked) and directly into Room 20. Walk between Nicolas Boileau's *Dit Despreaux* and Antoine Coysevox's *Jean-Baptiste Colbert* and turn left into the Cour Marly. Head up the stairs and pass between Guillaume Coustou's *Seine et Marne* (on the right) and Corneille Van Cleve's *Loire et Loiret* (on the left). When you get to the top of the stairs, go to the left and you'll find:

• • • • • • • • • • • • • • • •

1. **Einée et Anchise** by Pierre Le Pautre (date unknown). In this compelling piece Einée, the son of Venus, is fleeing the burning city of Troy. He carries his father, who holds the Palladium, the image of Pallas that would become a sacred Roman emblem. The little boy, Ascagne, is turning around, looking for Creuse, Ascagne's mother and Priam's daughter, who has disappeared.

    Head up the short flight of stairs and then upstairs again to the left side. The grouping of statues facing out into the courtyard—Antoine Coysevox's **Flore, Le Berger Fluteur et L'Hamadryade**—is charming. My favorite is the Fluteur, mainly because of the mischievous faun peeking out from behind the flute player. Other works here by Coysevox are the famous:

2A. **Renomée** *(Fame)* and 2B. **Mercure** *(Mercury)* (1699–1702). During his reign, Louis XIV focused on laying out parks and gardens that included monumental sculptures. The park at the Château de Marly was one of his projects, and this sculpture pair was designed to flank the horse pond there. After 1715 and during the Revolution, most of the sculptures decorating France's gardens, ponds, lakes, and waterfalls were moved to different locations. In this museum you can view more than 20 such pieces, as well as locate them on maps of the original Marly Park showing where the sculptures once stood. *Fame* and *Mercury,* astride regal winged horses rearing up above a trophy of arms, are among the most famous of the Marly sculptures. Before the Louvre acquired them, they were moved to the Tuileries Gardens. Replicas now stand where the originals once were (see Walking Tour 7, stop 9).

Turn around and head back to the *Faunes,* passing them (they should be on your right). On your right will be Room 9. As you enter, on your left you'll notice:

3. **La Vierge et l'Enfant** (*The Virgin and Child,* 12th century), a well-preserved wood sculpture. During the Romanesque period, the seated Virgin Mary with Child was a popular subject. Typical of Romanesque sculpture is the simplicity of line coupled with more detailed features, such as the complex drapery folds you see here. Many sculptures of this time were painted with polychrome colors, and some wooden pieces still show traces of the original paint.

Go around to the right into Room 10, at the center of which is the stunning:

4. **Tombeau de Philippe Pot** (ca. 1494). The tomb's monumental size, along with its unusually well preserved painted stone, sets it apart from the other sculptures on this tour. The dead knight's body is laid out in a prone position, feet resting on his trusted dog atop a stone slab carried on the shoulders of eight hooded mourners. The pallbearers' mode of dress obscures their faces and bodily features, making them appear to be Everyman; however, closer inspection of their faces reveals individual identities (each is illuminated by small lights sunk into the floor around the tomb).

The size and style of this tomb are indicative of the grand funeral processions held during the late 15th century. The shields carried by the mourners are a testament to the dead man's nobility. This tomb was commissioned by Philippe, Lord of La Roche-Pot, seneschal to the duke of Burgundy at that time. This sculpture, with its heavy colors and serious tone, is one you'll likely remember long after leaving Paris.

On the right side of the room, beyond the tomb, is the statue of a:

5. **Kneeling monk** (date unknown), dressed in traditional Burgundian robes (attributed to Antoine le Moiturier). This is thought to be a statue of Thomas De Plaine, 1st president of Burgundy's Parliament. The sculpture was commissioned for a Jacobean church in Poligny, De Plaine's birthplace. It's believed the original commission called for two pieces to be made; this is the only one remaining.

Head out of Room 10 into Room 11. Ahead of you will be the bas-relief:

6. *St. Georges combattant le dragon* (*St. George Fighting the Dragon*, 1508–9) by Michel Colombe (ca. 1430–1512). This piece marks the beginning of French Renaissance, which took its lead from the art coming out of 16th-century Italy. Apparently, French knights at war in Italy discovered works such as this one and transported them back to France. Michel Colombe is a French Renaissance master, yet very few of his works survive. He designed the Nantes Cathedral tomb for Anne de Bretagne's parents and is thought to have helped complete François II's tomb. In the piece in front of you, Colombe has depicted St. George (no longer recognized as a saint, by the way) fighting the dragon in order to free the princess.

As you continue around the room, note the terra-cotta bust of:

7. *Louise de Savoie,* mother of François I (artist unknown, early 16th century). This sculpture was found in a niche at the Château de la Péraudière in the Touraine and given to the Louvre in 1949. This sculpture is Italian in feeling (particularly in terms of the figure's size and bulk) and is somewhat unusual for France—although, as stated above, a growing Italian influence was felt in the 16th-century royal court. Louise de Savoie is wearing an interesting piece of headgear, the complexity of which (in terms of the sculpture's execution) testifies to the artist's skill.

Head through Room 12 (a short hallway connecting Rooms 11 and 13) into Room 13. On the right, beyond the doorway, is the:

8. *Retable de la résurrection et des apparitions du Christ* (*The Resurrection and Apparitions of Christ*, mid- to

late 16th century). This retable is particularly ambitious, boasting exacting details and numerous figures all individually rendered, with unique features. Sculpted out of fine limestone, this piece depicts Christ's resurrection and apparitions. At the top is God the Father surrounded by angels. The middle level's central "frame" shows Christ's resurrection. In the middle to the left is His apparition to the Virgin Mary; to the right He appears before Mary Magdalene. On the bottom, from left to right, is Christ's apparition to the three Marys, to St. Peter, to the Apostles, again to the Apostles, and finally to St. Thomas.

To your left, facing the door from Room 11, is:

9. **La Mort St. Innocent** (*The Death of St. Innocent*, early 16th century) from the Cimetière des Innocents in Paris. This work's rather macabre theme began to appear in French sculpture in the early 14th century, coinciding with the onslaught of the Black Death (bubonic plague). This black alabaster statue depicts a partially decomposed skeleton (flesh still hangs from parts of the torso). The effect is undeniably powerful, even though the figure is anatomically incorrect. Its right arm (restored in 1787) is raised and originally brandished a spear. In the left hand is a shield bearing this inscription:

> *Il n'est vivant tant soit plein d'art,*
> *Ne de force, pour résistance,*
> *Que je ne frappe de mon dart,*
> *Pour bailler aux vers leur pitance.*

> (*There's no living creature,*
> *Whatever his intelligence, his strength,*
> *Who can resist the thrust of my spear,*
> *To provide sustenance for worms.)*

Head into Room 14 where, directly in front of you, will be a series of:

10. **Stone bas-reliefs** (1547–49). The master of these strangely delicate pieces was architect/sculptor Jean Goujon (ca. 1510–65), and it was with these works he introduced the new form of bas-relief to the art world. The figures are completely contained within their frames and don't emerge as far from the background surfaces as those in *St. George*

Fighting the Dragon (stop 6). Although Goujon's idea was not to create a sort of "painting" in stone, this form of relief seems to bridge the gap between painting and sculpture.

Taken from Paris's Fontaine des Innocents, these bas-reliefs derive their unique beauty from the way in which the figures have been executed. No strong outlines delineate the body shapes; instead, drapery conveys elegant, even lyrical, forms. Note that Goujon contributed to the rood screen of St-Germain-l'Auxerrois (on which he worked with architect Pierre Lescot—see Walking Tour 1, stop 1, for more on this church). In addition, he collaborated with Lescot on the decoration of the Louvre.

In front of the window to your left is the:

11. **Trois Grâces** (*Three Graces*, 1560–66) by Germain Pilon (1535–90). In 1559 Henri II died from a wound received during a tournament. Shortly thereafter his widow, Catherine de Médicis, commissioned Pilon to do the funerary sculpture for Henri's tomb. Pilon executed one piece (group) for the tomb of Henri's body at the St-Denis church and another for the purpose of carrying the king's heart. The latter is the group shown here. Henri's heart was once encased in the gold casket "balanced" atop the heads of the three figures, or caryatids, known as the Three Graces.

Backtrack past Room 14's doorway to view the terra-cotta sculpture entitled:

12. **La Vierge du douleur** (*The Virgin of Sorrows,* ca. 1585), also created by Pilon for Henri II's funerary chapel at St-Denis. This glass-encased sculpture, personifying despair and solitude, is a model for a marble statue now housed in St-Paul–St-Louis (see Walking Tour 6, stop 9). Today you can still see some of the decorative paint. Originally, the top side of the virgin's cape was painted a rich blue, while the underside was done in a metallic paint. Notice the details on the seated virgin's lovely elongated hands and feet.

Pilon served as court sculptor under the Valois sovereigns and was controller of the mint under Charles IX; during that time he created medals, coins, and medallions that've since been described as the "finest of his time."

Continue around to the left as you face *The Virgin of Sorrows* and go right under the second archway. On your left are several works by Pierre Francqueville (1548–1615), including:

13. **David vainqueur de Goliath** (*David Conquering Goliath*, date unknown) and **Orphée charmant les animaux** (*Orpheus Charming the Animals*, date unknown). Francqueville's work represents the advent of Tuscan mannerism in Henri IV's court. In 1594, after the civil war and Henri III's death, Henri IV came to Paris and made the Palais du Louvre his principal home. He contributed to the palace's growth by augmenting the Grande Galerie, into which he installed a group of artists in 1608. Henri also lived in St-Germain-en-Laye and Fontainebleau, so the style of art that emerged from his court between 1594 and 1620 is known officially as La Seconde Ecole de Fontainebleau.

This period's sculptures reflect a complex composition (while remaining true to form and the realism of the human figure) and can often be characterized by their serpentine forms, implying movement. Henri appointed Francqueville to his court around 1598, after admiring his marble Orpheus surrounded by bronze animals in the center of a Parisian park. Francqueville was later promoted to Premier Sculpteur du Roi and lived at the Louvre, where he was in charge of creating several official court sculptures, including *David Conquering Goliath*.

Although the figure of David is beautiful by itself, the head of Goliath is something to behold. One thing that struck me about this sculpture is that at first glance it's possible to overlook Goliath's massive head. Amazing. Later, Francqueville was asked to collaborate on a statue of Henri IV commissioned by Marie de Médicis; it stands today by the pont Neuf at the tip of the Ile de la Cité (see Walking Tour 1, stop 27).

Straight ahead of you in Room 17 is Pierre Biard's:

14. **La Renomée** (*Winged Fame*, 1597). Biard (1559–1609) created this sculpture for the top of the duc d'Epernon à Cadillac's tiered funerary mausoleum. *Winged Fame* perfectly illustrates the second school of Fontainebleau's theories, which were less concerned with minute details than with the way a figure stands or appears to move. This robust figure's rendering is especially charming.

Balanced on one leg, she once held two trumpets, one of ill repute (held down at her side), the other of good repute, into which she was blowing.

Leave this room and head down the stairs. Exit to your right and go down another flight. Continue through Room 20 (where the tour began), to your left, into the Cour Puget. Directly ahead of you will be:

15. **Milon de Croton** (*Milon of Croton,* 1670–83) by Pierre Puget (1622–94). In 1670 Colbert commissioned this work as well as *Alexander and Diogenes* and *Perseus and Andromeda* (see below) for Versailles. *Milon* differs from other work done at the time since it's much more expressive and passionate. At 17 Puget traveled on foot to Italy, where he was able to work with Pietro du Cortona on the ceilings of the Barberini and Pitti palaces. He also did paintings for some Aix-en-Provence and Toulon churches, but eventually he devoted his attention entirely to sculpture. *Milon of Croton* is one of his best known. Puget captured human suffering in a way that will surely wrench at you. Viewers can't help but empathize with the plight of this man.

Go up the stairs to your left and, on your left, you'll find *Les Quatre Saisons (The Four Seasons)* by Pierre Legros (*Fall* and *Winter* are males, *Spring* and *Summer* are females). Also on this level at the top of the stairs is Puget's *Persée et Andromède (Perseus and Andromeda).* Note the detail in the Medusa's head at the bottom right of the sculpture.

Next, proceed through the courtyard's main level to the staircase on your left. At the top of the stairs, go right around to the opposite side of the courtyard, where you'll find:

16. **Orlando furioso** (1831–67) by Jean-Bernard (known as Jehan) Duseigneur (1808–66). In some ways I find this interpretation of the legend of Roland, a popular medieval French hero, even more moving than *Milon of Croton* (above). Roland was in command of Charlemagne's rear guard, which was under attack, when the situation turned desperate. However, Roland was too proud to blow his horn for help. Upon finally realizing he was outnumbered, he blew the horn—though in vain, for all were killed. This sculpture is a romantic manifesto: Instead of depicting events as they're believed to have occurred, it shows the symbolic

struggle of the man whose pride prevented him from saving his troops.

Backtrack to the entrance of Room 21 (you'll go up a short flight of stairs into this room). Go left though Room 21 into Room 22. Keep going into Room 23—note on the left between Rooms 22 and 23 the glass case with small Falconet and Lorrain sculptures. Proceed into Room 24, where you'll find an unusual, moving sculpture by Jean-Baptiste Pigalle (1714–85):

17. **Voltaire nu** (*Voltaire Nude,* 1776). This is, without question, one of my favorites in the Louvre. Its subject is impressive: Voltaire, the great philosopher, sits covered by only a small piece of drapery. He's depicted exactly as he appeared to the artist, with no pretenses. Pigalle has not wasted his opportunity to sculpt Voltaire by idealizing his physicality. The contrast between the old man's skeletal figure and his almost angelic face has an even greater impact than it would have had Pigalle beautified the body of the otherwise imposing philosopher. The result is truly mesmerizing.

Continue into Room 25, filled with small white marble sculptures that were admission pieces to the Académie Française. To your right in the glass case is:

18. **Mercure rattachant ses talonnières** (*Mercury Attaching His Wings,* 1744) also by Pigalle. He was fortunate to have learned the basic elements of his craft from Robert Le Lorrain (his neighbor at the time). In 1735 he traveled to Italy, where he had the opportunity to work at the French Academy in Rome. Six years later he returned to Paris and was accepted to the Royal Academy based on his presentation of a terra-cotta sculpture of Mercury attaching his wings. In 1744, for his reception to the group, he crafted the sculpture you see here. Under Louis XV, Pigalle became the country's most significant sculptor. This piece illustrates his understanding of the subtleties of physical movement. He later executed the same sculpture in monumental form—in 1748 a huge *Mercury* and a statue of Venus were sent to Frédéric II of Prussia, as a diplomatic gift. At that time, they stood in the gardens at Potsdam; today, they're housed in Berlin's Bode Museum.

Continue into the second part of Room 25. In the center of the room is the:

19. **Gladiateur mourant** (*Dying Gladiator,* 1779) by Pierre Julien (1731–1804). Neoclassical in feeling, this piece is extremely well executed. The heroic gladiator represented is dying silently, with strength and pride. The composition of the sculpture is perfectly balanced.

    You might want to look at some of the other works in this room, but note that alarms are easily triggered here.

    As you enter Room 26, note on your right the bronze statue entitled:

20. **Diane chasseresse** (*Diana the Huntress,* 1790) by Jean-Antoine Houdon (1741–1828). Known as a Neoclassicist, Houdon studied with Michelangelo, Lemoyne, and Pigalle and at age 20 took the Prix de Rome. Believe it or not, this sculpture, reminiscent of the mannerist tradition (remember Biard's *Winged Fame,* see stop 14), drew public criticism for its shocking "detailed nakedness." This wasn't the first sculpture of Diana executed by Houdon; he began working with this subject in 1774. He was later commissioned to execute the statue in marble by Baron Grimm, duke of Saxe-Goethe (who somehow had acquired a plaster model of the Diana). The marble statue was completed in 1780 and paid for two years later. Unfortunately, the sculpture would've been damaged had it been transported over land, so Grimm resold it to Catherine II, empress of Russia. Before the statue was shipped to Russia, Houdon cast it in bronze. That statue was purchased by a wealthy merchant. A second cast, the one you see here, was poured in 1790 and remained in the possession of Houdon until his death; his heirs sold it to the museum in 1829. The marble statue was placed in Tsarskoye Selo in 1786.

    Continue into Room 27, where you'll find:

21. **Psyché abandonée** (*Psyche Abandoned,* 1790) by Augustin Pajou (1730–1809). Student of Jean-Baptiste Lemoyne at the Academie-Royale, Pajou was a sculptor of all disciplines, dabbling in everything from portraiture to architectural decoration to monumental sculpture. In 1749, he won first prize in sculpture from the Academie. At the

Salon of 1759, Pajou gained Diderot's respect with a bust of Lemoyne that Diderot declared was the best bust ever executed of him. Three years later, Pajou became a professor at the Academie, then acquired a studio in the Louvre. In 1777 he became the custodian of the Louvre's royal sculptures. *Psyche Abandoned* was shown in plaster at the Salon of 1785, and (like *Diana the Huntress,* see stop 20) its explicit nudity created a scandal. The marble piece here was exhibited at the Salon of 1791.

When you enter Room 28, take note of:

22. **Houdon's portraits,** the sculptures in the case on the right. Here you'll find some portraits of Houdon's wife and two children, as well as a lovely 1777 bust of Louise Brogniart (âgée de cinq ans) (5 years old). Houdon became known for his portraiture and frequently received commissions from the United States. He made busts of various Frenchmen and Americans, including Washington, Jefferson, Franklin, Diderot, Rousseau, Lafayette, Buffon, Mirabeau, and John Paul Jones. To do studies for his portrait of Washington in 1785, Houdon came to America and stayed at Mount Vernon.

From Room 28, continue on through to Room 33, where you'll see:

23. *Jeune pêcheur napolitain jouant avec une tortue* (*Young Neopolitan Fisher Playing with a Tortoise,* 1831–33) by François Rude (1784–1855). A native of Dijon, Rude was a Bonapartist who left Paris after Napoléon's Waterloo defeat and spent 12 years in Brussels. His best-known work is the Arc de Triomphe's enormous *La Marseillaise* relief.

In the marvelous piece before you, Rude threw off the restraints of classicism and allowed himself to express a sort of naturalness. The boy's face, flashing a toothy grin, expresses pure joy at his play, and his posture implies movement. You almost feel like an intruder in his private game. Rude made an original study of this boy while visiting Italy in 1829. Two years later he did the piece in plaster, and in 1833 he executed it in marble.

Beyond the young fisher, to the right of the door opening onto the courtyard, is Pierre-Jean David d'Angers's:

24. **L'Enfant à la grappe** (*Child with a Bunch of Grapes*, 1837–1845). David d'Angers (1788–1856) is most famous for his portraiture, and this sculpture is a departure for him, coming directly from his own life experience. He had a son who stood eating grapes very much like this child; however, in reality, David d'Angers's son just missed being bitten by a viper. The incident had such an impact on the artist that he attempted to capture it in his work.

The first piece he did included the viper, though this one does not. The sculpture still manages to evoke the intended response—this beautiful little boy with his protruding belly and strong stubby legs reaches up on tiptoe to taste the sweet round grapes, and his innocence is striking. There's no need for the viper; David d'Angers achieves the result without being obvious. This is indeed a brilliant work.

Continue back out into the courtyard. The final three works on this part of the tour are in the Denon Wing, where the Italian sculptures are currently housed. To get to that wing, go downstairs into the lower courtyard. Pass through Room 20 again, backtracking to the museum's central pyramid. Look for the entrance marked DENON.

☕ **Take a Break** Although Part I is nearly over, you might want to stop for lunch or a snack under the pyramid before seeing the last three sculptures. If you plan to take both parts of the tour in one day, I suggest you finish Part I and then break for lunch. There are several restaurants as well as a self-serve cafeteria here from which to choose.

Go through the Denon entrance, past the *caisse* and the ticket takers. You've already had your ticket torn, so all you have to do here is show them that it's been torn and you'll be allowed to continue. Ascend the stairs on your right into Room 1a, the beginning of the Italian sculpture galleries. Immediately on your right will be:

25. **La Decente de Croix** (*Descent from the Cross*, Umbria or Latium, mid-13th century). Not only is this an emotional piece but also it's a fine example of Romanesque art moving toward a more naturalistic form (compare it with *The Virgin and Child* you saw at stop 3). The unknown

sculptor used the same Romanesque technique when depicting the clothing, while the figures exhibit more natural poses.

Continue through this room, take the stairs on your left, and enter the room housing Michelangelo's famous:

26. **Esclaves** (*Slaves,* 1513–15), the backs of which will be to you. Michelangelo (Michelangelo di Lodovico Buonarroti Simoni, 1475–1564)—Italian painter/sculptor/poet/architect—was born in Caprese, Tuscany, and showed artistic promise as a boy. Drawing quickly became his favorite pastime, so his father hired Ghirlandaio as the boy's teacher. Unfortunately, their working relationship was unproductive for the young genius, who moved on to be taught by Bertoldo di Giovanni, sculptor to the Médicis. Michelangelo even lived with the Médicis for two years. Though schooled in painting and drawing, he was primarily self-taught in the medium of sculpture. He first conceived of these sculptures as part of a monument for Julius II he was commissioned to sculpt. The original plans called for about 80 monumental pieces for the 36-foot by 34.5-foot by 23-foot tomb. However, the design was far too complicated and expensive. The final product was much smaller, with only one Michelangelo sculpture. *Slaves* was later given to Roberto Strozzi, who gave it to the king of France. It was never completed.

At the opposite side of the room, just before exiting, you'll find:

27. **L'Amour et Psyché** (*Eros and Psyche,* 1793) by Centonio Canova (1757–1822). This piece is impossible to ignore. Depicting Eros reviving Psyche from eternal sleep, this is one of the most magnificently executed sculptures on the tour. Canova's mastery of marble is obvious—Eros's wings are so finely crafted they're nearly transparent. In addition, the composition (with the bodies forming a pyramidal shape) is unusual.

You've now reached the end of Part I. If you don't wish to continue with Part II, exit through the doorway ahead. Go down the stairs and follow the signs back to the pyramid.

PART II: PAINTINGS

Start: Second floor in the Sully Wing.
Finish: First floor in the Denon Wing.
Time: Two to four hours.
Best Time: In the morning on Monday and Wednesday through Friday, just after the museum opens, or in the evening on Wednesday, when the museum closes at 10pm.
Worst Time: Tuesday, when the museum's closed, or weekends, when it's too crowded.

In Part II of the Louvre tour you'll explore the museum's painting galleries, including the famous Grande Galerie. Along the way will be French, Italian, Spanish, Dutch, and German works, representing such artists as Dürer, Fragonard, La Tour, Watteau, Ingres, Rubens, Rembrandt, Delacroix, Goya, El Greco, and Leonardo. In addition, you'll see the *Winged Victory of Samothrace,* the Apollo Gallery (which includes the Crown Jewels), and the *Venus de Milo.* Like Part I, I've designed Part II so it flows logically through the museum and takes you to the most famous pieces as well as some lesser-known ones, giving you a fairly comprehensive overview of European art from the 14th to the 19th century.

• • • • • • • • • • • • • • • •

Enter the Richelieu Wing and take the escalator up to the second floor. Head into the Sully Wing through the entrance leading into the French painting galleries. As you enter you'll see:

1. ***Jean II le Bon*** (*John II the Good,* ca. 1350). This piece is interesting since it's the first known individual profile portrait in all of Europe as well as one of the oldest works of the Academie Française. Jean II was the second king of the house of Valois, and it's thought the portrait was done before he became king, as he's shown without his crown. The inscription "*Jehan, roy de France*" (Jehan, king of France) was most likely added later.

Pass through Room 2 into Room 3. From here, go around to the right side (into French Painting). Ahead of you will be:

2. **La Pièta de Villeneuve-les-Avignon** (ca. 1455). The origins of this work were largely unknown until 1834, when writer Prosper Mérimée (also an inspector of historic monuments) found it in the Villeneuve-les-Avignon parish church. About 70 years later it was shown during a French Primitive Exhibition, then about a year later was offered to the Louvre. It took another 55 years and art historian Charles Sterling to determine that the man behind the work was Enguerrand Quarton, the most famous member of the 15th-century school of Provence.

Walk through Rooms 5, 6, 7, 8, 9, and 10. From Room 10, go left through the door marked Peintures Françaises (on the other side of the glass doors it's marked École du Nord). After entering the Ecole du Nord area, turn right into Room 8. On the left you'll find a well-known:

3. **Self-portrait of Albrecht Dürer** (1493). Dürer (1471–1528), painter/engraver/theoretician, was the most influential artist of the German school. Born in Nuremburg to a goldsmith, he worked as an apprentice in his father's workshop before deciding to work with painter Michael Wolgemut. He then journeyed throughout Europe, eventually returning to Nuremburg, where he settled permanently. Dürer went on to become the first German painter to gain notoriety outside the country. His sense of proportion was wonderful, his interest in art theory intense. Later in his career he became more concerned with the function of light and dark tones (chiaroscuro) in painting.

During his life he painted self-portraits and this one, the only Dürer known to exist in France, is his earliest painting. He's believed to have been 22 when he did this painting, and there are several theories about the nature of the portrait. Some say the thistle he's holding refers to Christ's crown of thorns, while others think the portrait was painted as a display of fidelity to his fiancée, Agnes Frey, who later became his wife.

On the wall to your right are three paintings. The one on the far right is Lucas Cranach the Elder's:

4. **Vénus debout dans un paysage** (*Venus Standing in a Landscape*, 1529). One of three German master painters of his time (the others were Dürer, above, and Holbein, below), Lucas Cranach (1472–1553) was the offical painter to the prince electors of Saxony. He was also a friend of Martin Luther, whose teachings are reflected in Cranach's paintings and engravings. Cranach took particular pleasure in painting mythological figures with a fanciful, almost mischievous twist. This painting is no exception: Venus stands nude in a landscape wearing only a wide-brimmed hat and a necklace. If you look closely you'll see the well-executed transparent veil she holds before her. Cranach never failed to include in his paintings his trademark symbol—a winged serpent holding a ring in its mouth. It's carefully concealed here.

Behind you, to the far left (as you face the exit), is Hans Holbein the Younger's:

5. **Portrait de Nicholas Kratzer** (1528). A German portraitist and religious painter, Holbein (1497–1543) was influenced by his artist father, Hans Holbein the Elder. Holbein was a friend of Erasmus (see the box on Erasmus in Walking Tour 5, Part I), of whom he did many portraits. He even illustrated one of Erasmus's works, *The Praise of Folly*. In 1519 he moved to Basel, where he did decorative work at the Town Hall. From 1526 to 1528 Holbein lived in England, where he did portraits of Sir Thomas More and Henry Guildford and his wife. He returned to Basel from 1528 to 1532 and resumed his work on the Town Hall. Finally settling in England, he was appointed court painter to Henry VIII. Holbein died of the plague in London at age 46.

Nicolas Kratzer, a compatriot who settled in England, was Henri VIII's astronomer, and he's shown here making astronomical instruments. In one hand he holds a compass, in the other the beginnings of a solar disk. We know without a doubt the identity of the sitter because his name appears on the piece of paper on the desk in front of him.

Go back through the glass doors and return to the French Paintings area (you'll finish the Ecole du Nord later in the tour), continuing to the left. Pass through Rooms 11 through 27 (when I wrote this tour Rooms 13 through 27 held a temporary exhibition) into Room 28, where directly ahead you'll find Georges de La Tour's:

6. **St. Joseph Charpentier** (*Christ with St. Joseph in the Carpenter's Shop,* ca. 1640). La Tour (1593–1652), painter to Louis XIII in 1639, is known for night scenes such as this. The scene depicts St. Joseph teaching the carpenter's trade to a young Christ.

Also in this room, to the left of the door as you entered, is one of La Tour's *Madeleines*. Currently there are four known versions of this work; however, the number of extant copies (by other artists) has led art historians to believe there are others still undiscovered. The subject matter here is not unusual, for it was frequently painted during the 17th century (especially by Caravaggiesque painters). But only Georges de La Tour could have painted her contemplative face illuminated by only the light of a candle. Note the skull, a 17th-century symbol of a person's inevitable destiny.

Continue around the room to Le Nain's:

7. **Famille de paysans dans un interieur** (*Peasant Family,* date unknown). There were three Le Nain brothers: Antoine (ca. 1588–1648), Louis (ca. 1593–1648), and Mathieu (1607–77). All were painters (considered today among the greatest French painters), worked in the same studio, and signed their paintings simply "Le Nain." They're also thought to have collaborated, making it difficult today to determine who's responsible for certain pieces. However, it's generally acknowledged that Antoine specialized in miniature family scenes; Mathieu in portraits of military men; and Louis in peasant portraits. The arist of this work is thought to be either Antoine or Louis. Most paintings of the time were allegorical, so the realistic use of peasant families was unusual. Originally from Laon, the Le Nains moved to Paris and became three of the founding members of the Royal Academy of Painting and Sculpture.

Continue through Room 31 into Room 32, where you'll notice two Le Brun paintings:

8A. **Entrée d'Alexandre en Babylone** (*Alexander's Entrance into Babylon,* 1661–65) and 8B. **La Bataille d'Arbelles**

(*The Battle of Arbela,* 1669). Painter/architect Charles Le Brun (1619–90) studied in Rome with Nicolas Poussin (whose works weren't on display when I wrote this tour) and worked with architect Louis Le Vau. In 1662 he became painter to the king and exerted control over the artistic development of France for more than 20 years. Le Brun, as Principal Director of the Arts, was responsible for the design of royal furnishings and the supervision of a large group of painters, sculptors, engravers, and decorators. He was also responsible for decorating the Galerie des Glâces (Hall of Mirrors) at Versailles.

Alexander's Entrance into Babylon was the first of four large canvases Le Brun painted between 1661 and 1673. Alexander the Great entered Babylon in 351 B.C. Here he's shown riding in a carriage pulled by an elephant. Just beyond Alexander is *The Battle of Arbela.*

Go through Room 33 and turn right into Room 36. At the center of the room are:

9. **Pierrot, dit autrefois Gilles** (*Pierrot, also known as Gilles,* ca. 1718–19) and, to the left, **Pèlerinage à l'île de Cythère** (*Pilgrimage to Cythera,* 1717), both by Jean-Antoine Watteau. The first was likely painted as a sign for the actor Bellini, who made a name for himself in the role of Pierrot, a popular character from the commedia dell'arte. Pierrot was a buffoon, a sort of clown, who dressed in loose white clothing. Here, the figure stands out so well from the background that you hardly notice the other figures in the lower third of the canvas.

Pilgrimage to Cythera exemplifies the *fête galante* style (a term coined by the Ecole Français to describe the genre of Watteau's work) with warm pastel tones and an airy, sensuous feeling. The figures here are represented in party dress, coming to Cythera seeking love. Watteau's works had a great influence on 18th-century garden and fashion design.

To Pierrot's right is an interesting study of hands by Nicolas de Largillierre. At the time it was usual for painters to paint various types of hands in different poses and use them in their more important works. You'll see several others like this in the next few rooms.

Move on to Room 38. On the left side of the room is:

10. **La Raie** (*The Skate,* before 1728) by Jean-Baptiste-Siméon Chardin (1699–1779). Known for his still lifes, Chardin was recognized as a great painter early in his career, even though he specialized in a genre of painting that was at the time not as respected as portraits or landscapes. On the day of his admission to the Academie Française (for which he submitted this piece), Chardin was made an associate *and* a member. As you can see here, Chardin had a particular genius for showing texture. The abstract nature of his paintings later influenced the modern schools.

In Room 39 is a wall of Chardin still lifes. From here, walk through Room 43 into Rooms 46 and 47 into Room 48; on the far right, the second painting is:

11. **Les Baigneuses** (*The Bathers,* date unknown) by Jean-Honoré Fragonard (1732–1806), who studied with Chardin and was also the recipient of the Prix de Rome. Fragonard enjoyed painting female nudes. Setting Fragonard apart from his rococo contemporaries are his feathery brushstrokes, which give the draperies on the bodies a light, delicate look and add a "sketchlike" quality to the painting. The arrangement of the bodies adds an ethereal motion to the painting.

Walk through Room 49, down the stairs, and through Rooms 50, 51, 52, and 53. Heading into Room 54, notice on the right the incredibly beautiful ***Portrait d'une Negresse*** *(Portrait of a Negress)* by Marie-Guillemine Benoist, who was a student of Jacques-Louis David.

Head out of this room and continue through to Room 60, where you'll find several works by Jean-Auguste-Dominique Ingres (1780–1867). First, in the center to the right, is:

12. **Le Bain turc** (*The Turkish Bath,* 1862). Ingres, son of a sculptor, won the Prix de Rome in 1801. Unfortunately, the French government was too poor to bestow the award, and he had to wait until 1806 to receive his honors. He lived in Paris until 1834, when he relocated to Rome and was made director of the Academie de France à Rome. Amazingly, Ingres was 82 when he completed this painting (five years prior to his death). He began studies of female bathers in 1807, and this is the final work in that series. Setting Ingres apart from all other painters is the quality

of color he uses in his nudes. The women's flesh is pale, almost to the point of translucence, with very little peach and pink toning. His nudes can be easily identified by this quality alone. If you look closely, you can tell that Ingres used the same model over and over. After his death the Ingres Museum was opened in Montauban, the place of his birth.

To the left of *Le Bain ture* is another Ingres painting, one of exceptional beauty and unusual charm:

13. **Angelique** (date unknown). Many people don't like this work because of the model's obvious neck deformity; however, I feel Ingres has transformed this otherwise freakish subject into a woman of great stature and beauty. The coloring of the nude flesh is similar to that in the previous painting.

Leave Room 60 and pass through Room 61 to Room 62, where you'll find some works by Delacroix. The most famous of his paintings are exhibited elsewhere in the museum; you'll see one of them later on this tour.

Continue into Room 63. To the left of the door heading into Room 64 is Théodore Chassériau's:

14. **La Toilette d'Esther** (*Esther at Her Toilette*, 1841). Son of a French father and Créole mother, Chassériau (1819–56) was born in Haiti. He left the island in 1821, and by age eight was showing remarkable talent as an artist. At 11 he was interviewed by Ingres, who was sufficiently impressed to admit the young boy to his studio. Ingres said of Chassériau, *"Ce petit-là sera le Napoléon de la peinture"* (This little one here will be the Napoléon of painting). Chassériau's first works were portraits of the family members showing great psychological insight. At the Salon of 1839, Chassériau's work was well received. In 1840 he left for Italy to attend the Academie de France à Rome.

Esther at Her Toilette was exhibited at the Salon of 1841. The influence of Ingres is clear; however, Chassériau combines what he learned from the master with Delacroix's color technique and his own passion for the exotic. What you see here is the young artist's rapidly developing personal style. In 1844 Louis-Philippe commissioned Chassériau to decorate the Cour des Comptes at the Palais d'Orsay, and he worked on it for four years. Unfortunately, much of it was destroyed by an 1871 fire. What survived is now housed at the Louvre, along with 77 paintings, 2,200 drawings, and 37 sketchbooks donated by Chassériau's heirs. It's truly a pity that Chassériau died at age 37.

Follow along through Room 64 into Room 65. Directly ahead of you is:

15. **L'Eglise de Marissel, près de Beauvais** (*Marissel Church near Beauvais,* 1866) by Jean-Baptiste-Camille Corot (1796–1875). Corot often visited a friend in the Beauvais countryside, and the Marissel Church (which stands today) became a favorite of his. For nine mornings he sat in front of this church working on this painting, which was exhibited in the Salon of 1867 and later bought by a tailor for 4,000 francs. Corot had an unusual talent for painting landscapes and was particularly skilled at the use of perspective. Note the reflection in the foreground pond.

Born in Paris, this landscape painter was one of the most influential of the 19th century. Until 1822 he worked in textile shops, then began to study painting with two classical landscape artists, Michallon and Bertin. Corot's works are known today for their simplicity of form and clarity of light.

☕ **Take a Break**   Follow the signs to this wing's exit, which will bring you back to the central pyramid. Here you might want to grab a bite to eat. There are several restaurants as well as a self-serve cafeteria from which to choose.

Now return to the Richelieu Wing and take the escalator back up to the second floor. Go into the Richelieu side of the escalators (the opposite side from which you began the tour). After you enter this wing, turn right into Room 18, where, on the entrance wall to your left, will be:

16. **L'Apothéose d'Henri IV et la proclamation de la régence de Marie de Médicis** (*The Apotheosis of Henri IV and the Proclamation of the Regency of Marie de Médicis,* date unknown) by Peter Paul Rubens (1577–1640). The foremost 17th-century Flemish painter, Rubens was born in Siegen, Westphalia, where his family was in exile because of his father's Calvanist beliefs. After his father's 1587 death,

his family moved back to Antwerp, where Rubens attended Jesuit school and became a linguist. Around 1591 he became interested in painting and subsequently apprenticed himself to several minor artists. Soon he made an eight-year trip to Italy (during which he was sent on a mission to Spain); while there he painted for the duke of Mantua. Five years following his return to Antwerp he was acknowledged as his country's greatest painter and overwhelmed with commissions, many of which were monumental in scale.

As a result, Rubens set up a workshop with scores of apprentices and associates. From 1622 to 1625 he received several French court commissions, including a series for Marie de Médicis' Luxembourg Palace that would document her life as wife of Henri IV and mother of Louis XIII. What you see here is one of those paintings. Rubens's assistants are thought to have done most of the work on the paintings churned out by his studio—Rubens added only the final touches. After his wife died in 1626, Rubens entered the diplomatic service and was eventually knighted for his peacekeeping work. He died of gout at age 63. More than 2,000 paintings are thought to have come from Rubens's studio.

Go through Room 18 into Room 17, then turn left out of Room 17. Proceed down and then up the stairs into Room 20 and continue straight ahead through Room 21 and into Room 24. Directly ahead of you is:

17. ***Charles Ier, roi d'Angleterre à la chasse*** (*Charles I, King of England, at the Hunt,* ca. 1635) by Anthony Van Dyck (1599–1641). Charles I was king of England between 1600 and 1649, and of all the portraits done of him, this is considered the most successful. The king's elegant clothing, the sheltering branches, and the servants waiting nearby in the background speak to his nobility. Like Rubens, Van Dyck spent much of his life working in Antwerp. These men collaborated for a few years, and in 1620 James I called Van Dyck to England to do his portrait. On returning home, he found he'd become nearly as popular as Rubens. In 1632 Charles I invited him back to England, where he was made court painter. It was at this time Van Dyck also received a deluge of commissions and was forced to utilize

assistants as Rubens had. However, Van Dyck still did most of the work.

Continue through Room 26 into Room 28. Directly before you, on the left side of the wall, is Frans Hals's:

18. **La Bohémienne** (*The Gypsy Girl,* ca. 1628–30). A Dutch painter of portraits and genre scenes, Hals (1580–1666) was born in Antwerp and spent most of his life in Haarlem, where he studied with Karel Van Mander. His early work focused primarily on military portraits. This painting of a jovial "gypsy girl" is typical of his later work. Hals used a variety of brushstrokes to illustrate texture—note that the face and breast are smooth, whereas the strokes on the clothing are much more animated. In addition, the unusual two-toned background implies movement. Hals spent most of his life impoverished; in fact, in 1652 his possessions were seized in order to pay his debts. Four years before his death the town of Haarlem graciously granted him a pension, and he was able to live the rest of his life in relative security.

Turn left and walk through Room 30 to Room 31. On your left is Rembrandt's:

19. **Bethsabée au bain** (*Bathsheba in the Bath,* 1654). The greatest master of the Dutch school, Rembrandt Harmensz van Rijn (1606–69) was a miller's son. He attended university for one year before leaving in 1621 to study painting. In 1624 he worked with Pieter Lastman in Amsterdam, returned home, then a year later went back to Amsterdam to develop his own style. Some of his favorite early subjects were portraits of the old and the poor. He also began a series of self-portraits that would eventually number close to 100 and today are an excellent documentary of his physical changes as well as the development of his artistic technique. In Amsterdam Rembrandt achieved high social status, due in part to his marriage to Saskia van Ulyenburgh, a burgomaster's daughter. In his time of wealth he became an avid collector of art and costumes, using the artworks to learn technique and the costumes to dress his sitters. He had a large number of students at this time as well.

His purchase of a large house in 1639 caused financial troubles, and in 1642, after the birth of his son, Titus, Saskia died. Rembrandt's interest then turned to landscapes, and he began painting for his own pleasure rather than for sale. This, coupled with his insatiable collecting, led to further financial straits, forcing his son and his mistress, Hendrickje Stoffels, to form a business partnership to shield him from debt collectors. During the last 20 years of his life his work was no longer considered fashionable; yet it is during this time he created some of his masterpieces, among them the one in front of you.

In the story of Bathsheba, King David cast an illicit glance at her while she was at her bath, then claimed her as his servant. This subject has been painted innumerable times, with most actually showing the king stealing a look at the bathing beauty. Rembrandt has taken a different approach: He doesn't show the king at all; instead, we see only a slightly crumpled "letter of request" in Bathsheba's hand. It's thought that Hendrickje Stoffels was Rembrandt's model for this painting. Hendrickje died in 1663; Titus died five years later. Rembrandt lived only one year longer than his son and was survived by his daughter (with Stoffels), Cornelia.

You should take a quick look around this room because it contains several of Rembrandt's famous self-portraits.

From here, continue through Rooms 32, 33, 34, 35, 36, and 37 to Room 38, where to the left of the exit will be:

20. **La Dentellière** (*The Lacemaker,* date unknown) by Jan Vermeer (1632–75). If you're not looking for this one you might walk right by it. The first time I saw it, I was shocked at how small it is—as if to emphasize the tediousness of the lacemaker's task. In fact, everything about this painting seems to emphasize the work at hand. The neutral background focuses our gaze on the lacemaker, who, as it turns out, is slightly out of focus. The focus is on the woman's hands and work, giving the painting a photographic quality. Vermeer, it seems, was a man well ahead of his time— though often confused with his contemporaries and relatively unknown during his life. Art historians are able to attribute only 35 paintings to this superb Dutch colorist. This is unusual enough without considering the fact that Vermeer had 11 children to feed. He couldn't possibly have supported them all on his painting alone.

By now you'll have made a large circle back to the escalators. Go down to the first floor and head into the entrance marked 1ER ÉTAGE. Just pass through the rooms here until reaching the Denon Wing. You'll know you're there when you begin to see a crowd of people walking to the right down a long hallway. Follow the crowd to the right and you'll find yourself in the:

21. **Galerie d'Apollon** (Apollo Gallery). This part of the building was destroyed in a 1661 fire and then rebuilt by architect Louis Le Vau. Louis XIV then asked Charles Le Brun to oversee its decoration. It was named the Apollo Gallery in honor of Louis XIV, the Sun King, whose collection of semiprecious stones is now displayed here. Other treasures in this gallery (at the far end of the room) are the 140.64-carat Regent diamond and the Crown Jewels. You can also view a Delacroix panel entitled *Apollo Vanquishing the Serpent Python.*

     As you come out of the Galerie d'Apollon (the way you entered), turn left and head down the stairs to reach the spectacular:

22. **Victoire de Samothrace** (*Winged Victory of Samothrace,* ca. 190 B.C.). I must admit I have a particular affection for this piece: After my first visit to the Louvre (when I was 12), the only thing I clearly remembered from the museum was the *Winged Victory,* which stood majestically in the same place it does today. A tour of the Louvre simply wouldn't be complete without a stop here. The *Winged Victory* is one of few sculptures of Greek antiquity whose origins are known. It was found with a group of fragments on a terrace overlooking the Cabires sanctuary on the island of Samothrace, in the northeast Aegean.

     The unknown artist obviously possessed an extraordinary knowledge of anatomy and was exceptionally skilled. The execution of the drapery on this piece is amazing. It's difficult to believe the marble-and-limestone statue dates from 190 B.C. The fact that she's missing her arms, feet, and head doesn't seem to detract from her appeal in any way. Note that the right wing is a plaster reconstruction. In 1950 her right hand was discovered—it's in the glass case on the other side of the landing at the Denon Wing's entrance.

     Continue past the *Winged Victory's* hand into the Denon Wing's paintings gallery. Pass through Rooms 1 and 2.

Enter Room 3 and go around the corner to the right, past a short partition. On your right you'll see:

23. **La Vierge, l'Enfant Jesus et Sainte Anne** (*The Virgin and Child with St. Anne,* ca. 1510) by Leonardo di ser Piero da Vinci (Leonardo da Vinci). More than a painter, Leonardo was a sculptor, an architect, a musician, an engineer, and a scientist. Born in Tuscany, this true Renaissance genius was the illegitimate son of a notary and a peasant girl. Like many of the other artists on this tour, Leonardo showed an early talent for drawing. In 1466 he moved to Florence and entered Verrocchio's studio, where he had the good fortune to meet Ghirlandaio, Botticelli, and Lorenzo di Credi. Beginning around 1482 he worked for Ludovico Sforza's Milan court for 16 years. It was there he wrote the better part of his famous notebooks.

    Around 1508 he developed a greater interest in science and by 1510 was studying anatomy. One of his paintings of that time is *The Virgin and Child with St. Anne.* Leonardo wrestled with this subject for some time before producing the painting you see here. Many sketches and cartoons that predate the finished work have been found—in fact, this painting, done on a wood panel, was never finished. If you look closely you can still see the underdrawing. Leonardo had this piece with him until he died.

    On the wall to the left of the entrance to the next room is:

24. **Vénus, Satyre et Cupidon** (*Venus, Satyr, and Cupid,* ca. 1525). Antonio Allegri (ca. 1494–1534), known as Correggio for his birthplace, was trained in basic artistic techniques by his uncle, Lorenzo Allegri. His work, in which he often used foreshortening, was strongly influenced by Leonardo. Correggio painted the ceilings of several churches in Parma. A characteristic feature of his work is a genius for chiaroscuro.

    Head into Room 5, the beginning of the museum's famous Grande Galerie. There probably will be a crowd not far down on your right, gathered in front of the:

25. **Portrait de Monna Lisa dite La Jaconde** (*Mona Lisa, called La Gioconda,* 1503–6), the world's most famous painting. Mona Lisa was the wife of a Florentine merchant. The

painting is a prime example of Leonardo's *sfumato* technique, "misty, subtle transitions in tone," used to blend the edges of the figure into the background so the face stands out from the rest of the painting. The sadness that seems to overwhelm the enigmatic smile on Mona Lisa's face is quite real—her son died just before Leonardo began her portrait.

A bit farther down the gallery, on the left, is Fra Angelico's:

26. ***Couronnement de la Vierge*** (*Coronation of the Virgin*, before 1435). Painted for the Dominican Convent of Fiesole, this predella documents Christ's entombment and six episodes from the life of St. Domenic, who founded the order to which Fra Angelico took his vows in 1425. In 1436 the Dominicans moved to St. Mark's convent in Florence, where Fra Angelico supervised the decoration. He painted religious subjects only and is known for using pure color. Note his excellent sense of perspective (most notably at the top of the panel).

Turn right and enter Room 6. On the right side of the room you'll find Titian's:

27. ***La mise au tombeau*** (*The Entombment*, ca. 1525), painted for the Gonzaga family at Mantira. Titian (Tiziano Vecellio, 1488/9–1576) was a Renaissance artist, born in Pieve de Cadore. He studied with Gentile and Giovanni Bellini and worked on many frescoes. After the Bellinis died, he became known as Venice's finest painter and received countless commissions and honors. In 1545 he traveled to Rome and stayed at the Vatican, where he began a portrait of Pope Paul III. Following 1552, he remained in Venice until his death. Titian's work is characterized by intense emotional expression.

Head back into the Grande Galerie, which is now Room 7. Turn right. Continue through Room 12 and turn right into Room 13, where you'll see Eugène Delacroix's:

28. ***La Liberté guidant le peuple, 28 juillet 1830*** (*Liberty Leading the People, July 28, 1830*). Though Delacroix (1798–1863) wasn't a participant in the events of July 1830 (three days known as Les Trois Glorieuses), he wanted to celebrate the day French citizens rose up in an attempt to restore the Republic (the events marked the end

of Charles X's autocracy and the start of Louis-Philippe's parliamentary monarchy). Carrying the tricolor, Liberty is shown leading the people to victory. This powerful work received mixed reviews at the Salon of 1837—conservatives hated it, but Louis-Philippe purchased it. The painting was later hidden for fear it would incite the people to riot. (See Walking Tour 10, stop 25, for more about Delacroix.)

Leave Room 13, walk through Room 16, and head right toward Room 21. Before you enter that room, examine the Goyas on the left. Then go through Room 21 to Room 20, into Room 19, and finally into Room 18. Here you'll find El Greco's:

29. **_Le Christ en croix adoré par deux donateurs_** (*Christ on the Cross Adored by Donors,* ca. 1585–90). Domenicos Theotocopoulos (known as El Greco, 1541–1614) was born in Candia, on Crete; he lived a great deal of his life in Spain and is known to have studied under Titian and painted in Rome. This dark, brooding painting shows many of El Greco's trademarks—elongated, sculptural, twisted bodies; flamelike lines; extreme highlights; and vivid color offset by a variety of grays. While alive, El Greco was unknown, and only in this century has he gained global recognition and appreciation.

As the climax of this tour, follow the signs from here to see the:

30. **_Venus de Milo_** (ca. 100 B.C.), accidentally discovered in 1820 on the Greek island of Melos. France's ambassador to Constantinople, the marquis de Rivière, later acquired it and then gave it to Louis XVIII, who gave it to the Louvre in 1821. The statue, which was made in two separate sections (the joint is visible), has been named the *Venus de Milo* in spite of the fact that no one really knows whom the woman is meant to represent.

From here, follow the signs back to the pyramid.

ESSENTIALS & RECOMMENDED READING

Paris may be one of Europe's largest cities, but you'll find it's a surprisingly easy metropolis to navigate. The following is an overview of the practical information you'll need to make your visit a hassle-free success. For fuller coverage, consult *Frommer's Paris* or *Frommer's France*.

TOURIST INFORMATION

At the main **tourist information office,** 127 avenue des Champs-Elysées, 8e (tel 47-23-61-72), you can secure information about both Paris and the provinces. It's open daily from 9am to 8pm.

Welcome Offices in the city center will also give you free maps, brochures, and *Paris Monthly Information,* an English-language listing of current events and performances.

City Layout

Paris is surprisingly compact. Occupying 432 square miles (6 more than San Francisco), it's home to 10 million people. The **river Seine** divides Paris into the **Right Bank** *(Rive Droite)* to the north and the **Left Bank** *(Rive Gauche)* to the south. These designations make sense when you stand on a bridge and face downstream, watching the waters flow out toward the sea—to your right is the north bank, to your left the south. Thirty-two bridges link the Right Bank and the Left Bank, some providing access to the two small islands at the heart of the city: **Ile de la Cité,** the city's birthplace and site of Notre-Dame, and **Ile St-Louis,** an oasis of sober 17th-century mansions. These islands can cause some confusion to walkers who think they've just crossed a bridge from one bank to the other, only to find themselves caught up in an almost medieval maze of narrow streets and old buildings.

Main Arteries & Streets

Between 1860 and 1870 Baron Georges-Eugène Haussmann, at the request of Napoléon III, forever changed the look of Paris by creating the legendary **boulevards:** St-Michel, St-Germain, Haussmann, Malesherbes, Sebastopol, Magenta, Voltaire, and Strasbourg.

The "main street" on the Right Bank is, of course, the **avenue des Champs-Elysées,** beginning at the Arc de Triomphe and running to the place de la Concorde. Haussmann also created **avenue de l'Opéra,** plus the **12 avenues** radiating like a starburst from the Arc de Triomphe. This design gave the square its original name: place de l'Etoile *(étoile* means "star"). Following de Gaulle's death it was renamed in his honor; today it's often referred to as place Charles-de-Gaulle-Etoile.

Haussmann also cleared the Ile de la Cité of its medieval buildings, transforming it into a showcase for Notre-Dame. Finally, he laid out two elegant parks on the western and southeastern fringes of the city: the **Bois de Boulogne** and **Bois de Vincennes.**

Finding an Address

The city of Paris is divided into 20 municipal wards called *arrondissements,* each with its own mayor, city hall, police station, and central post office. Most city maps are divided by these arrondissements, and all addresses include the arrondissement number (written in Roman or Arabic numerals and followed by "e" or "er"). For more information, see *Frommer's Paris* or *Frommer's France.*

Numbers on buildings running parallel to the Seine most often follow the course of the river—east to west. On perpendicular streets, numbers on buildings begin low closer to the river.

Maps   If you're staying for more than two or three days, purchase an inexpensive pocket-size book that includes the *plan de Paris* by arrondissement, available at all major newsstands and bookshops. Most of these guides provide a Métro map, a foldout city map, and indexed arrondissement maps, with all streets listed and keyed.

Getting Around

Paris is a city for strollers whose greatest joy in life is rambling through unexpected alleyways and squares. Given a choice of conveyance, make it your own two feet whenever possible. Only when you can't walk another step or are in a hurry to reach an exact destination should you consider the following swift and prosaic means of urban transport.

By Subway   The **Métro** (tel. 43-46-14-14 for information) is the most efficient and easy means of transportation. The lines are numbered, and the final destination of each is clearly marked on subway maps, on the trains themselves, and in the underground passageways. Most stations display a map of the system at the entrance. Figure out the route from where you are to your destination, noting the stations where you'll have to change. To make sure you catch the correct train, find your destination, then visually follow the line it's on to the end of the route and note the name—this is the *direction* you follow in the stations and see on the train. Transfer stations are known as *correspondances*. (Note that some require long walks—Châtelet is the most notorious.)

Most trips require only one transfer. Many larger stations have maps with pushbutton indicators that help you plot your route more easily by lighting up automatically when you press the button for your destination. A ride on the urban lines costs the same to any point.

On the Sceaux, Noissy-St-Léger, and St-Germain-en-Laye lines serving the suburbs, fares are based on distance. A *carnet* (ticket book) is the best buy. You can also purchase *Formule 1,* allowing unlimited travel on the city's network of subways for one day.

At the station entrance, buy your ticket, then insert it into the turnstile and pass through. At some exits tickets are checked, so hold on to yours. There are occasional ticket checks on the trains, platforms, and passageways, too.

If you're changing trains, get out and determine toward which *direction* (final destination) on the next line you want to head, then follow the bright-orange CORRESPONDANCE signs until you reach the proper platform. Don't follow a SORTIE sign ("Exit") or you'll have to pay another fare to resume your journey.

The Métro starts running daily at 5:30am and closes around 1:15am. It's reasonably safe at any hour, but beware of pick-pockets.

By Bus   Travel by bus is much slower than that by subway. Most buses run from 6:30am to 9:15pm (a few operate until 12:30am; a handful operate during early-morning hours). Service is limited on Sunday and holidays. Bus and Métro fares are the same, and you can use the same *carnet* tickets on both. Most bus rides require one ticket, but some destinations require two (never more than two within the city limits).

At certain bus stops, signs list the destinations and numbers of the buses serving that point. Destinations are usually listed north to south and east to west. Most stops along the way are also posted on the sides of the buses. To catch a bus, wait in line at the bus stop. Signal the driver to stop the bus and board in order. During rush hours you may have to take a ticket from the dispensing machine, indicating your position in the line.

If you intend to use buses frequently, pick up an RATP bus map at the office on place de la Madeleine, 8e; or at the tourist offices at RATP headquarters, 53 bis, quai des Grands Augustins, 6e, 75006 Paris. You can also write to them before you leave. For detailed information on bus and Métro routes, call 43-46-14-14.

By Taxi   It's impossible to secure one at rush hour, so don't even try. Taxi drivers are strongly organized into an effective lobby to keep their number limited to 14,300.

Watch out for the common rip-offs. Always check the meter to make sure you don't have your fare added onto the previous passenger's. Beware of cabs without meters, which often wait for tipsy patrons outside nightclubs—always settle the tab in advance. Regular cabs can be hailed on the street when their signs read LIBRE. Taxis are easier to find at the many stands near Métro stations.

By Car Don't consider driving a car in Paris—the streets are narrow and parking is next to impossible. Besides, most visitors don't have the nerve, skill, and ruthlessness required.

By Bicycle To ride a bicycle through the streets and parks of Paris, perhaps with a *baguette* tucked under your arm, might have been a fantasy of yours since you saw your first Maurice Chevalier film. If the idea appeals to you, you aren't alone: Paris in recent years has added many miles of right-hand lanes specifically designated for cyclists, plus hundreds of bike racks scattered throughout the city. (When these aren't available, many Parisians simply chain their bikes to the nearest fence or lamppost.) Cycling is especially popular within the larger parks and gardens.

One of the largest companies concerned with bicycle rentals is the **Bicy-Club,** 8 place de la Porte-de-Champerret, 17e (tel. 47-66-55-92; Métro: Porte-de-Champerret), which maintains at least half a dozen outlets within Paris's parks and gardens, usually on weekends and holidays between March and November. Two of the company's most popular outlets are a kiosk behind the Relais du Rois, route de Suresnes, in the Bois de Boulogne, and a kiosk in the Bois de Vincennes near the entrance to the Parc Floral.

FAST FACTS Paris

American Express Offices are located at 11 rue Scribe, 9e (tel. 47-77-77-07), close to the Opéra (also the Métro stop). Hours are Monday through Friday from 9am to 5:30pm. The bank window is open Saturday from 9am to 5pm, but you can't pick up mail until Monday. Other offices are at 5 rue de Chaillot, 16e (tel. 47-23-61-20; Métro: Alma-Marceau); 83 bis, rue de Courcelles, 17e (tel. 47-66-09-00; Métro: Courcelles); and 38 av. de Wagram, 8e (tel. 42-27-58-80; Métro: Ternes).

Area Code Paris's area code is 1. No other provinces have area codes. However, for long-distance calls anywhere within France, you must first dial 16.

Banks American Express may be able to meet most of your banking needs. If not, Paris banks are open Monday through Friday from 9am to 4:30pm; a few are open on Saturday. Ask at your hotel for the location of the nearest bank. Shops and most hotels will cash traveler's checks, but not at the advantageous rate a bank or foreign-exchange office will give you, so make sure you've allowed enough funds for *le weekend.*

Business Hours French business hours are erratic, as befits a nation of individualists. Most **museums** close one day a week (often Tuesday) and are generally closed on national holidays; usual hours are 9:30am to 5pm. Some museums, particularly the smaller and less-staffed ones, close for lunch from noon to 2pm. Most French museums are open Saturday; many are closed Sunday morning but open in the afternoon. (For detailed hours of individual museums, see *Frommer's Paris* or *Frommer's France.*) Generally, **offices** are open Monday through Friday from 9am to 5pm, but don't count on it. Always call first. **Stores** are open from 9 or 9:30am (often 10am) to 6 or 7pm without a break for lunch. Some shops, particularly those operated by foreigners, open at 8am and close at 8 or 9pm. In some small stores the lunch break can last three hours, beginning at 1pm.

Currency Exchange For the best exchange rate, cash your traveler's checks at banks or foreign-exchange offices, not at shops and hotels. Most post offices will also change traveler's checks or convert currency. Currency exchanges are also found at Paris airports and train stations. One of the most central currency exchange branches is at 154 av. des Champs-Elysées, 8e (tel. 42-25-93-33; Métro: George-V), open Monday through Friday from 9am to 5pm and Saturday and Sunday from 10:30am to 6pm. A small commission is charged.

Hospitals The American Hospital, 63 bd. Victor Hugo, Neuilly (tel. 46-41-25-25; Métro: Pont-de-Levallos or Pont-de-Neuilly; bus: 82), operates 24-hour emergency service.

Language In the wake of two World Wars and many shared experiences—not to mention the influence of American movies, TV, and records—the English language has made major inroads and is almost a second language in some parts of Paris. An American trying to speak French might even be understood. The world's best-selling phrase books are published by Berlitz— *French for Travellers* has everything you'll need.

Safety Whenever traveling in an unfamiliar city or country, stay alert and aware of your surroundings. Be particularly careful with cameras, purses, and wallets—all favorite targets of thieves and pickpockets.

In Paris, be aware of roaming child pickpockets preying on tourists around such sights as the Louvre, Eiffel Tower, and Notre-Dame; they especially like to pick your pockets in the Métro, sometimes blocking you from the escalator. A band of these young thieves can clean your pockets even while you try to fend them off. Their method is to get very close to a target, often ask for a handout, and deftly help themselves to your money or passport.

Useful Telephone Numbers Police, 17; fire, 18; emergency medical assistance, 15.

RECOMMENDED READING

General History

Bierman, John. *Napoleon III and His Carnival Empire* (St. Martin's, 1988).

Callaghan, Moreley. *That Summer in Paris: Memories of Tangled Friendships with Hemingway, Fitzgerald and Some Others* (Coward-McCann, 1963).

Carpenter, Humphrey. *Geniuses Together: American Writers in Paris in the 1920s* (Houghton Mifflin, 1988).

Collins, Larry, and Dominique Lapierre. *Is Paris Burning?* (Warner Books, 1991).

Cooper, Duff. *Talleyrand* (Fromm, 1986).

Duras, Marguerite. *The War: A Memoir* (Pantheon, 1986).

Febre, Lucien. *Life in Renaissance France* (Harvard University Press, 1979).

Fitch, Noel Riley. *Sylvia Beach and the Lost Generation: A History of Literary Paris in the Twenties and Thirties* (Norton, 1983).

Flanner, Janet. *Paris Was Yesterday 1925–1939* (Harcourt Brace Jovanovich, 1988).

Gibbings, Robert. *Trumpets from Montparnasse* (J. M. Dent & Sons, 1955).

Hampson, Norman. *Danton* (Basil Blackwell, 1988).

Hemingway, Ernest. *A Moveable Feast* (Macmillan, 1988).

Hibbert, Christopher. *The Days of the French Revolution* (Morrow, 1981).

Liebling, A. J. *The Road Back to Paris* (Paragon House, 1988).

Longstreet, Stephen. *We All Went to Paris: Americans in the City of Light 1776–1971* (Macmillan, 1972).

Lucas, E. V. A. *A Wanderer in Paris* (Methuen & Co., 1925).

McDougall, Richard. *The Very Rich Hours of Adrienne Monnier* (Scribner's, 1976).

Paul, Eliot. *The Last Time I Saw Paris* (Random House, 1942).

Phelps, Robert. *Belles Saisons: A Colette Scrapbook* (Farrar, Straus & Giroux, 1978).

Rearick, Charles. *Pleasures of the Belle Epoque: Entertainment and Festivity in Turn-of-the-Century France* (Yale University Press, 1986).

Russell, John. *Paris* (Harry N. Abrams, 1983).

Schama, Simon. *Citizens: A Chronicle of the French Revolution* (Knopf, 1989).

Sévigné, Madame de. *Selected Letters* (Penguin, 1982).

Thompson, J. M. *The French Revolution* (Basil Blackwell, 1985).

Thompson, J. M. *Napoleon Bonaparte* (Basil Blackwell, 1988).

Weber, Eugen. *France, Fin de Siècle* (Harvard University Press, 1986).

Wedgwood, C. V. *Richelieu and the French Monarchy* (Macmillan, 1965).

Zeldin, Theodore. *The French* (Pantheon, 1982).

Art & Architecture

Bernard, Denvir, ed. *Impressionists at First Hand* (Thames and Hudson, 1987).

Bernardac, Marie-Laure. *Picasso Museum Paris: The Masterpieces* (Réunion des Musées Nationaux, 1991).

Blunt, Anthony. *Art and Architecture in France 1500–1700* (Penguin, 1973).

Brassai. *The Secret Paris of the 30s* (Pantheon, 1977).

Delacroix, Eugène. *The Journal of Eugène Delacroix* (Crown, 1948).

Elderfield, John. *Henri Matisse: A Retrospective* (Metropolitan Museum of Art, 1992).

Freches-Thory, Claire, et al. *Toulouse-Lautrec* (Réunion des Musées Nationaux, 1992).

Friedrich, Otto. *Olympia: Paris in the Age of Manet* (HarperCollins, 1992).

Herbert, Robert. *Impressionism: Art, Leisure and Parisian Society* (Yale University Press, 1988).

Lecoque, A. L. *Renoir My Friend* (Editions Mona Lisa, 1968).

Reff, Theodore. *Manet and Modern Paris* (National Gallery of Art, 1982).

Rewald, John. *Post-Impressionism: From van Gogh to Gauguin* (Museum of Modern Art, 1978).

Sutcliffe, Anthony. *Paris: An Architectural History* (Yale University Press, 1993).

Van Gogh, Vincent. *Vincent van Gogh: Lettres à Théo* (Editions Gallimard, 1956).

Fiction

Bowen, Elizabeth. *The House in Paris* (Knopf, 1936).

Colette. *The Collected Stories of Colette* (Ward, Matthew & White, 1983).

Colette. *The Vagabond* (Ballantine, 1982).

Dickens, Charles. *A Tale of Two Cities* (Penguin, 1970).

Dumas fils, Alexandre. *Camille* (NAL Penguin, 1984).

Fitzgerald, F. Scott. *Babylon Revisited and Other Stories* (Macmillan, 1988).

Flaubert, Gustave. *Madame Bovary* (Random House, 1982).

Hemingway, Ernest. *The Sun Also Rises* (Macmillan, 1987).

Hugo, Victor. *Les Misérables* (Modern Library, 1983).

James, Henry. *The Ambassadors* (Penguin, 1987).

James, Henry. *The American* (Houghton Mifflin, 1985).

Krantz, Judith. *Mistral's Daughter* (Crown, 1983).

Laclos, Choderlos de. *Les Liaisons dangereuses* (NAL Penguin, 1962).

Maupassant, Guy de. *Selected Stories* (New American Library, 1984).

Miller, Henry. *Tropic of Cancer* (Grove, 1987).

Proust, Marcel. *Remembrance of Things Past* (Vintage, 1982).

Stein, Gertrude. *The Autobiography of Alice B. Toklas* (Random House, 1955).

Suskind, Patrick. *Perfume* (Knopf, 1986).

INDEX

Now Save Money On All Your Travels By Joining FROMMER'S™ TRAVEL BOOK CLUB The World's Best Travel Guides At Membership Prices!

Frommer's Travel Book Club is your ticket to successful travel! Open up a world of travel information and simplify your travel planning when you join ranks with thousands of value-conscious travelers who are members of the Frommer's *Travel Book Club.* Join today and you'll be entitled to all the privileges that come from belonging to the club that offers you travel guides for less to more than 100 destinations worldwide. **Annual membership is only $25.00 (U.S.) or $35.00 (Canada/Foreign).**

The Advantages of Membership:

1. Your choice of **three free** books (any **two** Frommer's Comprehensive Guides, Frommer's $-A-Day Guides, Frommer's Walking Tours or Frommer's Family Guides—plus **one** Frommer's City Guide, Frommer's City $-A-Day Guide or Frommer's Touring Guide).

2. Your own subscription to the **TRIPS & TRAVEL** quarterly newsletter.

3. You're entitled to a **30% discount** on your order of any additional books offered by the club.

4. You're offered (at a small additional fee) our **Domestic Trip-Routing Kits.**

Our **Trips & Travel** quarterly newsletter offers practical information on the best buys in travel, the "hottest" vacation spots, the latest travel trends, world-class events and much, much more.

Our **Domestic Trip-Routing Kits** are available for any North American destination. We'll send you a detailed map highlighting the best route to take to your destination—you can request direct or scenic routes.

Here's all you have to do to join:

Send in your membership fee of $25.00 ($35.00 Canada/Foreign) with your name and address on the form below along with your selections as part of your membership package to the address listed below. Remember to check off your three free books.

If you would like to order additional books, please select the books you would like and send a check for the total amount (please add sales tax in the states noted below), plus $2.00 per book for shipping and handling ($3.00 Canada/Foreign) to the address listed below.

FROMMER'S TRAVEL BOOK CLUB
P.O. Box 473
Mt. Morris, IL 61054-0473
(815) 734-1104

[ ] **YES!** I want to take advantage of this opportunity to join Frommer's Travel Book Club.

[ ] My check is enclosed. Dollar amount enclosed_____*
(all payments in U.S. funds only)

Name _____ _____

Address _____

City _____ State _____ Zip _____

Phone ( ) __ _____(In case we have a question regarding your order).

All orders must be prepaid.

To ensure that all orders are processed efficiently, please apply sales tax in the following areas: CA, CT, FL, IL, IN, NJ, NY, PA, TN, WA and CANADA.

*With membership, shipping & handling will be paid by Frommer's Travel Book Club for the three FREE books you select as part of your membership. Please add $2.00 per book for shipping & handling for any additional books purchased ($3.00 Canada/Foreign).

Allow 4-6 weeks for delivery for all items. Prices of books, membership fee, and publication dates are subject to change without notice. All orders are subject to acceptance and availability.

Please send me the books checked below:

FROMMER'S COMPREHENSIVE GUIDES

*(Guides listing facilities from budget to deluxe,
with emphasis on the medium-priced)*

	Retail Price	Code		Retail Price	Code
☐ Acapulco/Ixtapa/Taxco, 2nd Edition	$13.95	C157	☐ Jamaica/Barbados, 2nd Edition	$15.00	C149
☐ Alaska '94-'95	$17.00	C131	☐ Japan '94-'95	$19.00	C144
☐ Arizona '95 (Avail. 3/95)	$14.95	C166	☐ Maui, 1st Edition	$14.00	C153
☐ Australia '94-'95	$18.00	C147	☐ Nepal, 2nd Edition	$18.00	C126
☐ Austria, 6th Edition	$16.95	C162	☐ New England '95	$16.95	C165
☐ Bahamas '94-'95	$17.00	C121	☐ New Mexico, 3rd Edition (Avail. 3/95)	$14.95	C167
☐ Belgium/Holland/ Luxembourg '93-'94	$18.00	C106	☐ New York State '94-'95	$19.00	C133
☐ Bermuda '94-'95	$15.00	C122	☐ Northwest, 5th Edition	$17.00	C140
☐ Brazil, 3rd Edition	$20.00	C111	☐ Portugal '94-'95	$17.00	C141
☐ California '95	$16.95	C164	☐ Puerto Rico '95-'96	$14.00	C151
☐ Canada '94-'95	$19.00	C145	☐ Puerto Vallarta/ Manzanillo/Guadalajara '94-'95	$14.00	C135
☐ Caribbean '95	$18.00	C148			
☐ Carolinas/Georgia, 2nd Edition	$17.00	C128	☐ Scandinavia, 16th Edition (Avail. 3/95)	$19.95	C169
☐ Colorado, 2nd Edition	$16.00	C143	☐ Scotland '94-'95	$17.00	C146
☐ Costa Rica '95	$13.95	C161	☐ South Pacific '94-'95	$20.00	C138
☐ Cruises '95-'96	$19.00	C150	☐ Spain, 16th Edition	$16.95	C163
☐ Delaware/Maryland '94-'95	$15.00	C136	☐ Switzerland/ Liechtenstein '94-'95	$19.00	C139
☐ England '95	$17.95	C159	☐ Thailand, 2nd Edition	$17.95	C154
☐ Florida '95	$18.00	C152	☐ U.S.A., 4th Edition	$18.95	C156
☐ France '94-'95	$20.00	C132	☐ Virgin Islands '94-'95	$13.00	C127
☐ Germany '95	$18.95	C158	☐ Virginia '94-'95	$14.00	C142
☐ Ireland, 1st Edition (Avail. 3/95)	$16.95	C168	☐ Yucatan, 2nd Edition	$13.95	C155
☐ Italy '95	$18.95	C160			

FROMMER'S $-A-DAY GUIDES

(Guides to low-cost tourist accommodations and facilities)

	Retail Price	Code		Retail Price	Code
☐ Australia on $45 '95-'96	$18.00	D122	☐ Israel on $45, 15th Edition	$16.95	D130
☐ Costa Rica/Guatemala/ Belize on $35, 3rd Edition	$15.95	D126	☐ Mexico on $45 '95	$16.95	D125
			☐ New York on $70 '94-'95	$16.00	D121
☐ Eastern Europe on $30, 5th Edition	$16.95	D129	☐ New Zealand on $45 '93-'94	$18.00	D103
☐ England on $60 '95	$17.95	D128			
☐ Europe on $50 '95	$17.95	D127	☐ South America on $40, 16th Edition	$18.95	D123
☐ Greece on $45 '93-'94	$19.00	D100			
☐ Hawaii on $75 '95	$16.95	D124	☐ Washington, D.C. on $50 '94-'95	$17.00	D120
☐ Ireland on $45 '94-'95	$17.00	D118			

FROMMER'S CITY $-A-DAY GUIDES

	Retail Price	Code		Retail Price	Code
☐ Berlin on $40 '94-'95	$12.00	D111	☐ Madrid on $50 '94-'95	$13.00	D119
☐ London on $45 '94-'95	$12.00	D114	☐ Paris on $50 '94-'95	$12.00	D117

FROMMER'S FAMILY GUIDES
*(Guides listing information on kid-friendly
hotels, restaurants, activities and attractions)*

	Retail Price	Code		Retail Price	Code
☐ California with Kids	$18.00	F100	☐ San Francisco with Kids	$17.00	F104
☐ Los Angeles with Kids	$17.00	F103	☐ Washington, D.C.		
☐ New York City			with Kids	$17.00	F102
with Kids	$18.00	F101			

FROMMER'S CITY GUIDES
*(Pocket-size guides to sightseeing and tourist
accommodations and facilities in all price ranges)*

	Retail Price	Code		Retail Price	Code
☐ Amsterdam '93-'94	$13.00	S110	☐ Montreal/Quebec City '95	$11.95	S166
☐ Athens, 10th Edition			☐ Nashville/Memphis,		
(Avail. 3/95)	$12.95	S174	1st Edition	$13.00	S141
☐ Atlanta '95	$12.95	S161	☐ New Orleans '95	$12.95	S148
☐ Atlantic City/Cape May,			☐ New York '95	$12.95	S152
5th Edition	$13.00	S130	☐ Orlando '95	$13.00	S145
☐ Bangkok, 2nd Edition	$12.95	S147	☐ Paris '95	$12.95	S150
☐ Barcelona '93-'94	$13.00	S115	☐ Philadelphia, 8th Edition	$12.95	S167
☐ Berlin, 3rd Edition	$12.95	S162	☐ Prague '94-'95	$13.00	S143
☐ Boston '95	$12.95	S160	☐ Rome, 10th Edition	$12.95	S168
☐ Budapest, 1st Edition	$13.00	S139	☐ St. Louis/Kansas City,		
☐ Chicago '95	$12.95	S169	2nd Edition	$13.00	S127
☐ Denver/Boulder/Colorado			☐ San Diego '95	$12.95	S158
Springs, 3rd Edition	$12.95	S154	☐ San Francisco '95	$12.95	S155
☐ Dublin, 2nd Edition	$12.95	S157	☐ Santa Fe/Taos/		
☐ Hong Kong '94-'95	$13.00	S140	Albuquerque '95		
☐ Honolulu/Oahu '95	$12.95	S151	(Avail. 2/95)	$12.95	S172
☐ Las Vegas '95	$12.95	S163	☐ Seattle/Portland '94-'95	$13.00	S137
☐ London '95	$12.95	S156	☐ Sydney, 4th Edition	$12.95	S171
☐ Los Angeles '95	$12.95	S164	☐ Tampa/St. Petersburg,		
☐ Madrid/Costa del Sol,			3rd Edition	$13.00	S146
2nd Edition	$12.95	S165	☐ Tokyo '94-'95	$13.00	S144
☐ Mexico City, 1st Edition	$12.95	S170	☐ Toronto '95 (Avail. 3/95)	$12.95	S173
☐ Miami '95-'96	$12.95	S149	☐ Vancouver/Victoria '94-'95	$13.00	S142
☐ Minneapolis/St. Paul,			☐ Washington, D.C. '95	$12.95	S153
4th Edition	$12.95	S159			

FROMMER'S WALKING TOURS

*(Companion guides that point out the places
and pleasures that make a city unique)*

	Retail Price	Code		Retail Price	Code
☐ Berlin	$12.00	W100	☐ New York	$12.00	W102
☐ Chicago	$12.00	W107	☐ Paris	$12.00	W103
☐ England's Favorite Cities	$12.00	W108	☐ San Francisco	$12.00	W104
☐ London	$12.00	W101	☐ Washington, D.C.	$12.00	W105
☐ Montreal/Quebec City	$12.00	W106			

SPECIAL EDITIONS

	Retail Price	Code		Retail Price	Code
☐ Bed & Breakfast Southwest	$16.00	P100	☐ National Park Guide, 29th Edition	$17.00	P106
☐ Bed & Breakfast Great American Cities	$16.00	P104	☐ Where to Stay U.S.A., 11th Edition	$15.00	P102
☐ Caribbean Hideaways	$16.00	P103			

FROMMER'S TOURING GUIDES

*(Color-illustrated guides that include walking tours,
cultural and historic sites, and practical information)*

	Retail Price	Code		Retail Price	Code
☐ Amsterdam	$11.00	T001	☐ New York	$11.00	T008
☐ Barcelona	$14.00	T015	☐ Rome	$11.00	T010
☐ Brazil	$11.00	T003	☐ Tokyo	$15.00	T016
☐ Hong Kong/Singapore/ Macau	$11.00	T006	☐ Turkey	$11.00	T013
☐ London	$13.00	T007	☐ Venice	$9.00	T014

---

*Please note: If the availability of a book is several months away, we may
have back issues of guides to that particular destination.
Call customer service at (815) 734-1104.*